"Matt does an excellent job of providing clarity on many difficult issues every believer walks through on a daily basis. He does this by clearly articulating the scriptures to reveal the truth that really does set us free. This Volume, like the ones before, is an excellent devotional book to help any believer with their walk with God. Every page of this book is filled with the good news of God's unconditional love and grace. If you read one book this year, make it this one!" -*Amazon Customer*

"Another great book by Matt McMillen. The first two Volumes were amazing and this one doesn't disappoint. Written in a way that is so easy to understand. I highly recommend all of Matt's books." -*Amazon Customer*

"Matt McMillen has a God-given talent for ministry that reaches out to believers and unbelievers alike. His message is simple: you are a saved, perfect child of God through His New Covenant. Matt has the gift of bringing enlightenment to this and has saved me from a life of self-destruction! I am happy and feel truly loved by God through Jesus living within me every minute of every day!" -*Amazon Customer*

---

*Amazon customer reviews as of June 6th, 2018, courtesy of Amazon.com, Inc or its affiliates.

All rights reserved.

Matt McMillen is a bestselling Christian author and teacher of God's Word. His books and massive social media ministry has taught countless amounts of people their true identity in Christ. Matt's easy-to-understand biblical teachings have helped build confidence in his readers, break lifelong addictions, and find their true purpose for living: enjoying God's grace through Jesus Christ!

For more information on his ministry, visit:
www.mattmcmillenministries.com

60 Days for Jesus,
Volume 3

60 Days for Jesus, Volume 3

Understanding Christ Better, Two Months at a Time

Matt McMillen

Citation: THE HOLY BIBLE, Copyright © 1973, 1978, 1984, 2011 by Biblica, Inc.®
Used with permission. All rights reserved worldwide.

Copyright © 2018 Matt McMillen
60 Days for Jesus, Volume 3
Understanding Christ Better, Two Months at a Time

Published by: Matt McMillen Ministries
720 W. Karsch Blvd.
Farmington, MO 63640
matt@mattmcmillen.com

All rights reserved
Copyright © 2018 by Matt McMillen
All rights reserved. This book or any portion thereof
may not be reproduced or used in any manner whatsoever
without the express written consent of the publisher
except for the use of brief quotations in a book review.
First Printing, 2018

Printed in the United States of America

ISBN: 9780997153330
ISBN 10: 0997153334
All rights reserved.

For Mom and Dad. I love you.

Contents

Introduction xvii

Month 1

Day 1   Why I'm Thankful for Jesus Christ 3
Day 2   How to Keep the Commandments of Christ 9
Day 3   Why Should I Forgive Others? 17
Day 4   How to Deal with Your Spiritual Perfection 22
Day 5   The Truth About God's Anointing......................29
Day 6   What to do During Dormant Seasons of Life 36
Day 7   Why Should I Give Up My Addiction? 41
Day 8   How to Accept God's Timing..........................47
Day 9   Stop Killing Yourself..................................51
Day 10 You Don't Owe God Anything 56
Day 11 What to do When the Pain is Unbearable 62
Day 12 The Truth About "Faith Without Works Is Dead" 68
Day 13 Debunking Common Christian Myths 74
Day 14 Why You Should Get Rid of Your Back-Up Plan.........79
Day 15 Who is the Holy Spirit?.............................. 82
Day 16 Why Should I Have Good Behavior? 88
Day 17 You Are God's Ambassador..........................93
Day 18 A Conversation with an Atheist...................... 97
Day 19 How to Have Fun without Drinking Alcohol...........100
Day 20 You Were Planned By God 106
Day 21 What Is Sin?..109

Day 22 I Was a Victim of Religious Abuse 118
Day 23 Don't Listen to the Accuser. 126
Day 24 God Wants to Help You with Your Choices. 131
Day 25 How Can I Get Over My Past? 136
Day 26 What's the Difference Between Spirit, Soul, and Body? . . .142
Day 27 How to Confront Others in a Healthy Way. 149
Day 28 Why We No Longer Need Altars in Church. 156
Day 29 Dinner with a Former Drunk 162
Day 30 Why Christians Should Not Be Afraid of Hell 165

Month 2

Day 31 How to Change the World as a Christian 173
Day 32 The Truth About Tithing. 178
Day 33 God Does Not Care About Your Outfit. 189
Day 34 God Wants to Help You with Your Attitude 194
Day 35 How Suffering Can Be a Good Thing 199
Day 36 How's Your Relationship with Yourself?. 203
Day 37 How to Endure Like Jesus. 208
Day 38 How do I Know if I'm Going to Heaven?. 212
Day 39 Do You Worship the Bible or God? 216
Day 40 I am the Righteousness of God? 222
Day 41 The Truth About Speaking in Tongues 225
Day 42 Do You Feel Sorry for Yourself? 235
Day 43 It's Impossible to Get More of God 240
Day 44 How to Fight Like a Christian 245
Day 45 What Is the Unforgivable Sin? 250
Day 46 Smile! 258
Day 47 Christians Don't Have Wicked Hearts. 261
Day 48 Do You Feel Like You're All Alone? 272
Day 49 Am I Really Saved? 277
Day 50 How to Deal with Depression as a Christian 284
Day 51 The Truth About Baptism and Repentance 290
Day 52 When Praying for Your Enemies Is Hard 299

Day 53 Jesus Will Not Blot Out Your Name 304
Day 54 Debunking Christian Myths Part 2 .310
Day 55 Children: The Real Victims of Addiction. 315
Day 56 Why Should I Listen to God?. 321
Day 57 How Many Times Have You Been Saved? 326
Day 58 The Father Will Never Give up on You 332
Day 59 Don't Hide Any Longer. 337
Day 60 By His Stripes We Are Healed? 341

Additional books by Matt McMillen 349

"God made him who had no sin to be sin for us, so that in him we might become the righteousness of God."

2 Corinthians 5:21

I am the righteousness of God, and so are you, if you believe Jesus is your Savior.

INTRODUCTION

60 Days For Jesus

"God, I want to reach billions of people for you. Please, use me." My prayer is whispered softly as I let my Creator know my goals. The funny thing is, my goals have never been small. For whatever reason, God decided to create me with an inherent drive to be the best at whatever I was doing. This seems like a good thing, right? It is! The problem was, me wanting to be the best at everything was always out of balance. Soon enough, the Holy Spirit would teach me all about balance.

From the time I was a boy, I can remember wanting to overwork myself in order to achieve perfection of any particular objective. It didn't matter if I was putting together a puzzle, cleaning my room, or working on my jump shot, doing it "just right" was always my intent—and it still is. The difference is, now, I'm much more well-balanced.

With the skill-set the Holy Spirit has given me—along with being able to point out the enemy's lies and my old stinking thinking—I recognize it when I'm taking things too far. Stress, discouragement, and thinking I'm "less than" are red flags for me. When they pop up, I need to sit still and pray about what I'm feeling. Sometimes God says, "Take a stand against this. Be clear. Be respectful." At other times He says, "Let this go."

Once I hit my 30s I knew God wanted me to start my own personal ministry, so I did. However, my overly-passionate work ethic came along with it. Driven to learn more, so I can help others more, I became a sponge of the gospel. Studying Jesus in great depths, along with apologetic books and the epistles, this was my new obsession. I had been saved since I was a boy, but the life of Christ was starting to sprout out of me! It was exciting! Although I had read a lot of this stuff many times before, it was as if the Holy Spirit was turning each page! He started to reveal the infiniteness of His grace through the New Covenant! In turn, I felt like I could explode with love!

As time went on, my ministry grew unlike I could have ever imagined or planned. More and more people were paying attention to what I had to say, and it was helping them! That felt really good! Especially with all the time I was putting in. However, in the midst of this growth, God was trying to teach me two main things:

1. How to relax.
2. I wanted what He wanted.

This relaxing thing is a strange paradox. With my personality of "Work harder than everyone else—be the best!" as well as the world's teaching of "You get out of life what you put into it," I was bamboozled. God was trying to get me to sit still when I wanted to do more!

"What do you mean you want me to relax, God? There's more people to reach!"

"Matthew, I understand there are more people to reach, but I want you to stop stressing and straining. If you'll learn to simply be yourself and relax, you'll achieve more than you ever have before."

"But that makes no sense!"

"According to the world, yes. But according to me, it makes perfect sense. Trust me."

God wanted me to relax and be myself, but what did that mean? When He stitched me together in my mom's womb, He made me like I am, driven, so why was He wanting me to chill? Why not take advantage of my gifts? Soon enough, He taught me the answers: He wanted to teach me the art of doing nothing—which is almost impossible for me—and He also wanted to hone my talents by way of relaxation.

What I didn't know was that as Christians, when we are simply being our true selves, we never have to work hard. Just the same as an apple tree doesn't have to work hard to grow apples, I didn't have to work hard to "produce" for my Creator—I just "had to be." As I did so, He produced *through* me! This blew my mind! The Holy Spirit was informing me that it is in a state of rest, I can accomplish more!

In my heart I already knew this, but my mind was beginning to catch up! By way of relaxing, my gifts and drive would flourish on unprecedented levels! Which brings me to the second thing I was learning from God in bunches. I actually wanted what He wanted! All Christians do!

For so long, we've been incorrectly taught that we *don't* want what God wants. We've been misled to think there's a battle between us and our Creator. For believers, nothing could be further from the truth! We want exactly what God wants because we've been infused with His very own Spirit. His Spirit leads us away from the things which are not natural as His children. After we are saved, once, sin no longer matches up with us. An internal conflict happens each and every time we choose to act on sin. We want what He wants, no matter how long we deny it!

His Spirit in us constantly teaches us new things each day! His Spirit in us renews our attitudes and actions over time! Christians are not at battle with God! God is not "coming and going" based on what we do and don't do! He's committed to us for eternity! The Cross has completely reconciled us to Him! He's given us a new spirit! He's made His home *inside* of our new spirits, for good, never to leave again!

Once we come to the realization of these truths—which is the gospel—we start to actually *believe* that we want what God wants. Afterwards, everything changes because our focus changes. We no longer waste our time saying things like, "I gotta get closer to God!" because we know He's in us in full, and we're in Him!

So thank you for joining me once again! That is, if you've read my previous books! If not, that's no problem at all. The *60 Days for Jesus* series can be read in any order, and they're available on Amazon. Also, if you'd like to share or print out any of these devotionals, they can be found on my website for free! Simply search the title of the devotional on the home page! (www.mattmcmillen.com)

What God has done with this simple daily devotional book has far exceeded my imagination. Both, Volume 1 and 2, reached the number one spot on Amazon's best sellers in many different categories! The feedback I continue to receive from readers is extremely encouraging and humbling! How many volumes will I write? I don't know, but I will tell you this, I have no plans on stopping any time soon! As long as God allows it, and until He takes me home, I will continue to write devotionals to help set people free! What a blessing it's been so far! Let's keep going!

Month 1

"And that is what some of you were. But you were washed, you were sanctified, you were justified in the name of the Lord Jesus Christ and by the Spirit of our God."

1 Corinthians 6:11

DAY 1

WHY I'M THANKFUL FOR JESUS CHRIST

"But thanks be to God! He gives us victory over sin and death through our Lord Jesus Christ."

1 CORINTHIANS 15:57

There are many verses in the Bible about being thankful. Thankfulness is a characteristic which comes from the heart of every Christian. If we aren't being thankful we don't feel right, and that's because an attitude of gratitude is interwoven into our supernatural DNA. Why is this? This might shock some of you, but *God* is thankful! Our Creator is a thankful Person!

If you look at the short lifespan of Jesus while here on planet earth, He thanked the Father all the time. Further, the apostles thanked God in their letters—even in the midst of their deepest turmoils and stresses. We believers *bleed* thankfulness! We cannot deny being grateful! We can temporarily not *act* grateful, but the geyser from within will soon explode. It's impossible to muffle the Spirit of God, who is in us. We *always* find something to be thankful for.

Heck, even Paul stated that he delighted in his weaknesses—who does that? (See 2 Corinthians 12:10). Delight means *pleasure*, and everyone is thankful for pleasure. For Christians, we find thankfulness in nearly every situation because we know who holds all situations together...our Dad. In the end, and no matter what, Dad is still in complete control and He loves us unconditionally.

If I had to add a single "fruit of the Spirit" to the list in Galatians 5:22 and 23, it would be thankfulness. Paul reveals a list of spiritual fruit which will grow in our lives as we walk by our true selves. We will organically produce love, joy, peace, patience, kindness, goodness, faithfulness, gentleness and self-control. He sums these virtues up with, "against such things there is no law."

Why would he say that part? Because you can't legislate any of these traits. You can't force someone by way of punishment to be loving, patient, or joyous. You can't force someone to be *thankful* either. Thankfulness comes from within! It's either there, or it's not! For Christians, we can't get away from thankfulness, no matter what is happening in our lives, because the Spirit of God lives in us. But not only that, our *own* spirits have been reborn with thankful, heavenly DNA (see 1 John 3:9, John 3:7, 1 Thessalonians 5:18, Ephesians 5:20). How can this happen? How can we be reborn *of* God? Only by way of Jesus! He said so Himself:

> *"I am the way and the truth and the life. No one comes to the Father except through me." (John 14:6)*

I could write an entire book on why I'm thankful for Jesus Christ, but here are five reasons of mine:

1. **Jesus gave me a brand new, perfect spirit.** Until I began to go deeper into the knowledge of God's grace in my thirties, I didn't realize that Jesus had given me my brand new spirit in the 1980s, when I was a boy. Because of terrible, quasi-grace, double-talk teaching of "God leaves you when you mess up, so you better get to work so He'll come back," I didn't *know*

God had been with me—*in* my new spirit—nearly my whole life. This happened when I was just a small boy sitting in my mean-as-a-hornet Grandpa's church. I've molded my ministry to be the opposite of his, but even when I was sitting in his cold, nearly-empty church, on those hard pews—I believed. I believed that Jesus was who He said He was, and when that happened, my old spirit died—it was crucified with Him in the spiritual realm—it was buried, and then raised back to life as a new, perfect spirit! Nothing would ever be able to change this fact—not even me! (See Romans 6:6-7, Galatians 2:20, 2 Corinthians 5:17, Colossians 3:3, 1 Corinthians 6:19, 2 Timothy 2:13, Hebrews 10:14, 13:5).

2. **Jesus paid off my sin debt with the Father, once and for all time.** Again, because of believing false teaching, for so many years I thought I had to ask for forgiveness each time I messed up, and if I *didn't,* God would stay mad at me. This teaching is demonic because it takes away from what Jesus did at the Cross. It says, "Jesus' blood was not good enough!" I soon learned that *asking* never forgave anyone; the words, "ask for forgiveness" are not even in the Bible. Ask all you want, but until you place your faith in Jesus, you are not forgiven. Only belief in perfect blood forgives, not lip service (see Hebrews 9:22, John 3:16, Matthew 15:8). Further, the Jews got an entire year of forgiveness at the Day of Atonement, so the modern-day neurotic behavior of "asking to be forgiven" each time we sin is just plain stupid. We can't even keep up with each one of our sins *to* ask, and God does not grade on a curve—we must be perfect! (See Matthew 5:48). Only by receiving our new, perfect spirit can this happen, *not* by behavior or empty words of repeatedly asking (see Hebrews 10:10, 1 Peter 3:18, Romans 6:18).

3. **Jesus helped me get my priorities in order.** Since we are at peace with God through Jesus, He now counsels us. He doesn't

convict us, but *counsels*. The grace-confused person will yell, "Yes He *does* convict us! He convicts us of our sin all day long!" but that would be wrong because *what* exactly is the punishment of being convicted of sin? Death (see Romans 6:23). What did Jesus do at the Cross? He received *my* full conviction of *my* sin—as well as yours—and received death. Therefore, I'm not being convicted of any sin any longer, because Jesus was, once and for all time! (See Hebrews 10:12). Christ is not dying over and over in heaven each time I sin—IT'S FINISHED! (See John 19:30). God's wrath was satisfied completely by Jesus' obedience and willingness to take on my punishment (see Romans 5:9). So now, I'm being *counseled* each day by a loving, patient, kind Spirit, who keeps no record of my wrongs (see John 14:26, 2 Corinthians 5:21, Romans 5:1, 1 Corinthians 13). Once I began to understand this, the true Spirit of God *in* me began to help me trim the fat in my life. Nearly everything was shifted around as I began to understand what is important, and what is not.

4. **Jesus taught me my value.** If you know my story, then you know my childhood was not ideal, to say the least. In my youth, when I should have been being taught how valuable I am, I was being shipped from foster home to foster home. I was being beat up as the new kid in school, yet again, and ignored by my classmates. My addicted mother, who had no healthy parenting skills, caused me tremendous pain and insecurity. My self-worth was very low, and this spilled over into my adult relationships. My own addictions and codependency grew as I allowed unacceptable behavior from many people, just to keep them satisfied with me. Soon enough, Jesus revealed the *real* me *to* me: *an infinitely loved child of God!* As I began to flourish in the awareness of my identity in Christ, I grew in the knowledge of my value. Confidence began to spring to life as my relationships changed dramatically! I stopped putting up with such crap, and I put my foot down when it came to being taken advantage of. However, I was learning

how to do this properly, which is with love and respect—both for others *and* for myself. I'm still learning, but my goodness, I'm so much better than I was!

5. **Jesus taught me how to be content in my most difficult circumstances.** For so long, I thought I knew best when it came to making sure my life was in order. I'm an alpha male by personality, so I make quick decisions and I try to fix things as fast as I can. That won't work when you are being your true self as a heaven-ready saint. Patience with others *and* with yourself is the only thing that feels natural as a child of God. As my mind was being renewed to this truth, I struggled greatly. The pain and frustration of being still and allowing God to work things out *without* my help was tortuous. IT HURT. BAD. When the enemy wanted me to react in certain ways—to certain things and people—I told him to shut his face and I ignored his dumb butt. The quick fixes were over and I was beginning to understand Jesus' patience for me! In turn, He was teaching me the same thing He taught Paul about contentment, "I can do all things through Christ who gives me strength!" (See Philippians 4:13).

So today, my friends, let me ask you this: Why are you thankful for Jesus Christ? For many things I'm sure! Some of you might say, "Because He is helping me make it to heaven," but that would be wrong. If you love Him, He has *already* helped you make it to heaven! Heaven is in you, right now, today! (See Luke 17:21, Ephesians 2:6).

> **A prayer for you:** *Heavenly Father, I am so thankful for Jesus! What He went through, for me? Wow. I cannot express to you how much that means to me. All I can do to pay you back is simply allow Him to live through me each day. I plan on doing so until I get rid of this shell. Right now, I lift up all who are reading this, directly to you. So many of these dear readers feel as if they have nothing to be thankful for—they are in pain. Very tough times have hit them, and they feel defeated.*

Dad, please strengthen them today. Reveal yourself, and comfort them. Let them know you're with them. Let them know you love them so much, you gave them Jesus. Let them know you feel their pain on a deeper level than even they feel it—and that the pain will pass! These are promises for all who believe! We are thankful for you! We love you! In Jesus' name I pray, amen.

Day 2

How to Keep the Commandments of Christ

"And his commands are not burdensome..."

See 1 John 5:3

There are 613 commandments, not just ten. The modern church has turned what was meant to funnel people through a narrow gate of reliance on God's grace *alone*, into a buffet line. They've got their plates in hand, they scan the Scriptures, "Hmmmmm...let's see...I'll take this one, 'Do not commit adultery,' that looks good. Oh, and 'Do not steal,' I like that one."

Another walks up, "'Remember the Sabbath and keep it holy,' are you going to put that on your plate? If you're not a Seventh Day Adventist, like me, you are fooling yourself, because the Sabbath is from Friday to Saturday, not Sunday morning."

"Really? I didn't know that. My pastor told me to be in church on Sunday morning if I didn't want to end up in hell. So nah, I'll leave it. But I'll tell you what, since I'm not going to be obeying that commandment, I'll just substitute it with the tithe...there we go. Look at that! Ten! Viola! I'm going to go sit down and eat!"

If the apostle James was in line with these people, he'd give them a quick rebuke, "Hey! There's not just ten! There are 613! You gotta take *all* of them or *leave* all of them! You can't pick and choose—or replace!" Here's what James had to say about cherry-pickers of the Law:

> *"For whoever keeps <u>the whole law</u> and yet stumbles at <u>just one point</u> is guilty of breaking <u>all</u> of it." (James 2:10)*

The Law is an all or nothing proposition. The 10 Commandments *in* the Law are the same. God does not grade us on a curve when it comes to a person attempting to be justified *through* the Law—YOU HAVE TO EAT ALL 613. James' colleague, Paul, backs him up:

> *For all who rely on the works of the Law are under a curse, as it is written: "Cursed is everyone who <u>does not continue to do everything</u> written in the Book of the Law." (Galatians 3:10)*

Everything means *everything*. Continue means *continue*. And I'm about to hit you with a *major* shocker, are you ready for this?...Unless you are Jewish, you weren't even invited to *attempt* to eat 613 laws and commands—you are a Gentile, an outsider. You have no papers to prove you belong, therefore you'd be deported. Only Jesus has brought you in. *You* are only allowed to live by the *New* Covenant, not the Old. Here's proof:

> *"There is <u>no longer Jew or Gentile,</u> slave or free, male and female. For you are all <u>one</u> in Christ Jesus." (Galatians 3:28)*

A Gentile is simply anyone who isn't Jewish. So when a Gentile attempts to eat from the buffet line of Law, they are infringing on a family meal in which they don't belong. "Who are you and what are you doing trying to be like us?" they'd say.

But even they couldn't eat all 613! That's why Jesus came to give us a new agreement with God and to make the old agreement obsolete! The writer to the Hebrews—to the *Jews*—let them know about this Changing of the Guard:

> *By calling this covenant "new," he has made the first one obsolete (see Hebrews 8:13)*

The Old Covenant is obsolete, just like the pay-phone is obsolete. It's not needed because it's useless and something better is here! Further, as non-Jews, the *only* Covenant we *ever* had is the New one! When we read about the Law and the prophets—all of the Jewish patriarchs, matriarchs, events, and lineage—we are reading history books! As Gentiles, that was not written to us! It is all true and good, it belongs in the Bible, but it is not our mail. Our inbox begins after Jesus died—not when He was born—but when He died. Look:

> *"because a will is in force only when somebody has died; it never takes effect while the one who made it is living" (Hebrews 9:17)*

A will is a covenant, an agreement. We could not inherit anything from God in regard to the New Covenant until Jesus died. Why did He need to die? Because the entire sin of the world was on Him, and sin needed to be dealt with once and for all (see John 1:29, 2 Corinthians 5:21).

For the Jews of today who still attempt to live by the 613—less the bloody ones (cherry-pickers!)—they too are fooling themselves. Standing by, waiting on the Messiah to come, they are in limbo because they don't believe Jesus was He. They want to continue reading obsolete paperwork and wail at a wall! The internet is here, but they enjoy toting around a library of encyclopedias! It's silly! It's useless! WE HAVE

A NEW COVENANT OF GRACE! We have a New Covenant of God making His home *inside* of us for good! Not coming and going based on our performance and prayers!

So! If you read the four gospels—Matthew, Mark, Luke, and John—with *these* glasses on (New Covenant glasses), you will be able to decipher the crazy talk of Jesus when it comes to obeying Mosaic Law. For the legalist reading this, I'm here to tell you that you are right. Jesus *didn't* come to get rid of the Law but to make sure we knew the standard of it: *perfection*.

If you want to follow Law, you must do it flawlessly. The self-righteous Jews who thought they actually *were* following every single command, Christ upped the ante by showing them Law 2.0:

"You have heard, 'Do not murder,' but I tell you, if you even get angry with someone it is the same." (See Matthew 5:21-22)

"You have heard, 'Do not commit adultery,' but I tell you, if you even lust after a woman it is the same." (See Matthew 5:27-28)

"If your eye causes you to sin, pluck it out! If your hand makes you stumble, cut it off!" (See Matthew 5:29-30)

Every person listening to Jesus who thought they were following *all* of God's laws and commandments got a lump in their throat. They began to sweat, loosen up their collar, and gulp...they were beginning to realize it was impossible to crest the great Mountain of Law. All who attempted to do so, would die. Either that, or His listeners became angry and started to plot against Him because of their inability to realize living by the Law was not possible.

Jesus was making the "well behaved" folk look like complete failures by lifting the bar up so high *nobody* could vault over it. These religious people refused to see that there *had* to be another way. They hated the grace Jesus brought, even to the point of murdering Him. "That's too much grace! He is giving people a license to sin! We will put an end to that!"

Much to their frustration, Jesus never said, "Try your best and God will judge accordingly." Nope. He said, *be perfect like God is perfect* (see Matthew 5:48). He said, "If you think Moses gave you some tough stuff to do, try this on for size." Just look at how He talked to the rich, young ruler; a man who braggadociously claimed to follow *all* of the commandments for his entire life:

"All these I have kept," the young man said. "What do I still lack?"
Jesus answered, "If you want to be perfect, go, sell your possessions and give to the poor, and you will have treasure in heaven. Then come, follow me." (Matthew 19:20-21)

The man went away sad because he could not do it! Jesus pointed out that *one* thing which was keeping him from understanding grace! Grace is unearnable! Jesus wasn't against this fellow having money, He was trying to say, "You need me alone! Your observance of the Law, good living, and charity work will never get you to heaven! You will never know me until you know my grace alone!"

He was telling him about the gospel. The gospel is very insulting to those who think they can add to it or maintain it with works. *The gospel of grace*, Paul called it (see Acts 20:24), is Jesus plus nothing else. The gospel kicks our ego in the pants, slaps it on the back of the neck, and says, "Get outta here! You're not needed!"

The gospel *isn't* believing in Jesus plus obeying 9 commandments. It isn't a patch-job of 9 plus 1 to even them out. It's *just* Him. As insulting as it may seem to some, faith in Christ *alone* is the undiluted grace of God. It is us becoming His kids. It is God's commitment to us, not the other way around. It is us benefiting from the Father and Son's agreement, with open hands. It is Jesus *in* us, for good, which is our only hope of eternal glory! (See John 1:12, Hebrews 6:19, 7:25, 2 Timothy 2:13, Colossians 1:27, 3:3, Romans 6:6).

Jesus didn't come to abolish the Law but to show how much you need him *because* of the Law. The only reason why the Law was brought into play was to increase our recognition of our need for grace. The Law was given by Moses *just* to point out our dirty faces even more! Why? So that grace could increase even more! Read what Paul told the Roman Christians:

> *"The Law was brought in so that the trespass might increase. But where sin increased, grace increased all the more" (Romans 5:20)*

God's grace comes through our belief. For this reason, even *before* the Law was given by Moses, all relationships with God were built on faith alone—through belief! The animal sacrifices didn't justify people, but instead, reminded them of how badly they messed up (see Hebrews 10:4). God has always been interested in just *one* main thing: *do you believe Him?* Abraham, who lived way before Moses was born, he was justified by believing God and nothing more. It's in the first book of the Bible:

> *"Abram <u>believed</u> the LORD, and he credited it to him as righteousness." (Genesis 15:6)*

Friend, God wants us to believe Him. He wanted the Jews to believe Him before and after the Law, and now, He wants us to believe Him about Jesus. Keeping the commandments of Christ is not the problem. The problem is, for so many, *defining* His commandments.

Belief and love are the two new commandments we live by according to the agreement with God *Jesus* brought in at the Cross. If we believe God, we'll believe Jesus. That's first. Second is love. If we love someone, we won't kill them. If we love someone, we won't commit adultery. If we love someone, we won't be jealous of them. If we love someone, we'll forgive them! Do you see it? This is why Jesus said He is giving us a new command of love:

> *"A new command I give you: Love one another. As I have loved you, so you must love one another. By this everyone will know that you are my disciples, if you love one another." (John 13:34-35)*

To be clear, love is not helping us keep the Law. Love is not helping women stay in their houses during that time of the month. Love is not helping us resist pork-chops and shrimp fettuccine. We are dead *to* Law—all of it—so *that* we can be alive in Christ! We live by a new way of the Spirit leading us with wise counsel and love! (See Galatians 2:19, Romans 7:4-6).

The world will know that Jesus lives in us if we love! Sure, people will annoy us, and sure, we have to set healthy boundaries, but we still have a love inside our spirits which will never go away because we've been born of God by grace through faith! (See 1 John 5:4, Ephesians 2:8-9). The reason why our inherent love will not fade away is because love is a part of our supernatural DNA as reborn saints! The Spirit *of* love, God, lives in us and we in Him! (See 1 John 4:8, Colossians 3:3, 1 Corinthians 6:19).

So today, my friends, know this: To keep the commandments of Christ, be yourself. If you are a Christian, you already have love and belief intertwined with the fabric of your spiritual being. You *are* loving! You *do* believe! So be yourself today and let those who are around you enjoy Jesus Christ, who is in you!

A prayer for you: *Heavenly Father, thank you for teaching me so much through your Spirit. For so long, I thought that I had to be at a geographical location to learn about you, which was wrong. I am your location, and you teach me everywhere I go. I also thought that if I didn't constantly feel something, you had left me—that is a lie too. From your Holy Spirit, I've learned not to live my life from my feelings, but from my knowing. I KNOW that I am your child and nothing can change this fact! Not even me! In your Word, in 1 John, you tell us that* *your commands are not burdensome. The Law of Moses WAS burdensome. The Ten Commandments WERE burdensome. Thank you for the new commandments of belief and love! Thank you for freedom from the Law! Your Law is SO good and perfect, I had to turn to grace! Thank you. I am free. Right now, I lift up all who are reading this, directly to you. For those who think they need to sprinkle in some law with your grace, let them know it's not needed. Let them know a drop of law is a drop of poison. Let them know it is your Spirit who teaches us how to live our lives according to your approval, and according to our identity. We are heaven-ready, right now, in our spirits. Therefore, our spirits will guide us into proper living and morality—not tablets of stone or words on a page. It is YOUR Spirit who makes OUR spirit holy! It is your Spirit who guides us into all truth and counsels us! Set legalistic mindsets free today as we begin to live by Jesus' commandments of belief and love—only! In His name I pray, amen.*

Day 3

Why Should I Forgive Others?

*"Above all, love each other deeply, because
love covers over a multitude of sins."*

1 Peter 4:8

Many Christians have forgiveness all wrong. Because of bad teaching—mixing the Old Covenant in with the New—they think they *have* to forgive others or else God won't forgive them. As God's kids, we don't *have* to do anything, *and* we won't be punished if we don't. What do you think the Cross was for? Jesus took on *all* our punishment, once and for all (see 1 Peter 3:18, Hebrews 10:10).

"Matt, you're a liar! The Word of God says, forgive others or else your Father in heaven *won't* forgive you!"

Friend, I know it does. But this verse is before the Cross and it was spoken to the hypocritical people who thought their wonderful forgiveness was earning them righteousness with God. It wasn't. And that was Jesus' whole point. "You can't forgive your way to heaven, you need to be reborn completely. Faith in me *alone* is the only way that will happen." This was the gist of Jesus' teaching to the legalists.

God doesn't forgive us because we are wonderful forgivers. Just imagine if that were true, we'd all be doomed. So when you read impossible teachings of Christ, He was either A.) speaking spiritually, or B.) raising the bar on living by Mosaic Law.

Jesus was trying to teach us that we can't earn our spot with God through *anything* we do—even forgiving others. If we *do* believe that our forgiveness buys us favor with God, we become martyrs or hypocrites. There is no middle ground. The point of this impossible passage is to corral us into the narrow gate of grace.

"So Matt, you're saying we never have to forgive others? Apostate!"

No, that's not what I'm saying at all. I'm saying we *get* to forgive others because we are forgiving people at heart. And in Christianity, apostasy is impossible because the Father will never break His promise to Jesus (see 2 Timothy 2:13, Hebrews 6:19, 7:25, 15:5). You can't be un-born from God, just the same as you can't be un-born from your mom. You either *are* a Christian, or you never truly believed. Many people dress up and play church, but still, Jesus has never known them (see Matthew 7:21-23). But that subject will be for another time.

As for forgiveness on *this* side of the Cross, as *New* Covenant believers we are to forgive others because forgiveness is a part of our spiritual DNA. We've been born of God, God lives in us, so we have a natural desire *to* forgive, just like God. We even want to forgive those who don't deserve it—just like God.

However, we don't forgive to *get* forgiven, but instead, we forgive because we *are* forgiven. Just look at how Paul taught the early church:

> *"Bear with each other and forgive one another if any of you has a grievance against someone. Forgive as the Lord <u>forgave</u> you." (Colossians 3:13)*

See? Paul tells the Colossians to forgive because God *already* forgave them. Past-tense. He didn't say, "You *better* forgive or else!"

Let's look at another New Covenant epistle passage from Paul (tongue-twister there!):

> *"Be kind and compassionate to one another, forgiving each other, just as in Christ God <u>forgave</u> you." (Ephesians 4:32)*

Again he says, "forgave." We should be kind, compassionate, and forgiving because that's what we've already received from God through Jesus' sacrifice at the Cross. We don't forgive to get forgiven or to maintain our forgiveness but because we *are* forgiven people—and we know it! It makes sense to forgive others because Jesus forgave us!

"Matt, I'm *not* forgiving them! You just don't understand what they've done to me!"

Friend, I know it's hard. I know very well about the feelings you have. There have been times in my life when the enemy has convinced me that if I forgive someone who's hurt me, they'll just do it again—and they might. But that is a risk we have to take as heaven-ready saints. No, we don't want them to hurt us again but we have forgiveness built into us as a reflex. Just like we have the reflex of blinking and breathing, we can't stop forgiving others even if we wanted to. Our spirits would never allow us to deny forgiveness. An internal battle will continue until we do. Our hearts will cry out until the very moment we release them from their debt. Peace only happens in our minds when we choose to forgive.

When you forgive, you are exuding the character of God. Again, God is in you. He's meshed together with your spirit (see Colossians 3:3, Romans 6:6, Galatians 2:20, 1 Corinthians 6:19). Forgiveness is wise and it cleanses the palate of your soul from sour tastes. Forgiveness is an atomic bomb used in spiritual warfare, and we have our finger on the button at all times.

The problem is, even as Christians, so many of us have forgiveness confused with trust. Because of this befuddlement, we choose *not* to forgive because we don't want to be hurt again. However, forgiveness is *not* trust. Forgiveness is a choice. It is an act of our will. It has nothing to do with our feelings. It is instant, free, and for ourselves.

Trust, on the other hand, is none of those things. Trust is earned, expensive, and for the other person. Forgiveness is a gift you give to *you*. Trust is a gift you give to *them*.

When we learn to separate the two—forgiveness and trust—we can grow deeper into our relationships. Forgiving someone doesn't even require the other person to acknowledge what they've done was wrong. But for trust, they *need* to know that what they've done has pained you. With forgiveness, they don't *have* to know you've forgiven them. Although with trust, *it* requires healthy boundaries to be established and respected.

Since before time, God knew that humanity was going to need forgiveness, both with Him and with each other. This is why Jesus planned on coming to earth before it was even physically formed (see Colossians 1:15-17, Romans 5:8, John 1:1-5, 8:58).

How do you know if you've truly forgiven the other person?...You have peace. The pain they've caused is no longer a part of your life even if the damage is still there. Forgiveness separates your mind from your circumstances. How do you know if you can *trust* that person again?... You don't. We are human beings. Relationships are not static. So rather than gauge if you can trust them or not, allow the Holy Spirit to guide you each day. He'll not steer you wrong.

So today, my friends, if you are struggling with forgiveness—if you are in pain, torment, anger, and frustration—say this prayer with me to release the other person *and* yourself. I'm not saying trust them. I'm not saying reconcile. That may or may not happen. I'm saying forgive in full because *forgive* is what you do.

It could be a spouse, ex-spouse, coach, teacher, child, parent or relative. It could be the spouse *of* your child or their ex. It could be your in-law, an ex-boyfriend or girlfriend, or a current boyfriend or girlfriend. You might even need to forgive your actual neighbor, pastor, foster parent, step parent, step child, co-worker, boss, or *whoever*. Say this prayer of forgiveness with me and release yourself from pain. Say this prayer, and begin to *be* yourself as a child of God, a forgiving person:

> *"Heavenly Father, you see how much pain I'm in over what they've done to me. This person, _____, owes me big time. They've hurt me by _____, and I know you've seen it. But I also know that Jesus saw all of my mistakes and He still chose to forgive me in full with no strings attached. All I had to do was believe I was forgiven by Him, and I was. I'm so grateful for that! Through His example, and because I have His Spirit in me, strengthening me, I know I can forgive this person too! Today, I'm asking that you give me the grace to pull this off as I am making a conscious decision to forgive them completely—even if they do it again. Thank you for such peace! Remind me that I have forgiven them, and teach me how to establish healthy boundaries to protect myself in the future. In Christ's name I pray, amen."*

Day 4

How to Deal with Your Spiritual Perfection

> *"But now he has reconciled you by Christ's physical body through death to present you holy in his sight, without blemish and free from accusation"*
>
> Colossians 1:22

As a Christian, facing the truth about yourself is hard. For me, this juncture of my life was something that did not feel natural. "Who do you think you are, saying you are spiritually perfect?" the enemy whispered quite often.

However, facing the fact about having a perfect spirit was the turning point to enjoying a deeper relationship with God. I stopped hesitating as I stood on the cliff of religion, and instead, I jumped off into the ocean of God's grace.

Because I had been told that I'm a bad person for so long, by actual Christian teachers, I believed them. Satan works hard in the pulpits every Sunday morning as preachers beat people down, lying to believers about what God has truly done inside of them. Like so many others, I too was a victim of trash teaching, "You are a dirty sinner! You are rotten at heart! You need to feed the *good* part of you and starve the bad!" WRONG.

I have a good heart, all Christians do. How is this possible? Because God has made His home *in* my heart, after giving me a new one. Ezekiel foretold what our Creator would do in us, way before Jesus was even born:

> *"I will give you a new heart and put a new spirit in you; I will remove from you your heart of stone and give you a heart of flesh." (Ezekiel 36:26)*

God has given us a *soft* heart, a good heart. Stupid teaching will cause a preacher to pull a verse out of context from Jeremiah, which says we have wicked hearts (see Jeremiah 17:9). Nope. We *did* have wicked hearts, and now we don't. Jesus will not live in wicked places.

Therefore, we don't have a *good* part of us and a *bad* part of us—one to starve and one to feed. That's called schizophrenia. We are not at battle with ourselves! WE ARE COMPLETE! We simply need to *be* ourselves as heaven-ready saints, which we are in our spirits! (See Romans 1:7, 2 Corinthians 1:1). You don't need to "get out of Jesus' way," you need to be you!

Now, can we make bad choices that do not match up with our spiritual perfection? Absolutely. We still live on a fallen planet in which there are many players: the power of sin, Satan, his demons, poor choices of *other* people, flawed DNA, temptations for our flesh, so on and so forth. Lots of things, situations, circumstances, and people can influence us from *not* living organically. This is not heaven. Heaven is *in* us, but our physical bodies are not there (see Ephesian 2:6, Philippians 1:21).

But as for us believers in Christ, we have perfect spirits no matter what is going on in our environment. Despite what our attitudes and actions may be *because* of our environment's influence, we remain steady at heart. Choices do not change identity! Legalistic people hate this fact, but a spade is a spade! A child of God is a child of God!

It was Paul's goal to convince believers in Christ of their spiritual perfection, and he had a very difficult time doing so. As I learn more about this truth myself, I can see the soul of Paul spring from the pages of his teachings. He was passionate, to say the least, about informing people of what Jesus had really done for them. What's He done? Well, we Christians are ready for heaven, in full, right now! We have no reason to be afraid of God, and no part of us is bad! (See 1 John 4:18, Romans 8:1).

Again, can we make bad decisions? Yes! But those bad decisions do not surprise God, and they do not alter our everlasting genetic code. How is this possible?...Jesus.

Our problem is we are focused on our actions and attitudes and not on our identity. It is impossible for any of us to become more righteous than we are right now at this very moment. What Jesus did at the Cross, and our faith in that brutal punishment, *causes* us to receive from God, a new, righteous spirit! (See Romans 6:6-7, 2 Corinthians 5:17, Galatians 2:20, Ephesians 2:8-9). We are reborn! The spirit inside you has a new genetic code that is born *of* God! (See John 3:7, 1 John 3:9). This new birth of yours resulted in you being on the same level as Jesus, in your spirit! (See John 1:12, Romans 8:17, 1 John 4:17). Whether you felt something or not, this free righteousness by way of being spiritually reborn happened the very moment you believed it happened!

When this happened, what we owed God was paid for in full—DEATH! Sin requires death (see Romans 6:23). Why do you think Jesus *had* to die? Now, for those who think that what they are doing and not doing *completes* or *sustains* what Jesus did—I'm sorry, but you are wrong. If you could add to Jesus' sacrifice to complete it, or sustain it, the gospel would be based on "earned rewards." In turn, grace would not be grace. Paul tells the Romans this truth:

> *"And if by grace, then it cannot be based on works; if it were, grace would no longer be grace." (Romans 11:6)*

We don't "get" our salvation, we receive it. "Getting" means you are reaching out to take it, receiving means you are standing still with your hands open while saying, "Thank you." Just like you can't get or sustain your earthly DNA, you can't get or sustain your spiritual DNA. It's a gift! Paul explains how perfect we are in spirit, to the Christians in Colossae:

> *"But now he has reconciled you by Christ's physical body through death to present you holy in his sight, without blemish and free from accusation" (Colossians 1:22)*

Do you see that it was Jesus' physical body that reconciled us with our Creator? Why is that important? Because physical bodies die, because their *spirits* are sinful. Jesus' spirit was not sinful! Further, He never *committed* a single sin in His entire life! Therefore, He did not deserve to die. We did, He didn't.

The sin of the world had to be paid off with the Father once and for all, Jesus knew this. And because He loves us so much, He decided to take care of this problem which *would have* resulted in eternal separation from God. Jesus did not enjoy going to the Cross but He knew what would happen if He did! Therefore, He *became* sin so that *we* could become right with God!

> *"For our sake he made him to be sin who knew no sin, so that in him we might become the righteousness of God." (2 Corinthians 5:21)*

YOU ARE THE RIGHTEOUSNESS OF GOD! All of humanity now has the option to become one with God forever—by grace through faith! The power of sin and death has been dealt with for good! Christian, do you not know who you are?

To be clear, Jesus did not enjoy Friday, but He knew Sunday was coming! The author of Hebrews pens this truth:

> *"For the joy set before him he endured the cross, scorning its shame" (see Hebrews 12:2)*

What would compel Jesus to do such a thing? LOVE! HE LOVES YOU! God, the Father *loves* you! Jesus loves you! The Holy Spirit *loves* you! This is why the Trinity wanted to make you spiritually perfect just like them! Look!

> *"But God demonstrates his own love for us in this: While we were still sinners, Christ died for us." (Romans 5:8)*

C'MON PEOPLE, THIS IS *GOOD* NEWS! This is why the gospel literally means *good news*! God loved us so much He sent His only begotten Son to this planet, to play by His own rules, and to pay off a debt that we could never pay for ourselves! What a good God! What more could you possibly ask for?

The self-centered Christian will blurt out, "Yeah right, Matt! God is mad at us! His wrath is coming down hard on everybody!"

Bud, no it's not. Not on Christians. What in the *world* do you think the Cross was for? Partial payment? What a moronic idea, as if God decided to only take care of *some* of our sin at Calvary; as if He's yelling at us, "Those don't count!" The notion of us, created beings, having the power to add to Jesus' crucifixion by what we do and don't do? Wow. Sounds like pride to me. It actually sounds demonic. But anyway.

Listen, Jesus took on the wrath of God—completely—at that Cross. God's plan actually worked, believe it or not! He's not naive, He's a genius! So go ahead and try to add to what He's finished and Jesus might just say, "I never knew you," after everything fades to black. Please hear me, we are at *peace* with God, freely. Jesus' body took on the Father's wrath for good:

> *"Since we have now been justified by his blood, how much more shall we be saved from God's wrath through him!" (Romans 5:9)*

Do you see that? Paul asked a rhetorical question and didn't even put a question mark at the end of it. Instead, he yelled to get his point across.

We've been saved from God's wrath *through* Jesus' body...through His bloodshed. This is why we should have a mindset of peace:

> *"Therefore, since we have been justified through faith, we have peace with God through our Lord Jesus Christ" (Romans 5:1)*

So today, my friends, know this: You have peace with God. It's a peace which comes through Jesus. Yes, this peace is totally unfair, no matter how you look at it—grace *isn't* fair. It wasn't fair for Jesus, and it's not fair for us. But grace is good, so good! This peace allows us to be justified with God, which means you've been perfected in spirit. God requires sin-free perfection, and this only happens *once* and for all time (see Hebrews 10:10, 14).

"But Matt, how is this possible?"

By way of faith! Believe! From the beginning of Creation, God has been interested in one main thing: "Do you believe me?" Had Adam and Eve believed God, they would have never did what they did, same with us. If *you'd* believe God when He says you are perfected inside, you'd live that way! Begin to believe Him today! Begin to believe He's recreated you as a perfect individual! Believe Jesus! Believe what He's done for you! Believe what He's done *in* you!...Believing the truth changes everything.

> **A prayer for you:** *Good morning, Dad. Thank you for teaching me the truth of who you've made me to be. For so long, I kept insulting myself all the time because I thought those insults were the truth—you've taught me otherwise. I thought I was being humble, but I was actually lying. Insulting myself is not what you want me to do at all. Instead, you want me to be real, honest, talk about my struggles, and then stay focused on the real me, my spirit. My spirit is absolutely perfect just like you! You've killed off my old spirit, given me a new spirit, and then made your home IN my spirit! I'm forever grateful! Right now, I lift up all who are reading this, directly to you. So many of them have*

been lied to by the grace-confused Christians, they don't know what to believe. But if you live in them, you are already hard at work trying to convince them of who they are, which is spiritually perfect! Once they begin to actually believe this, they will live it out! Sure, they'll mess up, but they'll still know who you've made them to be and that those mess-ups don't define them in any way. Open up their hearts and minds today to this wonderful truth! The truth of what Jesus has done for us! FREE SPIRITUAL PERFECTION FOREVER! ABSOLUTE, HEAVENLY PERFECTION! In His name I pray, amen.

Day 5

The Truth About God's Anointing

*"But you have an anointing from the Holy
One, and all of you know the truth."*

1 John 2:20

Have you ever heard someone say, "I'm anointed to _____!"? You can fill in the blank because there are many flavors of people claiming to be anointed—and their "anointing" is always better than yours. That is, if you even *have* an anointing. I say this sarcastically because this is the gist of a lot of smoke-and-mirror teaching out there.

Some claim they are anointed to preach, and *some* preachers even claim they are anointed just so their congregations will give them more money. Isn't it amazing how the only people getting rich off of tithing are the anointed preachers who teach that tithing will get you rich?

"You just gotta have more faith and *give* more! If your tithing isn't working, give me—er, I mean *God*—give God, an offering above the tithe! Then He'll *really* open up the floodgates of heaven and pour out a blessing you can't contain! It will be all over your lap! *Test* Him in this and you'll see! If your faith is big enough, He'll pay you back a ten-fold portion!"

Trash. I'll stop my description of that teaching with one word.

Some people claim they are anointed to sing, and others even call themselves "anointed prayer warriors." Why do we need to be prayer *warriors*? As if we are at battle with our loving Heavenly Father, "fighting hard" to get Him to change His mind? Why not just ask Dad, and then trust Him? And who in the world anoints prayer warriors to *be* prayer warriors, other than themselves? Nobody.

Some people are even making the claim that they are anointed to prophesy, as if they are modern-day future-tellers like the prophets of the Old Covenant. New Covenant prophesying is meant to build people up and encourage them with God's truth, not freak them out by saying, "God told me to tell you to go to Antarctica and start an orphanage for baby penguins." BULLCRAP. God's Spirit talks to each of us directly, we don't need some yahoo to be our middle-man.

Are we blind to such stupid arrogance? Has our egos gotten in the way of the gospel? And have you ever noticed that those who claim to be anointed, claimed that anointing for themselves? That, or their momma did?...I'm kidding, but honestly, if this subject upsets you, you've fallen way off course. THE GOSPEL AIN'T ABOUT YOU—and I'm not sorry to say that. I love you, but please refocus on Christ. Only then will you see what I mean.

Friend, if you've experienced someone saying, "I'm anointed!" let me ask you, how did that make you feel? More than likely it made you feel like you *weren't* anointed, as if you were lacking something that only *they* had. The devil loves this. He loves it when we put on religious outfits with the goal of having people gaze toward our presence, thinking, "Wow, look at how holy they are." Lucifer loves it when we believe that God is treating *others* as if they are more important than us. He *loves* factions. He *loves* denominations. He loves pride.

Today, I plan on punching this idiot in his face with this devotional. I want to ease your mind and help you recognize his demonic lies. Here's the *truth* about God's anointing:

1. All Christians are anointed on the exact same level because we are anointed with God's Spirit. Our good, good Father does not have favorite kids.
2. God is not doling out "special anointings" on this side of the Cross. Old Testament anointings were meant to protect the line of Judah, which Christ came from. Now that Jesus is here, that stuff is over.

So what does *anointed* even mean? The definition is: *to smear or rub with oil*. So why are modern-day Christians hootin' and hollerin' up on stage saying they are anointed? I mean, after all, I don't see them drenched in olive oil. And aren't we supposed to be exuding self-control? (See Galatians 5:22-23).

Here's what's wrong with this insanity: they've taken their eyes off of the undiluted truth of the gospel. They might have started with it, but now they are trying to add to it, make it better, or sustain it.

When we take our eyes off the gospel—God freely making His home in us for good—and instead fixate on what we *think* our gifts are, bad stuff happens. *Arrogant* stuff happens. It's sad to say but we've switched the word "gift" with "anointing." This has thrown a huge monkey-wrench into the gears of our churches. It has created envy, resentment, hierarchies, and confusion, all of which is exactly what Satan wants for us. His desire is to cloud up the waters of God's grace with stupid crap that doesn't matter.

We have to stop this mess and refocus on what the truth is about Christians being anointed. We are all anointed the same! I'm not talking about your gifts and talents, I'm talking about God's Spirit living inside of yours! John attempts to explain this phenomenon as he wrote to the early Christians:

> *"But you have an anointing from the Holy One, and all of you know the truth." (1 John 2:20)*

We have an anointing from the Holy One! We've been *smeared* with His Spirit because we've been placed *inside* His Spirit! Unlike pre-Cross anointings of the Old Testament, we are not *being* anointed to *be* called to do great things, but we've *been* anointed with God's own Spirit, so we *are* called to do great things! Use-it-or-lose-it is a lie for New Covenant believers! Every Christian is equally called to act according to God's purposes because He is infused with our spirits! WE ARE ONE *WITH* HIM! Just look at what Paul told the Colossians:

> *"For you died, and your life is now hidden with Christ in God." (Colossians 3:3)*

Do you see that little two-letter word I've underlined—*in*? Your old spirit died, and now your *new* spirit's life is hidden with Jesus Christ *in* God! Ain't nobody gonna win a hide-and-seek challenge with the Creator of the universe! You are hidden away inside of Him for good! YOU ARE *INSIDE* OF GOD'S SPIRIT!

What does this have to do with anointing? Well, the only way you could be hidden in Him is if you were spiritually smeared with His Spirit. Friend, are you getting this? In the spiritual realm, Christian, you are inside of God! Smeared with! Anointed! But not only that, God is inside of you! It's hard to understand this because our minds are finite, but Paul still tries to put it in words when he wrote to the Corinthians:

> **"Do you not know that your bodies are temples of the Holy Spirit, who is in you, whom you have received from God? You are not your own"** *(1 Corinthians 6:19)*

Believer, the Maker of the heavens and earth is in you! God *is* Spirit and He is in you! In that physical body of yours God resides, and in that body, your spirit resides *with* Him. You've been mashed together with God Almighty and there is no difference between your spirits because you are one! You are separate, but you are one! How can this be? How can we be in God and God in us? How can Paul tell the Colossians they are *in* God, but then he tells the Corinthians that God is in *them*? HOW?

I've used some different examples in my writings of this anomaly, such as a handkerchief being immersed in a glass of water. Both the water and handkerchief remain separate, but both are now inside of each other. Here is a new one, the example of water and a tea-bag:

Let's say you have a glass of hot water, and you have a tea-bag, again, both are separate. You take the tea-bag and place it in the hot water and what happens? Does the tea-bag disappear? No. Does the water? No. They become *one*, yet they are still separate. The tea-bag and the water get mixed together and there is no changing it back. The combination is complete even though the elements of both are still individual.

This same thing happens with your spirit and God's Spirit from the very moment you first believe Jesus has forgiven you! The only difference is you, as a tea-bag, is that you have to be a new, resurrected tea-bag *before* you can be joined to Him! This happens *once* by grace through faith! (See Ephesians 2:8-9, John 1:12, Hebrews 10:10). Your old tea-bag spirit has to first be killed off so that God can give you your new tea-bag spirit! Only then can you be immersed in the water of Jesus Christ! (see Romans 6:6-7, 2 Corinthians 5:17, Galatians 2:20, 3:27).

THIS IS HOW YOU ARE *TRULY* ANOINTED!

"But Matt, what about James 5:14? That verse is from a New Testament letter, and it talks about anointing people with oil to be healed."

This is a very legitimate question, and if we read that passage in context, we will see the correct meaning. Crazy idea, right? To actually take Scripture to heart in context? I know, I know, it's not normal, but let's try it out. Here's the verse in full:

> *"Is anyone among you sick? Let them call the elders of the church to pray over them and anoint them with oil in the name of the Lord." (James 5:14)*

This verse is a call for church members to pray for sick people, it's not a gathering to perform an oily magic trick. It is in that *prayer*, from a group of God's children, that we have the *opportunity* to be healed. It's not in the oil, but in the prayer. That oil is but a symbol, in the same way that water in water baptism is a symbol. Neither have any supernatural power. If jugs of water and Wesson Cooking Oil had power, then Wal-Mart wouldn't be able to keep it on the shelves. Power from God doesn't come from *any* physical thing, it comes from His Spirit within us! *We* are the ones who are anointed with power, because *we* have the Holy One inside our spirits!

So today, my friends, know this: All Christians are equally anointed because all Christians have the Spirit of God in them. Do we have different gifts? Sure. Are we each individual body parts in the Body of Christ? Absolutely! We all have different functions! God likes variety and we all work together! However, we are *still* equal in His eyes. It doesn't matter if we are on stage singing and preaching, or if we are showing people where the restrooms are and helping in the nursery. It doesn't matter if we are writing books, or taking care of the kids after school. It doesn't matter if we are doing mission trips in South America, or reading the Bible with our teenager after dinner—WE. ARE. EQUAL. Our geographical location does not make us more anointed and neither do our gifts! We *all* have God's Spirit living in us and through us—equally! We *all* are anointed with God in full! Let's enjoy Him and live Him out!

> **A prayer for you:** *Father, thank you for your anointing. For so long, I thought that if I wasn't heavily involved in church work I wasn't anointed. That was a lie from Satan to make me feel not good enough. He always wants me to feel like I'm a two out of ten, but your Spirit always reveals the truth—that I'm off the charts with you! That's why you chose to live in me! Thank you so much! Right now, I lift up all who are reading this, directly to you. So many of them have felt inadequate because of the misrepresentation of the gospel from self-centered people. They've heard others proclaim that they are anointed to do certain*

things, and these lies have created stress for these dear readers. You don't want us stressed out, so reveal the truth—you don't have favorite kids! They've felt left out, so please let them know you've included them in full! Reveal that when Jesus was lifted up, He drew all people to Himself! HE INCLUDED US FOREVER! And by faith alone He makes His home in us, anointing us for good, with Himself. We are grateful for this! Take us deeper into the knowledge of such grace, and give us wisdom about our true anointing. In Christ's awesome name I pray, amen.

Day 6

What to do During Dormant Seasons of Life

> *He (Jesus) told them another parable: "The kingdom of heaven is like a mustard seed, which a man took and planted in his field. Though it is the smallest of all seeds, yet when it grows, it is the largest of garden plants and becomes a tree, so that the birds come and perch in its branches."*
>
> Matthew 13:31-32

"God, I know you're with me, but it hurts. It hurts so bad. It's been *so* long, and I'm still waiting. Please do something. I'm asking you again, please, change this for me. I hurt."

The prayers of a man who understands God's grace, compassion, good plans and love, flow out once again to His Creator's ears…yet… silence is all he feels.

"Father, I know I don't have to feel anything, I *know* you are with me and you love me, but I'm asking you again today to *please* fix this. I trust you, and I know that whatever you decide, I'll be more than fine. But I want this. I want this season to pass. I want you to answer this prayer how I'm asking you to, and please do it quickly. If you choose not to, for whatever reason, strengthen me. I love you."

The conversation continues for just a while longer, and then the man gets on with his day.

Prayer. Prayer is so important. Prayer allows us to communicate with God. Like a child who talks to their loving parent and *trusts* them, we too have this right with our Maker. However, this devotional isn't about prayer, but instead, it's about the cold, windy, dormant seasons of life. As we experience such, prayer keeps us warm inside. Each and every prayer is but a log on the fire in our souls.

Dormant seasons are necessary in the wilderness. Although we may not see anything happening, a *lot* is happening underground and in the plants, insects, and animals. Not on the outside, but inside, things are very busy—same with us as children of God. We don't like the cold seasons, we want to always be seeing and feeling growth. We want to constantly be enjoying a harvest.

But in order to be able to reap a harvest, sowing must take place, there is no way around it. To become fully mature, we must understand God's process of allowing the seed of His Spirit to germinate inside of us. If we are patient, we will benefit greatly. If we aren't, we will live in misery because we don't *see* or *feel* anything happening.

Paul knew such a season would come to the Christians in Corinth, he understood they would experience dry times. For this reason he wanted them to focus on the truth of what they *knew*, rather than on the dread of what they *saw*:

"For we walk by faith, not by sight." (2 Corinthians 5:7)

We have to focus on God's love for us, faith is what allows this to happen. Faith is a knowing, not a feeling. It is a knowing that no matter how trying times may be, we are *still* infinitely loved by God. As we continue to water our lives with this truth, dormant seasons can be used in a positive way. Even Jesus faced a dormant season as He begged the Father to come up with another way to save the world from sin...but God said, "No." (See Matthew 26:39).

So by looking to His example, and because He lives in us, during our own difficult seasons of life we must remember that God still cares. We must remember that He still has a good overall plan for *all* of humanity—the Cross proves this! What seemed like the darkest day in history was actually preparation for the most beautiful! That difficult event allowed the kingdom of God to be *inside* of us, right now, today! Not when we die, but now! (See Mark 1:15, Matthew 13).

Solomon, who was named by Jesus as a man filled with splendor (see Matthew 6:29), had wisdom that was unmatched. He wrote about the seasons of life in Ecclesiastes:

> *There is a time for everything,*
> *and a season for every activity under the heavens:*
> *a time to be born and a time to die,*
> *a time to plant and a time to uproot,*
> *a time to kill and a time to heal,*
> *a time to tear down and a time to build,*
> *a time to weep and a time to laugh,*
> *a time to mourn and a time to dance,*
> *a time to scatter stones and a time to gather them,*
> *a time to embrace and a time to refrain from embracing,*
> *a time to search and a time to give up,*
> *a time to keep and a time to throw away,*
> *a time to tear and a time to mend,*
> *a time to be silent and a time to speak,*
> *a time to love and a time to hate,*
> *a time for war and a time for peace.*

(Ecclesiastes 3:1-8)

Balance. Solomon was wise because he knew about being well-balanced. The seasons of life bring balance to us all. They are constantly changing but constantly causing growth *through* balance. On this side of the Cross, the Holy Spirit counsels us all day long...into balance.

Friend, give it time. God has not forgotten about you. He understands your situation deeper than even you do, and He loves you. You are His child. Allow this season of difficulty to teach you how to enjoy life as it is. Joy is inside you! It really is! Joy comes from within *all* children of God! I'm not talking about happiness, happiness is based on your circumstances. I'm talking about something which is a part of your supernatural genetic make-up: *joy*.

Paul tells the Galatians that joy will grow in their lives as they simply *be* themselves and walk by the Spirit of God! (See Galatians 5). You *are* a joyful person because God is enmeshed with your spirit! I'm not saying put on a fake smile and act like nothing is wrong—no way, be real! I'm saying remember who is *in* you, God. I'm saying remember who will never *leave* you, God. I'm saying, always keep things in perspective because the Creator of the universe uses all things together for good! Every single season of your life will produce something wonderful, even if you never get to see it on this side of heaven! (See Romans 8:28, Hebrews 11).

So today, my friends, do this: Enjoy your dormant seasons! *Enjoy* them! Major changes are happening beneath the surface! Stuff is moving around and getting shifted into place! A metamorphosis is occurring in your mind! What is *in* you is getting prepped to come out! Give it time, give it truth, and more than anything, ENJOY YOUR LIFE!

A prayer for you: *Good morning, Dad. Thank you for another day alive, I am grateful! As silly as it sounds to my own ears, I also want to thank you for dormant seasons because I know you are doing great things! Right now, I lift up all who are reading this, directly to you. So many of them are in deep pain, and you know that. They've been praying to you for a very long time and they want a breakthrough. Father, please give it to them. Let this season pass and a season of harvest come quickly. But whatever you decide, help them to understand you are with* *them and you'll never leave them. Help them to realize dormant seasons are vital for our maturity in you. We want to know more about our spiritual perfection, so teach us. Teach us how to respond to pain in the proper way. Teach us how to stay focused on your promises, and our heavenly heritage. Teach us who we really are as heaven-ready saints. But God, more than anything, teach us how to enjoy our lives in the midst of trouble. We want to be authentic and show the world what the Sons and Daughters of God really look like! We want to be well-balanced on the outside, because we know who we are on the inside! We love you and we trust you. During every season you bring us to, we will be positive, real, and patient. In Jesus' name I pray, amen.*

Day 7

Why Should I Give Up My Addiction?

> *"Do you not know that your bodies are temples of the Holy Spirit, who is in you, whom you have received from God? You are not your own; you were bought at a price. Therefore honor God with your bodies."*
>
> 1 Corinthians 6:19-20

"You're such a good boy," I say to my yellow lab, Harley, as I hold his face and scratch his head. "You are too, Charlie. I love you too, buddy." My Cavalier King Charles Spaniel needed to be reassured as he looked at me with jealous eyes because I was loving on Harley. I adore these two dogs. They are more like kids than dogs—they think they are anyway.

These two furry boys of mine always greet me in the morning when I get up. They want to be scratched all over and then let outside. So I do just that, and then I make my coffee. It's very early here on Saturday morning, the sun is still asleep as well as the rest of the neighborhood, but I like it that way. I like my mornings, a lot.

Used to be, I didn't get to see many mornings because I was only about 3 or 4 hours into my sleep at 5 am. And I know most people don't get up this early, but even back when I was still acting on my addiction of binge drinking, mornings were not an enjoyable time for me. They were painful.

Hangovers were a regular thing, denial *about* my hangovers—"Oh, it's not that bad today"—was an even *more* regular thing. "Why can't you just have some self-control?!" I'd say to myself, but I didn't know how to respond. The fact of the matter was, I *did* have self-control. I just wasn't allowing it to come to life.

As a Christian, the Spirit of God was in me. He had been in me from the time I first believed as a young boy. Therefore, I had quite a few heavenly characteristics on the inside of me which were dormant, and I *made* them dormant. I refused to let them grow.

Paul informed the Galatians about the truth of who they were inside *because* of Christ living in them. These same traits are embedded in the supernatural DNA of every believer in Christ, right now, today—because they're coming *from* Christ *in* them. Here they are:

> *"But the fruit of the Spirit is love, joy, peace, patience,*
> *kindness, goodness, faithfulness, gentleness,*
> *and <u>self-control</u>"* (see Galatians 5:22-23)

As you can see, we have wonderful attributes as Christ-indwellers! Paul calls these traits *fruit* because fruit never forces itself to grow. Fruit happens naturally. Same with us as Christians. Anything we produce in our lives should be happening from a state of rest. We are branches. Branches never *work hard* to grow fruit, neither do they *muster up enough self-discipline*. No, they simply *be* themselves, and that's what we are, branches, being who God made us to be! Jesus tells us this:

> *"I am the vine; you are the branches. If you remain*
> *in me and I in you, you will bear much fruit; apart*
> *from me you can do nothing." (John 15:5)*

Where do branches get all of their sustenance from? The vine. They can produce *no* fruit by themselves, they *need* the vine. If you think about it, the branch has it pretty easy. Its only job is to just be, to just hang out. It didn't create itself and it doesn't grow the fruit. The vine grows the fruit *through* the branch.

The confused person who thinks they're producing "amazing" fruit by their own efforts and gifts, they'll look at John 15:5 and immediately rebuttal, "Yeah Matt, the key word there is to *remain*! You gotta do your part to remain *in* Jesus! If you don't, you're out!"

Friend, from the very first time you are *in* Jesus, you can't *un*-remain. You're in Him for good (see Hebrews 7:25, 2 Timothy 2:13, Colossians 3:3, 1 Corinthians 6:17). Only those who have *never* been a part of Jesus "can do nothing" and we *have* become a part of Him through one step: *We've believed He's forgiven us (see John 1:12-13).*

But I want to stay on track here, this devotional is not about our salvation. This devotional is for the people who are struggling with an addiction. For me, it was quite a few things, but the most obvious was my alcoholism. If you glance back up at the verse I quoted from Galatians, I've underlined the last fruit of the Spirit, *self-control*, that's what I want to focus on today.

If you are struggling with an addiction and you believe Jesus has forgiven you, listen to me very closely…you *have* self-control.

"But Matt I've tried a thousand times to quit! How can you say I have self-control?!"

Because you do.

Why do you think you want to quit? Why do you think your addiction bothers you so much? It's because you weren't *made* for it. Your addiction will never be okay with you because your spirit is perfect and not addicted. The real you, your heaven-ready spirit, will be bothered until the day you die, letting you know you weren't made to be out of control when it comes to anything.

To understand this, you must separate your *who* from your *do*. To even be *able* to make this distinction, you must *also* understand that you're a three-part being: spirit, body, and soul.

As a Christian, your spirit is intertwined with God's Spirit like fabric. You and He are one. God only did this—became infused with you—*after* you allowed Him to kill off your old spirit and give you a new one. In the spiritual realm, you have literally been crucified with Jesus, buried, and resurrected as a new, holy being. *That's* who you really are! (See Romans 6:6, 2 Corinthians 5:17, 1 Corinthians 6:19, Colossians 1:22, Galatians 2:20)

Although you have new desires coming from your new spirit, your mind is being renewed over time (see Romans 12:2). It's exactly as it was *before* you received your new spirit. The good news is you are not your thoughts. Your thoughts can be matured. You can learn and grow!

Understanding this about myself changed so much! I am not what I do! I am not what I think! Neither are you! We are holy, set apart, and sealed with God's Spirit, right now! (See Hebrews 10:10, Ephesians 1:13). Over time, as I began to learn more about my true identity, the Holy Spirit began to reveal many things to me about my drinking:

> "Matthew, you weren't made to keep getting drunk all the time. I've got a better plan for you. Some people can drink, but for you, I don't want you to drink a single drop."
>
> "Matt, the reason why your hangover is so physically and emotionally draining is because you weren't made to be controlled by alcohol. Stop drinking so you can enjoy peace."
>
> "Son, you are right. You *have* tried to quit many times and you've failed. That's because you can't quit, but you *can* begin. You can begin living *out* who you really are inside, a self-controlled person. Self-control *is* there, you just have to trust me. Feel your pain and anxiety and choose not to drink. I'll help you."

The Spirit of God was teaching me who I really am and I was actually starting to believe Him! The religious people had taught me the opposite. If I was truly a Christian then I'd never get drunk. Therefore, my faith was fake. It's no wonder why so many people hate Christians; it's because of the lies from those who are supposed to be representing Jesus. We have to start telling believers who they really are: *self-controlled saints*! Once they begin to understand this truth, only then will they organically start living that way.

So today, my friends, know this: The reason why you should give up your addiction is because you have self-control. Self-control is a part of your heavenly genetic structure. Sure, there are many other reasons I could list off as to why your addiction should go, but those reasons will be in the drop-down menu of *Self-Control*. If you're saved, your addiction will never feel good or natural, no matter how long you deny it. So why not begin today? Why not begin being yourself?! In your spirit you are not addicted to anything! You are free! (See Galatians 5:1, John 8:36).

> **A prayer for you:** *Heavenly Father, I want to thank you for my sense of peace. I know that peace is a fruit of the Spirit and it's a very sweet fruit. You and I both know how non-peaceful so many mornings were for me when I was not living out my self-control. Thank you for teaching me who I am inside, sober and under complete control of my actions and attitudes.*
>
> *Right now, I lift up all who are reading this, directly to you. Lots of these dear readers don't have a drug or alcohol addiction, so they might not understand the agony of waking up the morning after a binge. However, if they knew about the torment we feel, they'd empathize. Some of them are dealing with an addicted person and they are DONE. They've had enough! I pray for them to be able to stand up and set boundaries. Help them to create new barriers of protection, and to make it very uncomfortable for the addicted person to continue. Teach them new ways to react. I ask that you remove any form of codependency or enabling. If they're addicted to the addicted, set them free.*

And God, for those who are in severe pain today because of acting on an addiction yesterday, help them begin to understand the truth of who they are inside. If they're believers they DO HAVE self-control, they just gotta let it come out! As they trust Jesus and allow Him to transform their thinking, they will learn to be themselves! Reveal that they ARE free, they just have to step out of the prison door! The door is wide open! Step out and be yourself! I pray these things in Jesus' name. Amen.

Day 8

How to Accept God's Timing

...God did not lead them on the road through the Philistine country, though that was shorter. For God said, "If they face war, they might change their minds and return to Egypt." So God led the people around by the desert road toward the Red Sea.

Exodus 13:17-18

After Pharaoh released the slaves, God had a promised land for them to inhabit and to flourish as a people. However, God knew they wouldn't be able to take the land away from those who currently occupied it—that is, immediately. Most of them still had a slave mentality and needed to first have their thinking changed.

Although they could have possessed the promised land sooner, it took forty years before they finally did. God's timing *wasn't* forty years, Israel's was because they kept hesitating. But God's timing wasn't *immediate* either. His timing was perfect.

We all have hopes and dreams, we have God-given desires in our hearts in which we are driven to accomplish. Sometimes the enemy talks us out of them, and other times it's people and even our own stinking thinking. But just because our aspirations don't come to life instantly, that does not mean they go away!

To be clear, there is no pressure on us. I'm not referring to salvation, but instead, human ambition. Our hearts are complete in Christ, but the other endeavors we long to come to fruition on a daily basis, *we* want to hurry up and happen already! God, however, is in no rush. To Him, time does not exist. One day is the same as a thousand years (see 2 Peter 3:8). So what we think is taking forever, He does not.

God also doesn't allow us to see the exact timing of His plan for *our* goals. God is not against our ambitions, He is the one who gave us the drive for them! His Spirit combined with ours has caused us to want what He wants, and vice versa! (See Psalm 37:4, 1 Corinthians 2:16).

That thing, that idea, that goal—He knows very well your eagerness and desire about it! Frustrating as it may be, not knowing how God will allow our passions to play out can become intense in our minds. His Holy Spirit wants us to *stay* driven, but to do it properly. First of all, with love. Love for God, love for others, and love for ourselves. If we have goals that cause us to *not* love, then we need to re-evaluate those goals.

The Spirit of God who inhabits us *woos* us to be motivated lovingly, peacefully, joyously, patiently, and under control. So when *un*controllable people and circumstances head our way, He speaks to us gently about those situations and people.

When we stop squirming, be still, and listen, sleepless nights turn into deep-sleep nights. Restlessness, fear, and anxiety, turns into a sense of strength and calmness. When we *know* that God is well aware of all our situations on a deeper level than even *we're* aware of them, solace comes to a troubled mind.

Friend, please be sure to realize one thing: the enemy will attempt to use our mistakes against us. He'll spout off, "Just look at how bad you screwed up today! It's no wonder God isn't answering your prayers!"

But our loving Heavenly Father will quickly rebuttal him, "My child, the more mistakes you make the deeper my love for you goes. Don't listen to those lies, my grace is infinite."

Vulnerability is not something that comes easily to most, but it's essential to trusting God's timing. When we think things should be changing a lot faster—even to the point of us stepping in to do God's job—humility will always lead us back into His loving arms. Not that we've left Him or that He's left us—we are one. But by way of *allowing* Him to embrace us in our deep times of pain—as we wait—we soon realize the unconditional love of the Father.

We get to swim in the ocean of His grace. We get to hear the whispers, "I'm here."

Like a loving parent with a baby who wants to run like the wind, yet cannot even stand, God knows what we are capable of in each stage of our lives. He protects us as we grow *through* His timing. He disciples us. He trains us. He hones our individual skills, gifts, and talents by way of one word . . . "Wait."

"Wait, Matt."

"Wait, Paul."

"Wait, John."

"Wait, Jesus."

"Wait, _____."

He's talking to you, too. He's saying, "Trust me. Wait."

So today, my friends, know this: Wait confidently! No matter how long it takes, wait for God's perfect timing with faith! Wait and *know* that He loves you more than your human mind can compute! Wait and know that He is in complete control and you are His child!

A prayer for you: *Heavenly Father, as I look back over the years of my life, at all of the different times of waiting, I can see that you were helping me grow into my true self—and you still are. When I thought my waiting was going to be the end of me, I can now see you were working everything out for a greater good! Thank you for teaching me how to wait! Right now, I lift up all who are reading this, directly to you. So many of them are tired, Dad. So many have been waiting a very long time for their goals to come to life. Reassure them today of who you are!*

The Great I Am! Alpha and Omega! God Almighty! Our Dad! Teach them how to trust you during their waiting periods! Teach them how to go deeper into your grace, and to GIVE this grace away to others! Help them to stay focused on the truth of their identity in Christ, as well as the bigger picture, eternity. This trip to planet earth is so short! You are currently preparing us for a life in heaven which we cannot comprehend! We trust your timing! We trust you, completely. In Jesus' name I pray, amen.

Day 9

Stop Killing Yourself

"For we are God's Masterpiece."

SEE EPHESIANS 2:10

We've been taught wrong in our churches. We've been taught that the word "self" is a bad word, which is not the case. Further, the words "Die to self" is an inaccurate translation of the original manuscript in regard to the verse which is normally taken out of context, 1 Corinthians 15:31. A more authentic translation is, "I face death every day." Why is this important? Because Paul wasn't talking about how he kills himself daily. Instead, he was explaining the dangers he encountered while traveling to spread the gospel; he even mentioned the threat of wild beasts in the following verse (see 1 Corinthians 15:32).

We've also been taught that we can't trust ourselves. Again, this is a lie. From the stages and pulpits, we get incorrectly educated to believe we have a Jekyll and Hyde complex—told to feed one part of us, and starve the other. This is wrong. Christian, you are not at war with yourself. Once you realize this, everything changes.

Paul knew full well that he was not at battle with *Paul*. God did not send Jesus here so that we may become schizophrenic, but instead, to give us a new self, a new spirit. One that lives temporarily in this flesh—but is still perfect. Paul was crystal-clear about this fact in several of his writings:

> *"Therefore, if anyone is in Christ, <u>the new creation has come</u>: The old <u>has gone</u>, the new is here!" (2 Corinthians 5:17)*

> *"For we know that our old self <u>was crucified with him</u> so that the body ruled by sin might be <u>done away with</u>, that we should no longer be slaves to sin" (Romans 6:6)*

There are many, *many more* identity verses, but these two highlight what *has* happened to Christians. Namely, we've been made brand new on the inside—*in our spirits.*

The grace-confused Christian will immediately attempt to point out Romans 7. Paul is speaking about a terrible battle he is facing, and it *appears* that he is talking about himself, but he's not. He's talking about his pre-saved self. He's talking about his old self who tried to live by the Law but couldn't seem to pull it off.

The subtitle of Romans 7 should be *I Fought the Law and the Law Won*. Why? Because this is a description of Paul as he struggled with the power of sin as he *attempted* to live by the Mosaic Law—which included the Ten Commandments (he uses coveting as the struggle, one of the Ten). Just look:

> *"For <u>when we were</u> in the realm of the flesh, the sinful passions <u>aroused by the Law</u> were at work in us" (See Romans 7:5)*

Do you see that? "When we *were*"? That is past-tense. This is referring to us *before* we received our new spirits and were still "in the flesh"—as in, still not forgiven. If you look deeper, *how* did sinful passions get aroused?...*By the Law*. Paul continues to explain what happens to our spirits once they become one with Christ:

> *"But now, <u>by dying to what once bound us</u> (Law), we <u>have been released from the Law</u> so that we serve in the <u>new way of the Spirit</u>, and not in the old way of the written code (Law)" (Romans 7:6, note added)*

We die to the Law so that we can live by a new way—the way of the Spirit! So many people think this idea of not living by any laws or commandments will cause us to sin, but I disagree completely and so did Paul. As he "tried to behave" his focus on what *not* to do (disobey "Thou shalt not covet") only caused him to covet. He struggled with jealousy because of being told, "Don't be jealous" (see Romans 7:8). He was told to *not* think of a pink elephant and guess what kept happening? Colorful elephants galore.

"So Matt, if we don't live by the Law and Commandments, then how do we know what is right and wrong?"

Simple...God's Spirit. The Spirit of God in you will never lead you to sin. That's why Paul said we live by the *new way* of the Spirit and *not* by the written code (see Romans 7:6). We don't *need* Mosaic Law, we have God inside of us! Therefore, we can trust ourselves!

Now, this brings me to the main point of this devotional. If we are new—that is, our spirits—then why would we want to constantly think we gotta die daily? We only die *once* in our spirits, it's not a daily thing. Even Jesus isn't dying daily, so why should we think that we are? As a matter of fact, our salvation stays secure because Christ will never die again! (See Hebrews 7:25).

"Yeah Matt, but you still gotta pick up your cross and follow Christ!"

We aren't following Christ, the people on earth were, literally, when He was here in the flesh. Instead, on this side of the Cross, we have something so much better—HE'S IN US! His Spirit, the Holy Spirit, is inside us!

If you look even deeper into that statement of us needing to pick up our crosses every day, let me ask you this, is Jesus still on *His* Cross? No. He only went to the Cross and died *once*. Same with you. You're not toting around an invisible cross everywhere. Jesus wanted you to follow Him into *belief* in His forgiveness—and you did. Hopefully, anyway. This message is mainly for believers, but if you're not a Christian you can become one this very moment by simply believing Jesus has forgiven you.

Anyway, I want to help you understand that you are *not* at battle with yourself. Friend, you are perfectly compatible with the Spirit of God in you! He likes you, a lot! He likes your style, your personality, your goofiness, your elegance, your quirks—all of you—whatever, He likes you!

"But Matt, I still struggle with _____!"

He knows. You are no surprise to Him. He knew what He was getting with you before time began. He loves you *exactly* as you are. Don't worry, He will continue to counsel you, comfort you, teach you, and coach you—but no matter what, your spirit is absolutely secure and perfect in Jesus. Sure, your mind is constantly being renewed *into* this spiritual perfection, but *you* are okay. Paul tells the Christians in Philippi this truth:

> *"And I am certain that God, who began the good work within you, will continue his work until it is finally finished on the day when Christ Jesus returns." (Philippians 1:6)*

We are all learning and growing, we are all trying to figure out how to walk by our perfect spirits like wobbly babies. The glory which will be revealed in us when this is complete in heaven is unfathomable (see 1 Corinthians 15:52). But for now, by us making decisions the Spirit leads us to make—and having attitudes the same—our immature thoughts are being put aside.

But no matter what, I want you to know that God is not mad at you, and He's not disappointed in you. So if *He's* not mad or disappointed in you, then you shouldn't be either. You don't need to "kill yourself" all the time, that is a demonic thought. God loves you because you are His child and He is more than happy to call you His own.

As time goes on, and you realize that you are not at battle with *you*, life will become abundantly fruitful and joyous. Contentment in all circumstances will happen. Thankfulness will be a normal thing for you because you will know that God *is* good, that He lives *in* you, and most importantly, He loves you unconditionally.

So today, my friends, know this: God doesn't want you to kill yourself, not literally or figuratively. He wants you to *be* yourself! Just be you! Sin will never match up with you, because sin has nothing to do with you—your spirit that is, who *is* you. God isn't looking for any type of martyrdom or overachieving, He just wants you to know that He's your Dad and He cares for you. Good dads don't expect their kids to die daily. Instead, they want them to *live*, to enjoy their lives, and to be who they were created to be: *beloved children.*

> **A prayer for you:** *Dad, I love you. I'm grateful that you are my Dad. I appreciate all you do for me, and I want to thank you for teaching me I'm your masterpiece. Right now, I lift up all who are reading this, directly to you. For those who have been lied to about you, help them. Help them come to know your true heart, your true and unconditional love. I ask that you remove any fear from their minds, when it comes to their relationship with you. Let them know you are glad to have them as your child. Let them know you love all of us equally. Let them know this short lifetime is but a prequel to our real life at home in heaven with you. But also give them the revelation that heaven is already in them right now, because you live in them. Give these dear readers the peace of knowing that you are always there for them, no matter what. You'll never leave them, forsake them, or hurt them—you love them. In Jesus' name I pray, amen.*

Day 10

You Don't Owe God Anything

"But now he has reconciled you by Christ's physical body through death to present you holy in his sight, without blemish and free from accusation"

Colossians 1:22

What does it mean to be reconciled with someone? Rather it be a spouse, business partner, parent, child, neighbor—whoever—when you hear a person say, "We've reconciled," what immediately comes to your mind? More than likely you'll think, "So you guys are cool with each other now? That's good."

Webster defines reconcile as this: "To restore to friendship or harmony." "To check a financial account against another for accuracy."

When you reconcile a relationship or a checkbook, what are you doing? You are releasing the balance and evening things up. You no longer owe. A few years ago, the title of this devotional would have ticked me off, "I don't owe God? You're crazy! I owe Him everything! After all He's done for me? How dare you say that I don't owe God!"

Yeah, my knickers were a little too tight. But why? Why would I be so upset about somebody saying that I don't owe God a thing?...Because I didn't fully grasp what He had done for *me*. My life had been changed by Him in such a drastic way—because I was finally living *out* my relationship with Him—but still, I was on the treadmill of "Gotta pay God back! Gotta pay God back!" and all along, I didn't *have* to pay God back. All I *had* to do was be myself.

A grace-confused Christian might bark at me, "Matt, you can't say that all you had to do was be yourself! You are a sinner on the inside! Your heart is *still* wicked!"

Friend, no it's not. My heart is perfect. My heart is one with God. So many Christians today don't understand this fact because they've been taught they have two natures, we don't. Christians have one nature, that of God (see 2 Peter 1:4).

When a pastor tells someone, "Come to Jesus and be made completely new!" but then the next Sunday, "Repent! You wicked sinner!" people are going to be bamboozled—rightfully so. This is called *doubletalk*, and it will either make you frustrated and angry, or self-righteous due to denial. There is no in-between because this type of teaching makes no sense. We must be clear about what has happened in us *once* we first believed.

Christian, you received a new heart the moment you realized Jesus has forgiven you. You have a heart that is good. The religious Christian will pull an Old Testament verse out of context and try to slap it on the New Covenant to prove we are bad inside:

> *"The heart is deceitful above all things and beyond cure." (See Jeremiah 17:9)*

And sure, this is correct, but only for non-believers. Once we place our faith in Jesus, we get a new heart—a heart that is one *with* Jesus. Ezekiel prophesied this heart transplant would happen, hundreds of years before Christ was born:

> *"I will give you a <u>new heart</u> and put a <u>new spirit</u> in you; I will <u>remove from you</u> your heart of stone and give you a heart of flesh." (Ezekiel 36:26)*

Do you see that? Do you see what God's plan was all along? It was wiping your slate clean and making you new inside. This happens through the New Covenant! The New Covenant of what? *Complete reconciliation with God by grace through faith in the Messiah.*

After the Cross, the author of Hebrews explains what happens in our hearts by believing in Jesus. We go from being judged by Mosaic Law, to understanding God's "laws," as in, "What God really wants," from the inside of us. Just look:

> *"This is the covenant I will make with them after that time, says the Lord. I will put my laws in their hearts, and I will write them on their minds." (Hebrews 10:16)*

The legalist will immediately shout, "See Matt! Law! God wants us to obey His Law!" and I'd say, "Ah, ah, ah, now wait a minute. This does not say Law, as in the Mosaic Law, but instead, *laws,* as in, knowing what God expects from us through His Spirit *in* us. That's why it says hearts *and* minds."

God's Spirit is not trying to get us to stop eating shellfish and porkchops—part of the Mosaic Law. The writer of Hebrews deliberately changed this word to a *lowercase* "law" and added an "s" to make it "laws." He wanted to be clear with the Jews who were still attempting to live by Law (all 613, not just 10), to know that God will teach them right from wrong, organically, from the heart. Law was no longer needed because God was *in* them! Here's proof:

> *"No longer will they teach their neighbor, or say to one another, 'Know the Lord,' because <u>they will all know me</u>, from the least of them to the greatest." (Hebrews 8:11)*

WE ALL KNOW GOD ONCE HE COMES TO LIVE IN US! And how could God possibly come and live in us if we have a wicked, sinful heart? He won't! That's why He *removes* our heart and gives us a new one! Your spirit is brand new! Believer! Inside you, you are *new*! You really *do* want what God wants! This is why sin never feels good permanently! You weren't made for it! Your flesh might get a temporary thrill from acting on sin, but *you* hate sin! Paul tells the Romans:

> *"But now, by dying to what once bound us, <u>we have been released from the Law</u> SO THAT we serve in the <u>new way of the Spirit</u>, and not in the old way of the written code." (Romans 7:6, my emphasis added)*

This is your identity. You live by the new way of the Spirit of God in you, guiding you, counseling you, and comforting you. You are led by a heart that is reconciled with God *not* by Jewish rules and commands—you don't need them! You've got God's Spirit! That is, if you've believed Jesus has forgiven you. If you have, you are new. This could have happened decades ago, but you just *now* are realizing it!

YOU. ARE. NEW.

YOU. ARE. NEW.

YOU ARE NEW!

You are new because you've been reconciled with God for good! Paul informs the Colossians, "You have been reconciled with God through Jesus' body! You are holy! You are without blemish! You are free from all accusation!" (See Colossians 1:22).

Friend, we don't owe God anything because Jesus paid everything off for us. If He didn't, then what was the Cross for? Was it not good enough? Does the Messiah need *your* help? No, He doesn't. The answer is *no*. He did what He did as a free gift. When someone gives you a gift, you don't help them give it to you. Instead, you open up your hands and say, "Thank you."

God doesn't have you on a scale, waiting for you to make your good side rise higher than the bad side—YOU DON'T HAVE A BAD SIDE! You've got some old stinking thinking and immature coping mechanisms, but as you walk by your perfect spirit, those things will be a non-factor (Galatians 5:16, Philippians 4:8). And when they are *temporarily* a factor, God's grace is a much *larger* factor (see Romans 5:20).

This is the only thing we are qualified to preach...the ministry of reconciliation with God. We aren't supposed to be yelling at people to start living right, we are supposed to let people know that they *are* right with God. As a matter of fact, this is the *only* ministry we are qualified to preach, and that is, "Christian, you are okay with God. You're *okay*." Just look at what Paul told the Corinthians:

> *"Now all these things are from God, who <u>has reconciled</u> us to himself through Christ and <u>gave us the ministry of reconciliation</u>" (2 Corinthians 5:18)*

"Gave us the ministry of reconciliation." This is the purest form of ministry we can have! Which is letting people know they don't owe God! Once a person knows and believes this fact, they will begin to enjoy a loving relationship with their Creator. You can't savor an intimate union with someone while knowing you owe them—the debt has to be released. Jesus did that for us, with God, at the Cross.

So today, my friends, know this: We don't even have the *ability* to pay God back. All of our efforts are but filthy rags, no matter how "amazing" they appear to be. Your best gifts to God will not come from effort, but from simply being yourself. He's your Daddy who enjoys the scribbly drawings you've made for Him. Further, God doesn't need anything from you—He's God! He just wants you to live your life as His child. Good dads don't hound their kids to pay them back, instead, they let their debts go because they love them. God, is a good dad. He's the best one ever. Believe this because it's true, and be who He has made you to be in your heart: *a heaven-ready saint*.

A prayer for you: *Heavenly Father, your Word says in Acts 17 that you are not served by human hands because you are in need of nothing, and I believe that. It took me a long time to realize this as I tried to keep* *my spot with you, but all along it was mine for free because I'm your son. Thank you for teaching me who I am in my heart. I'm completely reconciled with you and you love me unconditionally. Right now, I lift up all who are reading this, directly to you. For those who are working their hardest to be good for you, let them know that they ARE good. Let them know that on the inside, you live there and they are complete. Help them to realize their actions and attitudes cannot change their identity in you—let them know who they are! You stay with us and we keep our identity because you love us, and because you're our Dad. You don't do this for us to pay you back because Jesus paid it all. Give these dear readers peace in knowing who they really are inside, that is, Children of God! In Jesus' name, amen.*

Day 11

What to do When the Pain is Unbearable

"Cast your cares on him because he cares for you."

1 Peter 5:7

P ain. We all feel it at some point in our lives. Sometimes our pain is a 2 out of 10, and at other times the pain is so severe, we feel like we no longer want to live. Death would be a respite—or so we think. Many people believe that suicide is a selfish act, and to an extent it absolutely is. But for those who take their own lives, they do so because they want relief. The enemy convinces them the unbearable pain they feel will never go away, so they act on those feelings one last time.

When pain is not noticeable in my own life, and someone asks me, "How are you doing?" sometimes I'll reply with, "Enjoying a season of blessing," and honestly, I am. I'm milking it for all it's worth because I know full well, with the life I've lived, when the seas are calm it's time to enjoy smooth sailing—but it won't last. Does that seem pessimistic? Why would I say such a thing?...Because I'm being real. Because I know a hurricane can come in at any point in time, causing the waves to crash all around me, trying to throw me off the boat so that I may drown.

I'm not saying that I look forward to the hurricanes, or that I even *worry* about the hurricanes, but I *know* that a season of pain will eventually head toward the panhandle of my life. It happens to all of us. This is why we should always smile, close our eyes, and breathe in deep when we are sailing through seasons of ease.

This world is fallen. Because of our original ancestor, Adam, when he chose to act on the power of sin, this planet crashed. It's broken. It's not what God *wanted*, but what God knew would *happen* because of the option of *choice*. Without choice, we can't love. Without love, we can't have a relationship with God. But that's not what this devotional is about. It's about being punched in the stomach with crippling pain, and what we should do about it.

With us being in Adam's loin at the time of his first sin, we not only inherited a terrible planet, but we also bequeathed sin-filled DNA—by no fault of our own (see Romans 5). By being born *into* this fallen place, we must now face whatever painful trials come our way—and it's Adam's fault. But honestly, even if it was me who was in the Garden, it would have been my fault too. I'd make a choice that God did not agree with, eventually...we all would. So, if God is rich in mercy and full of love, what are we to do when the pain of this place becomes unbearable?

Refocus...refocus on our thoughts.

Pain is a feeling. Feelings are dictated from our thoughts. Whatever you are constantly thinking about is what you are going to constantly be feeling *about*. For this reason, Paul told the Philippian Christians:

> *"And now, dear brothers and sisters, one final thing. <u>Fix your thoughts on</u> what is true, and honorable, and right, and pure, and lovely, and admirable. <u>Think about things</u> that are excellent and worthy of praise." (Philippians 4:8)*

Twice he said what they should do—THINK DIFFERENTLY!

"But Matt, I can't help what I think!"

I'll give you that, you are right. We can't always help what we think, but we *can* always help what we are *deliberately* thinking of. This is why we allow God to transform our lives by the *renewing* of our minds—renewing means ongoing. Further, it doesn't say *renew our feelings* because we have no control over how we feel, just look:

> *"Do not conform to the pattern of this world, but <u>be transformed by the renewing of your mind. Then you will be able to test and approve what God's will is—his good, pleasing and perfect will.</u>" (Romans 12:2)*

Where our mind goes our emotions follow. Some of us have worried ourselves sick about something happening to us that has never even happened! Why? Because we've been *thinking* about this fear for a very long time! This is why Paul told the Romans to *be* transformed by the renewing of their minds. He didn't say you *are* transformed. In their spirits, yes, they *had been* transformed because they received a new spirit from God the moment they first believed (see Romans 6:6, 2 Corinthians 5:17, Galatians 2:20). But our minds are not our spirits.

And notice what he told them to be transformed by?...God's good, pleasing, and perfect will! You might immediately say, "Well, what is God's will?"

It's Jesus.

It's Christ *in* us (see John 6:40, Colossians 1:27). God's will is His Spirit *in* you transforming your mind! Paul never said, "Be transformed by the renewing of your feelings." He said be transformed by the renewing of your mind in Christ! (See 1 Corinthians 2:16). Once we begin to do this *everything* changes, no matter how unbearable a time of trial may be!

Friend, God knows about your pain, He gave us feelings for a reason. There is nothing wrong with your feelings, God has feelings too! He knows what you feel deeper than even *you* feel it, and He's with you! That is, if you've believed Jesus has forgiven you.

The agony you feel could be a financial turmoil that keeps you awake at night—THEY SAID ALL YOU HAVE TO DO IS TITHE, BUT YOU ARE STILL STRUGGLING! "The pastor just bought a new boat! I saw him on Instagram taking a family trip to Paris, and I can't even pay my bills! Why did he lie to me about tithing? I even gave above and beyond the tithe!"

You might be suffering from the abuse from when you were young—IT WASN'T YOUR FAULT! THEY SEXUALLY ABUSED YOU OR BEAT YOU TO NO END! They stole your innocence! "WHY WOULD THEY DO THAT TO ME? I WAS JUST A CHILD!"

Your pain might be from an addicted or absent parent. They left you! They loved their addiction, or their new relationship, more than you! You cried in those foster homes while they were out getting drunk and high! "THEY DIDN'T CARE ABOUT ME! ALL THE OTHER KIDS HAD THEIR PARENTS BUT I DIDN'T!"...It *wasn't* your fault. *They* were the messed up ones—not you.

Or maybe it was a parent who kept you from your *other* parent. You were brainwashed into thinking they were a bad person, and they weren't! They *wanted* to see you all along, and they fought for you! You were robbed of a relationship! You were lied to! "HOW DARE THEY DO THAT TO ME!"

An addiction might be the pain in your life right now—YOU ARE DONE LIVING! You think, "I can't beat this! I hate myself because I'm so weak! I've tried a thousand times to get rid of this! I don't *want* it! WHY CAN'T I QUIIIIIIIIT?"

The suffering you are facing could be coming from a spouse, they've done the unthinkable and their vows were lies to you and God. They enjoy seeing you in pain because it gives them pleasure—"IT HURTS SO BAD!" Or maybe a child has refused to speak to you, they are making decisions which are tearing you apart—"WHY ARE THEY DOING THIS? I DIDN'T RAISE THEM THAT WAY!"

Your pain might be coming from a sickness—"WHY AM I SICK, GOD? WHAT DID I DO TO DESERVE THIS?" Or maybe someone close to you has died, it was too soon and it's not fair—"MY WHOLE BODY ACHES WITH PAAAAAAAAAAAAAIN!"

IT'S UNBEARABLE!

Maybe it's religious abuse that has caused you to suffer so much. The graceless Christians have kicked you out and told you you're not good enough, "Go somewhere else! You weren't quick enough to repent! Your kind doesn't belong here! You are going to hell!"...when all along you just wanted some help with your pain.

Whatever or whoever is causing you unbearable pain, Jesus wants to help you. He wants you to refocus on Him. He wants you to refocus your *thinking*.

> *"You, dear children, are from God and have overcome them, because he who is in you is greater than he who is in the world." (1 John 4:4)*

You, dear child, are an overcomer! Do you see what John wrote? YOU ARE AN OVERCOMER! How? Because Jesus lives in you! He who is in you is greater than he who is in this fallen world! Who is the *he* who is in this world? The devil. The enemy. Satan. His demonic crew. Jesus said this idiot only has three main goals: *steal, kill, destroy* (see John 10:10)—and he does this in your mind...in your thinking.

But what does Jesus do in your mind? He transforms it! As you allow Him to transform your mind into the truth of who you are and *whose* you are—YOU WILL BE ABLE TO OVERCOME *ANY* UNBEARABLE PAIN! You will *feel* the pain and Jesus will comfort you! You will *feel* the pain and He will strengthen you! You will *feel* the pain and you will grow! You will feel the pain and know that it won't last forever because He who is in you is greater than *all* pain! He who is in you took on the painful sin of the entire world and you and He are one! (See Colossians 3:3, 1 Corinthians 6:19).

So today, my friend, refocus your mind on these truths. When you do, you will realize that God works all things out together for good, even our pain. Just look at the Cross. The most painful day in the history of the world turned out to be the most beautiful. Jesus, who did that, lives in you.

> **A prayer for you:** *God, you know about the unbearable pain so many of us are in, you KNOW this. And at the same time, you know what we are truly capable of through you. The very same Spirit of Christ who took on the pain of the world lives in us, and we are grateful. Remind us of this fact as we get beat up and hurt, yet we don't respond how the devil wants us to. If we've decided to allow you to live through us, we know that our pain will get even worse at times because the population of hell is threatened by us. As our enemy holds over the flames whatever, or whoever, we've placed our identity in, remind us who we are! YOUR KIDS! Help us change our thinking and teach us more about our identity as we move forward, changing this world for you, with love. We are focused on Jesus! Amen.*

Day 12

The Truth About "Faith Without Works Is Dead"

"So also faith by itself, if it does not have works, is dead."

JAMES 2:17

Martin Luther was a very controversial figure, to say the least. In the 1500s, the Catholic church was called out by Luther in a memo named, *95 Theses*. In this letter, he wrote 95 things the church was doing that went against the gospel. He then nailed it to the front door of the Wittenberg Castle Church. If you think that I'm a grace guy—ha! Martin Luther would put me to shame!

Based on his study of Scripture, as well as his own personal religious burn-out, Luther felt the church had the gospel all wrong. Isn't it amazing how the harder we try to earn God's approval and acceptance, the more we realize we can't?

For this reason, Martin Luther thought the Book of James shouldn't be in the canonization of the Bible. Why? Because James' epistle appeared to go *against* grace. I disagree with Luther, I think James is just fine where it's at. But here is an example in James in which Luther thought a Sharpie was needed:

> *"What good is it, my brothers, if someone says he has faith but does not have works? Can that faith save him?" (James 2:14)*

Now, at first glance, and if you take it out of context, this verse will insight one of two things in you: *fear or self-righteousness*. This is a go-to verse for the Christians who don't understand what God has really done for us by sacrificing His Son. They will use James 2:14-17 to manipulate new believers, as well as be hyper-critical of seasoned Christians.

For so long, I read this verse as, "You better have works or you're not saved!" That makes no sense because grace would then be void. The very definition of grace is "unearnable favor." Anything we work for is earned. Plus, how do we know if we've done enough works to tip the scales in our favor? We don't, because that's impossible.

This ideology is demonic and anti-gospel. It creates hierarchies of Christianity, which is exactly what Satan wants. His desire is to get us to believe we are a 2 out of 10 because of our lack of good works, or a 6 or 7 at best *because* of our good works. But truth be told, we are an 11! We are off the charts because of *Jesus'* work, not ours!

After I realized *working* to stay saved wasn't true, I began to see this passage in James as such: "Sure, you still *have* faith, but you need to revive it by doing something! You gotta do more! You gotta *be* more! Get to work and stop being a passive Christian!"

However, that theology evolved as well because such a mindset creates severe stress. God is not a God of stress. He is a God of peace, comfort, and a sound mind—and He lives in me (see 2 Timothy 1:7). If I feel pressured, that is *not* coming from God. Instead, it's coming from old, unrenewed thinking, from religious people, or from the enemy—but not from God. I am a branch who produces fruit of the Spirit. Branches are never pressured to grow fruit from the vine (see John 15:5, Galatians 5:22-23).

So if I'm not being pressured to "work up" some fruit, then what is James talking about? Context is key. If we don't look deeper into this passage—all around it—it will not make sense. Without a frame of reference, Paul would be arguing with James to this day, because he told the Romans the *opposite* of what James wrote:

> *"And if by grace, <u>then it cannot be based on works</u>; if it were, <u>grace would no longer be grace</u>." (Romans 11:6)*

And again, he said the same to the Christians in Ephesus:

> *"<u>For it is by grace you have been saved</u>, through faith—and this is not from yourselves, it is the gift of God—<u>not by works</u>, so that no one can boast." (Ephesians 2:8-9)*

So which is it? Is it works or faith?...The answer is *yes*. No, they are not combined, that would nix grace completely (see Galatians 3:1-3). However, James is letting us know that a *decision* must be made when it comes to your salvation. He uses two examples of people who made *one* choice to become righteous with God—a choice of faith—once and for all.

To build his case, James claims, "Even the demons believe!" (See James 2:19). And that's true, those who are in the spiritual realm have their doctrine correct: *Jesus is the Messiah*. They know that! They have head-knowledge of God! But the difference between us and them is *they* are already damned to hell, we aren't. We still have time to make a decision to believe Christ *has* forgiven us.

Also, notice James doesn't say, "*Salvation* without works is dead," no, he says *faith* without works is dead. He is saying we must make a decision by faith about *who* Jesus is. James is no fool! As Jesus' own brother, he knew that works never saved anyone! He understood the New Covenant and what the blood of Jesus did for us. Works didn't save anyone *before* Jesus, and works definitely can't save us *after* His new agreement was put in place (see Hebrews 8:13).

This is why we must look at James' examples of people making a one-time decision *to* believe. First, he talks about Abraham:

> *"Was not Abraham our father justified by works when he offered up his son Isaac on the altar?" (James 2:21)*

Do you see what completed Abraham's faith?...*A decision*. Abraham had done *many* works, but James only lists a *single* action, a *single* decision. Being willing to sacrifice Issac didn't *make* Abraham righteous, he was righteous before that. James recites Old Testament Scripture to be clear about this point:

> *"Abraham <u>believed</u> God, and it was <u>credited to him as righteousness</u>" (see James 2:23, Genesis 15:6)*

Belief is what gives us our credit as righteous people! The *moment* of belief is a decision! Abraham believed God *before* Issac was even conceived, so he was already righteous before this particular act at the altar (see Genesis 15). This proves that the New Covenant is older than the Old Covenant because Abraham was before Moses. God has always been interested in one main thing: "Do you believe me?"

James then lists one other person, a "matriarch" of our faith, Rahab the prostitute. Yes, a woman of the night is one of James' examples of faith being brought to life through a decision. She wasn't even a Jew! This was *before* the Cross! Hmmmmmm...makes me think. But I'll stay on track here.

Rahab was a Gentile call girl, so why would James mention such a person? Why not pick someone else regal, like he just did Abraham?... He listed this harlot to prove our righteousness with God is based on a one-time decision of believing God! It's not about *who* we are according to the world or religious people!

"Matt, how can you say it's one time, based on this Scripture?"

Let's look at it in context. Does James say, "Rahab did *this* good thing and *that* righteous work, then she stopped prostituting and became a pioneer of Christianity by all she had done."? No! She was an outsider! A non-Jew! She wasn't even included in God's original chosen people to carry His Oracles! So what made her righteous? *One* act of faith that involved works! James writes:

> "*And in the same way was not also Rahab the prostitute justified by works when <u>she received the messengers</u> and <u>sent them out by another way</u>?*" (*James 2:25*)

What did Rahab do to be justified? She encountered the spies, and then made a decision to open a door.

1. Received the messengers.
2. Sent them out by another way.

Two *works,* one *action*. And if you look at Abraham's example, the same case is made. Abraham had to load up his stuff, make a trek up the mountain, and bound Issac—multiple *works* yet one action of faith!

But as for Rahab, in the Book of Joshua, the Israelites were promised the city in which she lived, Jericho. When she encountered the spies who were doing recon work, she could have easily had them captured and killed, but she didn't. She made a decision to help them! She made a one time choice of faith *for* God, and God noticed!

Friends, James is letting us know that just because we have knowledge about Jesus, that doesn't mean we've made a choice to place our faith in Him. When we *do* make that choice, we get new desires on the inside of us because He now lives *in* us and *we* live in Him (see Colossians 3:3, 1 Corinthians 6:19).

You might be thinking, "How is that even possible? How can we be in Jesus and Jesus be in us?"

Only when you see it spiritually will you understand. It is not the physical Jesus we become one with, but the Spirit of Jesus—the Holy Spirit. Let's look at it this way: Say you have a handkerchief and a glass of water. You take that handkerchief and you push it down into the water. What happens? Does the water go away? Does the handkerchief disappear? No. They become one, even though they are still separate. The handkerchief is in the water and the water is in the fabric of the handkerchief. This is what happens with you and the Spirit of God when you *decide* to believe you need Jesus' forgiveness—once.

In Romans 6, Paul calls this "baptized into Christ," yet not once does he mention water. Baptized simply means *placed inside of*. The grace-confused Christians have taken this part of the gospel—baptism—and retrofitted a law of being immersed in a liquid in order to be made right with God. No amount of *any* liquid in all of the universe can place us inside of Jesus, only our one-time faith in Him can. Water baptism is simply a celebration of your spiritual rebirth, it's not the actual day you are born again unless that was the day you decided to first believe.

But to get back on subject here, faith without works *is* dead. A choice must be made! James gives us *two* examples of people who made one-time decisions to go from the sideline of viewing God's goodness, to jumping in and playing!

Do you want to do that today? Do you want your spirit to be born again? Do you want to go to heaven? Do you want God to come live inside of you, right now, and never go away? If so, repeat this prayer with me and believe it as true. This decision will change everything inside you because God Himself will be joined with you forever:

God, I believe. I am deciding today to believe you for the forgiveness of Jesus. I want it. I admit that on my own I am a sinner. I don't want to be a sinner anymore in my spirit, so please give me a new, perfect spirit. I want to be just like you, right now. I believe that by me making this decision today, I am your child forever, and you're my Dad. I believe you will make your home in me and we will become one. So come on in, I'm inviting you! I'm ready! Teach me more about yourself, and teach me more about my new self! I want to grow in love with you! In Jesus' name I pray, amen.

DAY 13

DEBUNKING COMMON CHRISTIAN MYTHS

"Then you will know the truth, and the truth will set you free." ~Jesus

JOHN 8:32

Here is something I heard from a well-known Christian teacher:

"God doesn't require us to be perfect—He made us, and He knows we're human and will make mistakes. Our job is to get up each day and do our best to serve God with the gifts He has given us. And when we makes mistakes, we must get right with God, receive His forgiveness, and go on."

Now, at first glance, this statement looks great, doesn't it? A lot of people would say, "I don't see anything wrong with it at all."

For the Type A personality like myself, it actually looks awesome! It gives us goals to strive for, it leaves room for mistakes, and it even says God doesn't require us to be perfect. For a time in my life, I would have eaten this up with a spoon, stood to my feet, and clapped with all vigor. But—everything about this statement is incorrect when you begin to understand the New Covenant, which is the only Covenant available to the world. With all due respect to this teacher, here's what's wrong:

1. **God *does* require us to be perfect.** We not only have to be perfect, but we have to be perfect on God's level. Jesus said so: "Be perfect, therefore, as your heavenly Father is perfect" (Matthew 5:48). The problem is, if you don't understand the New Covenant, you will think Jesus is referring to *your* actions and attitudes—He's not. Jesus is talking about your spirit. Your spirit must be perfect like God is perfect. After this happens—once—your actions and attitudes will catch up to your spiritual perfection over the course of your lifetime. Rest assured, you will not reach the finish line of perfect actions and attitudes until you shed this shell of flesh (see Philippians 1:6, 1 Corinthians 15:52). You can only become perfect in spirit by having God kill off your old spirit—by grace through faith—and then at the same time, He gives you a *new* spirit which is connected to Him forever. When this happens you become a slave to spiritual perfection because your spirit can never be changed once it's born again; just like your flesh can never be changed once it's born the first time (see John 3:6-7, Ephesians 1:13, 2:8-9, Romans 6:6-7,18, Galatians 2:20, 2 Corinthians 5:17).

2. **Our job is not to serve God, but to enjoy being a member of His family.** Again, Jesus debunks this servant/master mentality with the disciples: "I no longer call you servants, because a servant does not know his master's business" (see John 15:15). We are on a higher level than servants! We are children of God! (See John 1:12) What kind of good father would call his children servants? Not a good one! Good fathers love their kids and don't expect them to "serve" them. They expect them to enjoy being their child! They expect them to be confident in their lineage! And yes, I get it, He is Lord—that's a no brainer. But for us, He's so much more. He's Daddy! (See Romans 8:15).

3. **We are to use our gifts to build up the Body of Christ, not serve.** Yes, I'm picking at words here, but the word *serve* has a connotation of *requirement*, of "Do this or else!" Jesus served *us*, and we have a heart to do the same for others because He lives in us. But when we create a law out of servitude, the good news of the gospel goes out the window and duty is created. Religious manipulation is created...*resentment* is created. Do you see where legislation *to* serve can lead? Friend, remember, the entire reason Jesus came and went was to give you freedom! (See John 8:36, Galatians 5:1). We don't *have* to do anything! What would happen if we didn't? Punishment? NO! What do you think the Cross was for? *Our* punishment! Therefore, use your gifts however you want, whenever you want—and enjoy your life! Yeah, enjoy your life! There's no pressure on you! The Holy Spirit will lead you into a healthy balance, trust me. You won't go crazy with this or sit passive.

4. **We get right with God one time, not each time we make mistakes.** What is a mistake according to God? A sin. And what does God require for sin to be paid for? Death (see Romans 6:23). And what did Jesus do at the Cross? He died. By my amazing math calculations we no longer have to pay for our sins. If we do, then God is a liar and the Cross was a waste of time. This subject—getting right with God, once, through faith in the Cross—can be tied into number one on this list. Our spirits are perfect because we get new ones (Hebrews 10:14). They *stay* perfect because Jesus will never die again (Hebrews 7:25, 10:10). Remember, it's death that must happen when we sin, and Jesus already died. He isn't dying again and again for each mistake we make. So *when* we sin, rather than feel condemned for a week, or work hard to get back into rightness with God, why not do something radical? Have some remorse. Remorse over sin is healthy. Not guilt, not denial, not condemnation, but remorse (see Romans 8:1). Secondly, turn away from it. Ask God for help

with it. You can even say sorry if you want to, but you are not getting more righteousness with Him by repenting and apologizing. You are right with Him for good because of who you are! (See 2 Corinthians 5:21, Colossians 1:22). Begin to separate your *who* from your *do*, thank God for His commitment to you, and move on. Form these habits and you'll be amazed at how much *less* you sin—not more.

5. **You *have* received God's forgiveness.** Every believer has. This is a past-tense event. God is not handing out new forgiveness to you each day. Why? Because forgiveness requires blood. "Without the shedding of blood there is no forgiveness" (see Hebrews 9:22). Is this starting to make sense? Where did the blood come from that you needed for God's forgiveness? Jesus! Your spotless lamb! It was Jesus' blood shed at the Cross that forgave you once and for all time! You believed He forgave you and He actually did! You are spiritually perfect and completely forgiven! The only way this can be reversed is if Jesus dies again and that ain't happening! (See Hebrews 7:25).

A prayer for you: *Good morning, Dad! It's a great day today! I know that every day is a great day because it's a gift from you, but I'm feeling really good! Thank you for another chance to enjoy life on planet earth! Right now, lift up all who are reading this, directly to you. Many of them might be taken back by what I've written today, and I understand that. Even I would have been, at one point. But as you've taken me deeper into the truth of the New Covenant, you've taught me that your Spirit brings rest, unconditional love, and easiness. That was hard for me to grasp! I want something to do! And I want to be the best at it! But all along, you wanted to use this personality of mine to teach people how to strive to rest—but first, I had to learn it for myself. I think I'm doing it. I think I'm using my gifts and calling properly. In this rest, you've motivated me the most! It's a strange paradox what you've done! Please begin to teach these dear readers that you motivate us from the heart,* *organically, without stress! Take them deeper into the knowledge of your grace. Take them deeper into the knowledge of your unconditional love through Jesus. It's so amazing. Amen.*

Day 14

Why You Should Get Rid of Your Back-Up Plan

"As for me, this is my covenant with you: You will be the father of many nations." ~God

Genesis 17:3

I would like for you to think of the oldest person you know. It could be a relative, neighbor, friend—whoever—but picture a person who looks to be knocking on heaven's door. They are *old*. Now, just imagine if that person was told:

"I will surely bless you and make your descendants as numerous as the stars in the sky and as the sand on the seashore."
(See Genesis 22:17)

That happened. That really happened! God said this to Abraham, who was already enjoying the senior citizen discount at Denny's! At 99 years old, He said, "I will make you fruitful!" (see Genesis 17:6) and Abraham knew there was no more fruit to be grown!...Or so he thought.

God even took it a step *further* and told Abraham it would be his wife, Sarah, who'd give birth! Abraham couldn't hold back any longer, he burst out in laughter, "Will a son be born to a man a hundred years old? Will Sarah bear a child at the age of ninety? If only Ishmael might live under your blessing!" (See Genesis 17:17-18).

Who was Ishmael? Ishmael was Abraham's back-up plan, a child who was conceived by way of Sarah's helper, Hagar. When it came to the promise of countless descendants, God wasn't moving fast enough for Abraham and Sarah. So they concocted a plan for Abraham to sleep with Hagar…and he did, resulting in Ishmael.

Have you ever done that before? Tried to rush God through human effort? You are praying, and hoping, and living the life God wants you to live—but you *feel* like what God has promised hasn't happened fast enough, so you come up with an idea to *help* God? What happens when we do this? We get a microwaved blessing. We get an Ishmael. We get *our* back-up plan, which is not as good as God's original plan, had we been patient!

Now, Ishmael was still loved by God and God had a plan for even him. God uses all of our choices together for good—even our forced choices—so there is never a need to worry. However, Ishmael was not the promise God had for Abraham and Sarah. He wanted Issac to be born. The lineage God had planned for Israel was in Isaac, not Ishmael.

Abraham and Sarah couldn't see that. So when death was knocking on their door, Sarah suggested Abraham sleep with Hagar to keep their family going. He obliged, and then Sarah got mad at *Abraham* for doing so…I'm going to move forward.

Although it was her idea, she resented Hagar and Ismael, and had them sent away. Her back-up plan blew up in her face and did nothing but cause her to be resentful and bitter. GOD HAD A BETTER PLAN HAD SHE JUST BEEN PATIENT! Had she just *trusted* Him, strife and division in her family could have been saved.

BUT! At just the right time, when God wanted her to conceive, she did!

> *"Sarah became pregnant and bore a son to Abraham in his old age (Issac), <u>at the very time God had promised</u> him." (Genesis 21:2, my note added)*

"At the very time God had promised!" Do you see that? Do you see that God was right on time with *His* promise? All along, they didn't *need* a back-up plan—they just had to wait!

Friend, God is faithful. God knows what you want, He knows what you need, and He knows what's best! You are His child! He loves you! He knows about every detail of your life on an even deeper level than *you* do! Today, give yourself permission to get rid of your back-up plan. Talk to God about it. Let Him know you trust Him. Let Him know that no matter *when* He decides to fulfill the promise He's placed in your heart, you will be who He has created you to be on the inside: *a grateful child with a wonderful attitude.* This is the peace He has planned for you! Trust Him today!

A prayer for you: *God, we know you love us. We know that your plan for all of us, ultimately, is Christ in us, and we have that promise today! We have all we truly need, right now! However, you also know we have individual desires for our lives, relationships, careers, finances, and our health. We don't want to force anything and get an Ismael, we want our Issac. Give us wisdom to make the right choices. We want what you want, we honestly do! So we are going to trust you, we are going to get rid of our back-up plans, and we are going to be who you have created us to be, your children. We love you! We know your promises are never late! In Jesus' name, amen.*

Day 15

Who is the Holy Spirit?

"Flesh gives birth to flesh, but the Spirit gives birth to spirit. You should not be surprised at my saying, 'You must be born again.' The wind blows wherever it pleases. You hear its sound, but you cannot tell where it comes from or where it is going. So it is with everyone born of the Spirit." ~Jesus

John 3:6-8

I was watching a movie this past weekend and in one of the scenes a dance was happening at a Catholic school. It was chaperoned by priests and nuns, so "awkward" would be the best way to describe it. Each time a couple got too close to one another, a priest or nun would scamper toward them, pull them apart, and then look at each person with shame and disgust. After about the fifth or sixth break-up session, one priest said to the duo, "Make room for the Holy Spirit!" and he pushed them apart.

As I lay there on the couch, the Holy Spirit immediately spoke to my heart, "That man just lied about me. I'm not trying to break up that dance."

Another time I was scrolling through Facebook and I saw a video of a well-known televangelist on stage preaching; there was a line of people in front of him, so I clicked on it. As I watched, one by one, he put his hand on each person and said, "*Receive* the Holy Spirit!" As he did, the people reacted as if he had dynamite in his hand. They exploded away from him and then onto the floor, lying still like they were asleep. The bodies quickly piled up as he went through the long line of men, women, and children.

Again, the Holy Spirit spoke to me, "That's weird, isn't it? That's not me. You know that, right?"

But the false advertising of the Holy Spirit didn't end there. When I was a young boy, I had an uber-religious, aggressive relative who caused me to believe the Holy Spirit was out to get me—that is, "If I wasn't careful." They sold my young, impressionable mind on the lie that He'd do some serious damage to me and that I'll "Get exactly what I deserve from the All-Seeing Eye!"

On and on, I could continue with the world's incorrect idea of God in Spirit form. And that's what the Holy Spirit is—or I should say *who* the Holy Spirit is...God in Spirit.

The Holy Spirit is not an *it*, but a *Him*. He is a Person. Just imagine if we called Jesus an it, or the Father an it. Well, the Holy Spirit is equal to the Son and the Father, so He's not an it either. He's not a nebulous force, but an actual Being who has no physical form (see John 3:8). This is how He indwells all Christians all at once (see John 12:32).

Paul called Him the Spirit of Christ (see Romans 8:9). Jesus said He and the Father are one (see John 10:30). Therefore, He rounds out the Trinity perfectly. Jesus is the physical part of God, the Father is God in Spirit form, and the Holy Spirit is God in the Spirit form, in us!

Before Jesus' sacrifice, the Holy Spirit never made His home inside of any human being. Instead, He came and went, He was *with* people and *upon* people, but never *in* people—that is, in their spirits. This is the difference in the New Covenant and the Old (see Hebrews 8:12-13). God is now *in* us—*fused* with us, for good—because of our faith in Jesus' sacrifice. Without Jesus' sacrifice this would not have been made possible (see 2 Corinthians 5:11, John 1:12, Ephesians 2:8-9).

If you look back in the Old Testament you'll see the Holy Spirit coming "upon people" to give them great power, and then He'd leave. For example, Samson. In the book of Judges, the Holy Spirit came upon him to *give him* the strength to slay 1,000 enemies of God with the jawbone of a donkey. He also came upon him once again, to push over the pillars in order to kill the Philistines. So as you can see, the Holy Spirit came and went. He was not infused with Samson's spirit like He is with Christians! (See John 14:23, Revelation 3:20).

Let's look at David. David begged God, "Please don't take your Holy Spirit from me!" (See Psalm 51:11). But as for us, we don't have to beg God any longer because of the Father's promise to the Son at the Cross, and vice versa. As New Covenant believers, God will never leave us nor forsake us! (See Hebrews 13:5). Our old, sinful spirits have died, and our new, perfect spirits are actually hidden inside of God's Spirit! (See Romans 6:6-7, Colossians 3:3, 1 Corinthians 6:19).

As a matter of fact, once we believe Jesus is our Savior, we are sealed up forever inside of the Holy Spirit! (See Ephesians 1:13). Even if we are faithless He remains faithful! Why? Because the Father will never turn His back on the Son (see 2 Timothy 2:13, Hebrews 6). The Cross solidified our salvation (see Hebrews 7:25).

The people of the Old Testament did not have perfect spirits like we do on this side of Calvary. For this reason, the Holy Spirit could never make His home in them. Their spirits were still in Adam and not in Christ. Their spirits were still in sin, and not cleansed (see Romans 5&6). As for us, those things are not true. We've been perfectly cleansed forever! (See Hebrews 10:14, 1 Corinthians 6:11, 2 Peter 1:9). Not our actions and attitudes, but *us*! Our identity has changed! We've been re-born *of* God's Spirit! (See John 3:6-7, 1 John 3:9).

So what is the Holy Spirit like? What's His personality like? If you look at Jesus, you'll find your answers. Jesus personified the Father *and* the Holy Spirit! They are not playing good cop, bad cop, dumb cop. All three are God, all three are equal, and God is love! (See 1 John 4:8).

A grace-confused person will be quick to get mad at me for pointing this out. The self-centered individual, who is focused on all of their "amazing" religious behavior and church work, will cherry-pick *different* Bible verses, attempting to create fear. They don't like 1 John 4:8 very much, or John 3:16. They lean more toward Scriptures to make us think what *they* are doing is more holy than what *we* are doing. Little do they know, anything that begins with "I do" or "I don't do" is anti-gospel. The Message is not about us, it's about what Jesus has done *for* us. We are receivers and reflectors, not producers.

They want us to be legalistic like them and they can't stand grace. They want us to believe the Holy Spirit is on their side and not ours. Here's one of their favorite lines: "The Holy Spirit is here to convict you of your sin! He isn't here to make you feel good or tickle your ears!"

Friend, who's really having their ears tickled? Those of us who are saying we are nothing without the Spirit? Those of us who are claiming God's grace is enough? Or is it *you* who is claiming "your part" is completing the Spirit's work? Is it *you* who is making the assertion that grace is just a license to sin—as if without grace *you* have a license? That sounds a lot more like ear-tickling to me.

With all due respect, the pastor who pats a person on their religious little head—and then scolds the world in front of them for not being like them—*that* seems more like music to the ears of a person who doesn't know God's Spirit. But who am I to judge? I'm just a branch.

Yes, Jesus said the Holy Spirit will convict the world of sin (see John 16:8), but *we* are not of this world! (See John 17:16). We are already seated with God in heaven, in the spiritual realm! Christian, that's where your spirit is right now! (See Ephesians 2:6).

If you think about it, what is the punishment for the conviction of sin? DEATH! (See Romans 6:23). What did Jesus do? He died! God's wrath over your sin was satisfied completely at the Cross! (See Romans 5:9).

Therefore, the Holy Spirit is not convicting *Christians* of sin! Jesus was already convicted and killed! So now, instead of God's wrath over our sin, we get something so much better: a God who is satisfied (see 1 John 2:2).

Believer, the Holy Spirit counsels us, guides us, disciplines us (with love and patience), and He comforts us (see John 14:6, 14:16, Hebrews 12:6). But be sure, He is not convicting you of sin. People might attempt to convict you, the enemy might try, and even your old unrenewed pockets of thinking—but God isn't. Jesus' conviction and death was more than good enough. You're now okay with your Creator. You're *okay*.

So if the Holy Spirit isn't mad at us, if He's not disappointed, and if He's not convicting us, then what is it that causes us to change our lives? HIS GOODNESS! It is the *goodness* of God that leads us toward any type of repentance! (See Romans 2:4). Really, all we are repenting from is the stuff that's not a part of us anyway—that is, as heaven-ready saints.

We are connected to God's Spirit, so He'll always lead us into the truth of ourselves and Himself! Here are the true characteristics of His personality:

1. He gives you freedom.
2. He's loving.
3. He's joyful.
4. He's peaceful.
5. He's patient.
6. He's kind.
7. He's gentle.
8. He's humble.
9. He keeps no record of your wrongs.
10. He doesn't dishonor you.
11. He's not pompous.
12. He's not too busy for you.
13. He feels your pain.
14. He doesn't get enjoyment from bad things happening to you or others.
15. He delights in His truth—the *only* truth.

16. He protects your spirit at all times.
17. He trusts you.
18. He doesn't allow Satan or any demon to touch you.
19. He has hope in you.
20. He never fails you.

(See 1 Corinthians 13:4-8, Galatians 5:1,22,23, Matthew 11:29, John 11:35, 1 John 5:18).

So today, my friends, know this: The Holy Spirit *is* your life! Because of your faith in Jesus' sacrifice, you are in Him permanently! (See Colossians 3:3-4, John 10:10, 14:6). You can't even admit this without it being true! (See 1 Corinthians 12:3). You live by the Spirit, you pray by the Spirit, you walk by the Spirit, and you love by the Spirit! YOU AND THE HOLY SPIRIT ARE ONE, FOREVER! He is God, you are in Him, and He is in you!

A prayer for you: *Heavenly Father, thank you for your Holy Spirit. For so long, I was afraid of Him, but He's taught me the truth of who He is, and I absolutely love Him for it. Right now, I lift up all who are reading this, directly to you. So many of them have been lied to about the Holy Spirit. They think He's far off, angry, unattainable, or unreliable. They even think they need to have some special gift to get a second portion of Him, please, reveal these lies today. The Holy Spirit is not only NEAR them, but IN them! He's not only in them, but He's in them in full and He'll never go away! Begin to open up their minds to the truth of who you are! Let them know that if they feel relaxed and loved, it's you. Everything opposite is a lie! That is, for all who believe in Jesus. In His name, I pray. Amen.*

Day 16

Why Should I Have Good Behavior?

"And that is what some of you were. But you were washed, you were sanctified, you were justified in the name of the Lord Jesus Christ and by the Spirit of our God."

1 Corinthians 6:11

"*Why should I have good behavior?*" The short answer to the title of this devotional is: Because good behavior is authentic, as a Christian.

When you behave properly, and you are a child of God—a believer—you are working *out* who is in you, Jesus. Paul told the Christians in Philippi about *allowing* Jesus to live through them:

> "work <u>out</u> your salvation with fear and trembling" (see Philippians 2:12)

First off, about this verse, it has been used for centuries by the grace-confused Christians to scare people. However, there's nothing to be afraid of when you read this passage. Why? When you read the whole of Scripture, you can decipher what Paul was saying through a little-used word: context.

1. **Paul said work *out* your salvation, not work *for*.** He was emphasizing, "What is *in* you, a saved person, work it out." Like squeezing toothpaste out of a tube, in order to *use* God in you, work Him out *through* your actions and attitudes.
2. **In regard to the words "fear and trembling," John told us in 1 John that we have nothing to be afraid of as Christians.** He said, God's love for us is perfect and it casts out *all* fear. He even goes on to say why: "because fear has to do with punishment" (see 1 John 4). As Christians, we are not going to be punished by God, ever, for anything. What do you think the Cross was for? Jesus took on our punishment once and for all (see 1 Peter 3:18, Hebrews 10:10). Sure, God *disciples* us, but punishes? No way. Therefore, fear and trembling is more of a way of saying "respect and awe." It's having a mindset of, "Wow, I have the God of the universe *in* me, and He is living *through* me."

So obviously behavior does matter. Behavior mainly matters because people are watching, and behavior is all they see. However, behavior cannot change our perfect spiritual identity or *keep* our perfect spiritual identity—only Jesus does that because He will never die again (see Hebrews 7:25). Therefore, when our behavior is good, it is simply an outward sign of an inward truth.

Behavior matters because it's impossible for someone to *see* our faith. For example, when I was getting drunk all the time, I'd hang out at bars and get toasted quite often. People *saw me* in public exuding alcoholic *behavior*. Is drinking a sin? No. Obviously it's not because Jesus' first recorded miracle resulted in the creation of alcohol, and Paul advised Timothy to have some wine for his stomach issues (see John 2, 1 Timothy 5:23). But, getting *drunk* is a sin, and as a Christian I wasn't made for sin (see Ephesians 5:18, Romans 6:1-2). This is why I was so miserable doing it—even if my flesh got a temporary thrill—*I* couldn't stand it.

I'll tell you what else is a sin, being a bad example for my daughter by coming home sloshed, *that's* a sin. Being controlled by a liquid, *that's* a sin. I'M NOT MADE FOR SIN! I'M A SAINT IN MY SPIRIT! Every Christian is! Thankfully, those sinful behaviors would never be able to change who I am. No matter how often I practiced them, I'd never be able to get better at them. My supernatural identity is *sinless*. This is why John said:

> "*No one who is born of God will continue to sin, because God's seed <u>remains</u> in them; they <u>cannot go on sinning</u>, because they <u>have been</u> born of God*" (see 1 John 3:9)

Do you see that? We don't have the ability to go on sinning because we've been reborn! God's supernatural sperm—for lack of better description—remains in us just the same as our earthly father's physical sperm remains in us! IT IS WHO WE ARE! So when we choose to *act on* sin, we are acting on a trait that is not *of* us! The word "sin" is not a part of our supernatural DNA! We are cats who bark when we sin! Dogs who are meowing! It makes no sense for us to do so! This is why we must *be* our true selves!

My incorrect behavior of alcoholism didn't change my perfect spiritual identity back then—and even if I decided to go temporality stupid and pick up a 12-pack on the way home tonight, I'd *still* be a holy saint, right now. BEHAVIOR DOES NOT CHANGE IDENTITY!

For this reason, Paul made sure the early Christians knew who they were, no matter *how* they acted. He told the terribly-behaved Corinthians they were saints! (See 1 Corinthians 1:2). Corinth would make Las Vegas look like Sesame Street! No matter! Paul *still* addressed his letter, "To the saints in Corinth"! They didn't *act* like saints, that's for sure!

But even still, Paul continued to repeat himself, letting them know that unholy behavior is silly because it's not authentic as heaven-ready people. After writing out a laundry-list of atrocious behaviors and attitudes, Paul tells them this, which blows my mind:

> *"And that is what some of you <u>were</u>. But you <u>were</u>*
> *<u>washed</u>, you <u>were sanctified</u>, you <u>were justified</u>*
> *in the name of the Lord Jesus Christ and by the*
> *Spirit of our God." (1 Corinthians 6:11)*

A person reading this letter might have said, "But Paul, how can you say they *were* washed, they *were* sanctified, and they *were* justified? They sure as heck aren't living that way! They are still doing the same disgusting stuff!"

…It's because they were not being themselves *in* spirit. They weren't working *out* who was in them, the Holy Spirit. Paul was formerly the most well-behaved Jew of his time (see Philippians 3), so he knew how important outward actions were to those around him. However, he also knew that authentic proper behavior could only come from the Spirit of God (see Romans 6:6, Colossians 1:10). *And* he knew that once the Spirit of God came to live inside a person, He'd never leave them because of what Jesus did at the Cross (see Hebrews 7:25, 13:5, Matthew 28:20, 2 Timothy 2:13).

So when Christians weren't acting like holy people, Paul always reminded them that *only* holiness would make sense to them—even if they fell off track. Just look at how he spoke to the Colossians:

> *"But now he <u>has reconciled you</u> by Christ's physical body*
> *through death <u>to present you holy</u> in his sight, <u>without</u>*
> *<u>blemish</u> and <u>free from accusation</u>" (Colossians 1:22)*

Paul, once again, is speaking in past-tense. He's saying, "Look at who you really are! You are completely settled-up with God because of Jesus! You are holy! You are blemish and accusation free! Choosing to sin is childish! Show the world your true selves!"

Not *once* did he say, "Your phony, improper, sinful behavior will cause God's grace to run out," no, not ever. Paul knew this would never happen because of what Jesus went through. As a matter of fact, he said poor behavior and legalistic attitudes will only cause God's grace to increase, *not* decrease (see Romans 5:20).

Why would we choose to abuse such amazing grace? Why would we *not* act like the perfect people He's made us to be inside? It makes no sense! So Christian, behave authentically. Behave like God's child, who you are (see John 1:12).

So today, my friends, know this: Good behavior matters because you are a good person with good behavior. Even when your unrenewed, stinking thinking *temporarily* convinces you otherwise, that does not mean you are a bad person. YOU ARE A SAINT! YOU ARE SEALED WITH GOD'S SPIRIT AND SET APART FOREVER! Let's show the world who Jesus really is by showing them who *we* are! Let's make them want Him too, with our love, because we *are* loving people!

A prayer for you: *Heavenly Father, I want to thank you for your guidance. Even when I get shipwrecked and make stupid choices that don't match up with the real me, you stay committed to me. Also, I want to thank you for teaching me that you are never convicting me, but instead, counseling me. Conviction creates stress and guilt, counsel creates hope through correction—and that's what you do! You are hopeful even while correcting our poor behaviors and attitudes! Keep doing it! Right now, I lift up all who are reading this, directly to you. For the saints, keep teaching them they are saints! Remind them that every believer in Christ is a saint on the exact same level! Let them know your Spirit in them will never lead them to sin—Satan and his demons will, so will the power of sin itself—but their true selves don't even want to sin! They want what you want! Keep reminding them that when others see us choose improper behavior, we are misrepresenting our Family, and we don't want to do that. We want to show the world the truth of who we are in Christ! Holy saints! Amen!*

Day 17

You Are God's Ambassador

"We are therefore Christ's ambassadors, as though God were making his appeal through us."

See 2 Corinthians 5:20

The plane just touched down in a foreign country, glancing out your window, the airport looks odd. It's not what you are used to, but you expected this. Your first trip to represent your country's leader has brought you to a culture outside of the norm.

As the roar of the engines cause the vessel to stop, you look down at your notes. A finely crafted bullet-point your leader has personally typed up, you've studied the whole way. You know exactly what he wants you to discuss with the people of this foreign nation. But all of the sudden, you crumple the pages, rip them up, and shove them in the trash as the flight attendant walks by for a final garbage pick-up.

"I'm doing this my own way. I'm saying what *I* want to say, and I don't care what my leader wants. This country will hear *my* opinions, get *my* policy ideas, and I will express my own beliefs!"

What just happened?…Unfortunately, you decided to no longer represent what your dignitary and home country stands for. Even though the place you are visiting *thinks* you are, you're not.

This happens to us "Christian representatives" every day. We've been included in the gospel, assigned a spot in God's Cabinet, but yet we often go rogue in our actions and attitudes. Now, do our incorrect choices, words, and body-language make us *not* a member of God's country? No. Nothing can change that. But sadly, the people of this world *see us* misrepresenting God when we act out incorrect ideas.

Paul said we are Christ's ambassadors, that He is making His appeal *through* us! And what is it exactly He is trying to appeal? RECONCILIATION! HE WANTS US TO BE RECONCILED WITH GOD! (See 2 Corinthians 5:20).

Reconcile is defined as: restore friendly relations between; cause to coexist in harmony; make or show to be compatible.

It means, kiss and make up! It means, you are back in the black! It means, bury the hatchet! Declare a truce! It means become *one* with! This is what we are called to represent as Christ's ambassadors!

We've touched down on planet earth and our main objective is to let the world know *everyone* has the opportunity to be completely reconciled with God! How? Through faith in Jesus Christ!

This is the *only* type of representation we are truly qualified to express! Paul calls it the ministry *of* reconciliation! He informs the Christians in Corinth—some of the worst behaved people, ever—about the ministry they are all qualified to now preach:

> *"All this is from God, who <u>reconciled us to himself</u> through Christ and <u>gave us the ministry of reconciliation</u>" (2 Corinthians 5:18)*

Here Paul is, writing to the Corinthian Christians—a group of believers who would make today's porn industry look PG—telling *them* that they have a ministry of reconciliation? HOW CAN THIS BE? It's because Paul *knew* they were already reconciled with God through their faith in Christ! So now *they* had the same ministry as he did!

A self-absorbed person will read this and yell, "Matt! Stop lying! We gotta repent! We gotta make ourselves living sacrifices!"

Friend, I would agree with you. But we must *define* repent, and we must understand what "living sacrifices" truly means. First, in regard to repentance, let's establish a biblical fact: all that is required to become reconciled with God is repentance of unbelief in Jesus' forgiveness.

The book of Hebrews was written primarily to the unbelieving Jews. They were Mosaic Law-abiding citizens. They didn't have the problems of obvious carnal sins—like those dirty Corinthians, Ephesians, Galatians, and other Gentiles—so the author doesn't even bother talking about such stuff. However, they still had a *major* sin issue. They rejected the idea of Jesus being the Messiah. They taste-tested the gospel and said, "No, thank you. I'll choose Law and animal blood, not grace and Jesus' blood."

They were very well-behaved but they lacked one thing, Jesus. The first ten chapters of Hebrews speaks of only *one* sin, the unforgivable sin: unbelief.

Once we believe Jesus is the Messiah, that He's forgiven us for free, we've repented. We've changed our mind about Jesus. Afterwards, repentance of incorrect actions and attitudes happen organically as Christ in us teaches us who we are in our spirits—holy saints. But make no mistake, repentance of incorrect actions and attitudes didn't save us in the first place. Jesus did, and we *let* Him through our faith (see Ephesians 2:8-9).

As for making ourselves living sacrifices, I completely agree with that too. Paul even tells us to do this very thing! (See Romans 12:1). However, we must understand that we are to be *living* sacrifices—not dead ones. We are not killing ourselves off! Sure, our minds are being renewed day by day, but our old spirits have *already* been killed off from the moment we first believed! When this happened, we got a *new* spirit—a perfect spirit—which is connected to Christ for good! (See Romans 6:6-7, Galatians 2:20, 2 Corinthians 5:17, 1 Corinthians 6:19, Colossians 3:3, 2 Timothy 2:13, Hebrews 7:25).

We are not martyrs! We are *living* holy saints! WE ARE ALIVE! So when we represent God in our actions and attitudes, all we need to do is be ourselves! We can be confident! We can look people in the eye and let them know what God will do for them for free! What will He do?

HE WILL RECONCILE EVERYONE TO HIMSELF THROUGH THEIR FAITH IN JESUS! (See Colossians 1:20-22, 2 Corinthians 5:19).

So today, my friends, know this: You *are* an ambassador for God, if you believe you are. What Jesus did at the Cross gives you this right! The foundation of your representation is reconciliation. Reconciliation is expressed easily through two things: *belief and love*. Belief and love are the two requirements to *be* reconciled with God through Christ. First, believe this truth of His forgiveness for your own sin. Second, embrace the love of the Father *through* your belief in Jesus Christ. Afterwards, you too have become an ambassador! Welcome!

> **A prayer for you:** *Heavenly Father, thank you for teaching me the one true ministry, reconciliation. For so long, I was distracted by stuff that doesn't matter—and sometimes I still am. But even still, you gently guide me back toward what matters the most, belief and love. I want to thank you for your patience with me as I continue to learn more about representing you properly. I love you, and I'm so happy to be able to do this. Right now, I lift up all who are reading this, directly to you. So many of them have been distracted by the lies of the enemy and ill-informed Christians. They think they need to force the world to change, and they don't. That very sentence causes strife in their mind, but that's because you want them to be purged of such frustrations. There is no pressure on them to be your ambassador, as they simply live life they'll do it effortlessly—even when it's difficult. Put their minds at ease by letting them know all they have to do is be themselves. As they do so, you take care of everything! Give them peace today! Give them confidence! Teach them more and more about just HOW reconciled they are with you, because of the Cross! COMPLETELY! As they go deeper into the knowledge of this truth, the easier it will be for them to tell others about it. Sometimes, they'll even have to use words. In Jesus' name I pray, amen!*

DAY 18

A CONVERSATION WITH AN ATHEIST

"The Son is the image of the invisible God, the firstborn over all creation. For in him all things were created: things in heaven and on earth, visible and invisible, whether thrones or powers or rulers or authorities; all things have been created through him and for him. He is before all things, and in him all things hold together."

COLOSSIANS 1:15-17

Who made the sun, moon, planets, and stars? Something or someone had to make them. And further, something or someone has to *keep them* where they are. The sun, moon, planets, and stars are not randomly in the sky—neither is this planet. The question is, "Where'd they come from?" If you're truly seeking, you'll find the truth.

"Matt, all of those things just appeared at the Big Bang. There is no *real* God, if that's what you mean."

"Okay. But who or what *caused* the Big Bang? How can anything happen without something already being there to cause it *to* happen?"

"NOTHING CAUSED IT! It just happened!"

"So it looks like you have a problem of origin, that is, if you don't know where the Big Bang came from."

"No I don't! I don't have a problem! I just believe it!"

"So you simply *believe* in something, and that's how you develop your truth? Hmmmmmm...sounds very familiar to me. And as far as 'nothing' causing the Big Bang, that's impossible. Something *had* to cause the Big Bang—something or someone. Matter can't come from nothing."

"Says who? And what makes *your* god the truth, Matt?"

"What makes anything the truth? I don't know why the God of the Bible is the truth, but I do know that I've searched every nook and cranny to find out *why* we are here and *where* we came from, and it's all funneled into Jesus."

"WHAT MAKES YOUR JESUS THE TRUTH?"

"Grace. Grace is what makes Him the truth. No other religion is based on grace."

"Bull!"

"Okay, search for yourself. I've got a library of books I can loan you that I've compiled during my quest to find out why I'm here. Not all of the authors agree with each other, but Jesus is the one cornerstone they stand on equally. Can you get to the bottom of where all of this came from for yourself, and then give me your opinion?"

"NO! I choose to believe in NOTHING!"

"Then your god is nothing. 'Nothing' is literally your god. As a human being with an everlasting spirit, it's impossible to *not* believe in something creating you. You can't *not* believe this, just like you can't *not* breathe. Our Creator made us this way. Pondering our origin, and where we will go when we die, is what makes us different than all of God's other creations. We are spirits, nothing else is. So even when you believe in nothing, you are still making nothing your creator."

Friends, the Bible says God has placed eternity in the heart of every human (see Ecclesiastes 3:11). So we *will* look up at the sun, moon, and stars, and think, "Why is that there? Where did it come from? Why am I looking at it in awe?"

The answer is love, God's love. Because of what Jesus did at the Cross, we now have free access to God's love by believing Christ is our Savior from sin—our Savior who doesn't need our help (see John 3:16, Acts 17:25). This love is tapped into by grace through faith (see Ephesians 2:8-9).

The reason why this planet is here—why the sun, moon, stars and *you* are here—is because God has a permanent place for your spirit with Him in heaven after your physical body wears out. This short trip here is but a blip on the radar screen of eternity.

So today, my friends, ask God this, even if you don't know who He is just yet: "Why did you create everything? Why did you create me? God, who are you? Reveal yourself to me." Make no mistake, He will answer all of these questions! He promises! Keep asking and keep seeking the truth! The mystery of God is over!

A prayer for you: *Heavenly Father, thank you for teaching me the truth of your love. You and I both know, that for a time, I was trying to disprove your existence. But as I kept seeking, you kept revealing yourself. It all makes sense now. Jesus' life, death, and resurrection—His miracles and love—has taught me everything I need to know about you. All in all, Creation is a stage, this was a rescue mission, and Jesus is the hero. Keep teaching me more about your grace, and give me wisdom so that I can represent you properly. Right now, I lift up all who are reading this, directly to you. For those who want to believe in you but there is that ONE THING that keeps them from doing so, let them know that one thing is no big deal. Nothing is a big deal to you, you are God! Help them to believe! From the beginning of time, you've simply wanted us to believe you. I do, and I know that many more will, before this story is over. Thanks for making us a part of it! In our Savior's name I pray, amen.*

Day 19

How to Have Fun without Drinking Alcohol

*"I have the right to do anything," you say—but
not everything is beneficial. "I have the right to do
anything"—but not everything is constructive.*

1 Corinthians 10:23

"It's 1:30, let's just head home," I say to my brother as we stumble into my car.

"The heck with that! I want to keep drinking!" he replies, once we are sitting inside the vehicle.

"No, man. I'm tired," I retort, then lean back in my seat as he begins the 45-minute trip home from the bar we were at.

"Fine. But let's get some Taco Bell."

As we pulled off from the bar parking lot, Mark didn't even get fifty feet down the road before he started to run off into the ditch, so I sat back up in my seat to "monitor" his drunk driving. It was my car, but I already had two DWI's, so throwing my keys at my drinking partner was always backed up by my selfish excuse *not* to get another citation.

After binge eating, I dozed in and out—then suddenly, I start to notice a white light getting brighter in front of us. Soon enough, it went from *one* bright light to two.

"Oh my God, it's a caaaaaaar! Stooooop! Mark! Turn around!" I looked over at him and his eyes were nearly closed.

"What!" my brother yelled! Mark was so drunk he had gotten on the northbound lane of the interstate, going south! He immediately slammed on the brakes, the car screeched and swerved as he started to turn around. So smashed, it took him *way* too long and *another* car goes buzzing by!

"MARK! GOOOOOOO! We are going to die!"

...I'll never forget the look of sheer terror on his face as he scrambled to twist the steering wheel. We finally made it to the off ramp, crossed over the highway, and began driving home in the proper direction.

"Real fun, wasn't it? Idiot. You almost got you and your brother killed last night." I say to myself the next morning in disgust. My conversations were always influenced by the enemy when I was hungover. I was mean to *me*, and the devil heaped on the condemnation. Of course it wasn't me *me*, it was my old, stinking thinking.

"You could have died! You and Mark, both! But you *had a blast*, didn't you? Totally worth it, right? Some Christian you are!"

This sarcastic, demeaning conversation would continue for the rest of the day as I nursed a hangover on the couch in the den.

This is just one of many stories I could write about my life of drinking; a 300-page book of just drunken episodes could be typed up by me, easily. As a matter of fact, I have to try to keep my writings balanced when it comes to talking about my former addiction. Why? Because I know that not everyone has a problem with alcohol, and further, there is nothing *wrong* with alcohol. Brace yourself for what I'm about to say: *alcohol is not the enemy.*

Our enemy is the enemy. The temptations he dangles in front of us, is the enemy. Stinking thinking is the enemy. Old coping mechanisms is the enemy—but alcohol is just a liquid. It is a liquid I allowed myself to be controlled by for a long time.

I saw a meme the other day which read something like this:

> "No, you don't need alcohol to have fun. You also don't need running shoes to run, but it sure F*@%ing helps."

Does it? Does it *really* help us have fun? Again, I'm speaking to those who act as if they *can't* have fun without it. For just a moment, I would like for you to think of all the stories *you* could write, just like I wrote in the opening of this devotional. Were *your* stories really that spectacular? Or did some end with a near-death experience? Maybe someone has actually died or been seriously injured, but the enemy has convinced you it was fun up until that point, so drinking isn't the problem. Maybe you've made some of the most regrettable choices while drunk, choices so diabolical you don't even want to *speak* of them. So tell me, how fun is your drinking life?...Be honest. Is it or was it *really* that fulfilling? No...not at all. The cons far outweigh the pros.

Now, for those of you who think our issue is simply a will-power deficiency, do this: for yourself, think about something that controls you... go ahead...right now, if alcohol doesn't have any effect on your self-control—you can take it or leave it—think of *one thing* you can honestly say, "I have no control over that part of my life." Whatever it may be, that *thing* is controlling *you*, not the other way around. That's us with drinking.

Sure, we might be able to pull off a normal-drinking episode now and again but we know, we *know* it's like walking on the edge of a cliff. Drinking alcohol in excess is simply a control issue for us. It is *being* controlled by a liquid that alters our feelings. As Christians, the Holy Spirit in us has given us self-control—so we have it—we just have to let it come to life! (See Galatians 5:22-23). We are not to be controlled by anything or anyone, but instead, we are to be led by the Spirit of God in us. Paul had a few things to say about alcohol, here's one verse:

> *"Don't get drunk on wine, which leads to debauchery. Instead, be filled with the Spirit"* (Ephesians 5:18)

First of all, for those who think that alcohol in the Bible was *not* fermented, you will have to get a Sharpie and mark through this verse. Paul said, "Don't get *drunk*." How do you get drunk? Drumroll please...

dadadadada…fermented alcohol! Ta-da! Amazing how that works, isn't it? You can only get drunk on fermented juice, not unfermented.

Pardon my sarcasm. I've just had way too many run-ins with grace-confused Christians who say alcohol was not actual alcohol in the Bible—that it was grape juice. You can't get drunk on grape juice. Moving on.

Second, Paul didn't say, "*Don't* drink wine," he just said, "Don't get drunk." So for those of us who know we can't drink without getting drunk because our off-button is broken, we shouldn't drink a single drop. Godly wisdom needs to come into play. Also, Paul *advises* someone to *drink* wine, Timothy, a preacher (!), for his frequent stomach issues (see 1 Timothy 5:23). So obviously fermented alcohol isn't the problem here, it's being controlled by such.

Next, what does Paul say getting drunk *does*? It leads to debauchery. What is debauchery? It's pretty much what Mark and I were doing that night at the bar: *stupid, nasty stuff*. Getting drunk leads us to doing some of the stupidest things, but we're drunk, so we don't care! Oh, the next day we care. The embarrassment sometimes is so severe, we hide from people for long periods of time. *Awkward* would be a good description of how we feel, after saying and doing bone-head things. Then we gotta go into clean-up mode, making sure we didn't burn any bridges.

Lastly, what does Paul say we *should* do, *rather* than getting drunk on wine? Be filled with the Holy Spirit! Being filled with the Holy Spirit is a one-time event that happens the very moment you believe Jesus has forgiven you. So this verse is more of a "be *being* filled," as in, enjoy Him because He's in you! God's Spirit doesn't "come and go" based on our good or bad behavior—no way! That's what He did according to the Old Covenant. According to the *New* Covenant which Jesus created and we are under, He never *ever* leaves us!

We read about David begging God, "Please don't take your Spirit away" (see Psalm 51:11), but now, on this side of the Cross, He *won't* take His Spirit away because we are one *with* His Spirit! (See Hebrews 8:13, Colossians 3:3, 1 Corinthians 6:19, Romans 6:6, 2 Timothy 2:13,

Hebrews 13:5). So if you are going to get drunk, you are taking Him with you.

Friend, Paul is saying, "Instead of getting drunk, enjoy the Holy Spirit!" He's saying, "Get your enjoyment from who is already in you! You don't need an outside source!" Just look at what he wrote in the following verses:

> *"speaking to one another with psalms, hymns, and songs from the Spirit. Sing and make music from your heart to the Lord, always giving thanks to God the Father for everything, in the name of our Lord Jesus Christ."* (Ephesians 5:19-20)

SING! LAUGH! DANCE! SOCIALIZE! Have a good time! The Holy Spirit knows how to have fun and He lives in you! If you are allowing yourself to be controlled by alcoholic beverages, you don't *have* to! And, you don't have to shut yourself off from the world! You just have to have fun organically through God *in* you! Be yourself! Buy someone a beer, but *you* don't need that booze!

"Matt, you are just trying to get people to ruin their witness! A true man of God would never drink alcohol!"

Really? What about Jesus? Was He a true man of God? The Messiah *created* alcohol for a party—the best alcohol ever (see John 2). God-made wine would put all other wine to shame! Alcohol is *not* the problem. *Drinking* alcohol is not the problem. The problem is being *controlled* by something.

We are free. God sent Jesus here to free us (see Galatians 5:1). Since we are free, we shouldn't use that freedom to allow ourselves to be controlled, yet again. Not by a liquid, a needle, a plant, a pill, a pretty face, an attractive body, a box of donuts, a gym, or the approval of a pastor. WE ARE FREE. WE ARE FREEEEEEEEEEEE!

So how do you have fun without drinking alcohol? By understanding your freedom. When you truly understand just *how* free you are as God's own child, you won't allow anything to control you. You won't be waiting on Friday to have fun because you know that Friday is *inside* of you. Friend, not only are you free, but you are a *slave* to righteousness! Imprisoned for life! (see Romans 6:18). You can never get away from being spiritually perfect no matter how un-free your choices may be! So be yourself and *be* free! Be free! You *are* free, so live that way!

A prayer for you: *God, today I want to thank you for showing me the prison door was wide open to freedom on May 8th, 2014. Oh my goodness, the time I spent in that cell was so stupid, sobriety was right there! The whole time the door was open! Thank you for giving me the wisdom to stop being controlled by alcohol. I had some relearning to do, but it's been worth it! Right now, I lift up all who are reading this, directly to you. For those who are addicted to anything, help them. If they are believers, let them know they are already free! Let them know the fun begins when they simply be themselves in you! Reassure them that you are not disappointed in their behavior in any way, and that their choices have not altered their identity: child of God! Let today be the first day they understand who they truly are inside as they walk out of the prison doors of addictions, once and for all! In Jesus' name I pray, amen.*

Day 20

You Were Planned By God

"For we are God's masterpiece. He has created us anew in Christ Jesus, so we can do the good things he planned for us long ago."

Ephesians 2:10

God has created some pretty amazing things! If you've ever seen the spectacle that is a blue whale bursting up out of the ocean, high into the sky, and then slamming right back into the vortex it just made, you can appreciate its size! It's massive! Being the world's largest animal, it could easily crush a small boat if it landed on it after doing what is called, *cetacean behavior*, or *surface breaching*. (That cool thing it does when it jumps out of the water!)

A blue whale can weigh as much as half a million pounds! A baby blue whale gains up to a *ton* of weight in a month! That makes me feel better after gaining a few pounds each weekend. The heart of an adult male can tip the scales at over 1,000 pounds! And the length of a full grown blue whale can span three buses! That's huge!

On the very opposite "size side" of the animal kingdom is a mammal that could easily be mistaken for an overgrown bumblebee. The hog-nosed bat is the smallest recorded animal on the planet. If you walked into a cave full of these little bats, you'd think you just stirred up a hornet's nest! They are so small that when it rains it's hard for them to fly. That's *really* small!

But what I think is the most amazing thing about both of these animals—what's most intriguing—is that God thought of both of them. They were God's ideas! And He didn't just think up how different their sizes would be, but also, their bone structure, what cells would make up their bone structure, how they'd look, what they'd like to eat, so on and so forth—GOD THOUGHT OF THAT!

God loves variety! No two things are the same! Even twins, their genetic make-up which matches, *still* can't produce two of the exact same people. They have different souls and spirits. They have different likes, styles, hobbies, personalities, and goals. God wanted to make all of us different, He planned it this way.

What baffles my mind is that the very same God who thought of and *created* enormous blue whales and tiny hog-nosed bats, He thought of you and me too. He even planned us before He created this vast universe! (See Ephesians 1:4). He personally stitched us together in our mother's wombs! (See Psalm 139:13).

However, the most exciting news, the very thing that should make you feel absolutely spectacular is this: you are His most prized possession! Out of all of His creations, from the sun, the planets, and the stars, to the fish in the sea, the birds of the sky, and the lions of the Serengeti—*even* compared to the biggest mountains, lush rainforests, and vast deserts—*YOU* ARE HIS MASTERPIECE! (See Ephesians 2:10). He created all of this for you to enjoy with Him!

So today, my friends, know this: By simply placing your faith in Jesus, you can begin to enjoy this relationship right now; a relationship so great, God just *had* to create you!

A prayer for you: *Good morning, Father! Wow! What a beautiful, crisp morning you've given me! Thank you! Thank you for the sound of* *the birds! Thank you for the good health you've given me! Right now, I lift up all who are reading this, directly to you. I ask that you help them to understand why you created them, which is to have a loving relationship with you. Teach us more about your unconditional love through Jesus Christ! Amen.*

Day 21

What Is Sin?

"But if you do not do what is right, sin is crouching at your door; it desires to have you, but you must rule over it."

See Genesis 4:7

"So Matt, you're saying that we don't ever sin? How dare you! We sin all the time!"

"No, I'm not saying that we don't *commit* sins. Christians sin, a lot. I'm saying our spirits are perfect and have a sinless nature because we have *God's* nature."

This conversation would continue for a while, as I tried to explain how we've been given new spirits by grace through faith. "Yes, perfect spirits," I said, which quickly enraged this gentleman. Even after giving him tons of Scripture to back up the facts of our spiritual perfection, he was mad as a hornet (see Romans 5:1, 6:6-7, Galatians 2:20, Colossians 1:22, 3:3, 2 Corinthians 5:17, and more).

If you want to upset a legalist, tell them they are completely forgiven for all time. I'm not saying *try* to upset them, I'm saying they will *become* upset. As for you, always be prepared to give an answer for the hope you have, but do so with gentleness and respect. Let all of your conversations be seasoned with grace (see 1 Peter 3:15, Colossians 4:6).

When I decided to start my social media ministry back in 2011, I would try to keep up with every angry person and respond, but that's impossible. So now, if I decide to go down that road with someone, in regard to responding to their attacks, it is rare and I'll usually continue for one main reason: *I want to help them relax.* I've been there. I know what it's like to try to work to keep what I've already been given for free. It's madness. God does not need our assistance in maintaining our salvation, Jesus is doing a fine job (see Philippians 4:7, Acts 17:25, Hebrews 7:25).

However, when I tell someone, "Your spirit is perfect," thems fightin' words! That is, *if* they are a self-centered person. I mean no disrespect by saying self-centered but this is true. They are centered on what *they* are doing—or not doing—rather than on what God *has* done through Jesus. They don't think the Cross really worked. Therefore, they have to add to it to make it suffice.

Fortunately, it is Jesus who keeps us forgiven, not our great behavior or lack of poor behavior. And why is that?...Can I get a drumroll please?... Because Jesus will never die again! When we sin, a death is needed, resulting in perfect blood needed to pay *off* that sin with God! The Jews got an entire year of sins paid for at the Day of Atonement with animal blood. However, *we* got something so much better! An entire lifetime of forgiveness by way of Christ's *final* sacrifice! That's exactly what the New Covenant is all about! Why do you think He said, "It is finished!"? (See John 19:30).

Jesus is not dying over and over again, up in heaven, every time we choose to sin. It's finished. He's chillin', and ain't worried about nothin' in regard to a Christian's sin problem. As a legalist, that sentence will enrage a person. As an individual who understands what Jesus has really done, it will give you extreme confidence.

If you want to live by the obsolete Mosaic Law (see Hebrews 8:13)—613 laws, not just ten—try to remember that *only* animal blood forgives the sins of breaking them. Not asking for forgiveness, not confessing, but only blood. The author of Hebrews explains:

> *"In fact, the Law requires that nearly everything be cleansed with blood, and <u>without the shedding of blood there is no forgiveness</u>." (Hebrews 9:22)*

When the Law was brought in by Moses, blood became God's currency to pay off sin with Him. *Asking* did not forgive people, neither did confessing—only blood.

"But what about that verse in 1 John that says if we confess our sins God will forgive us?"

That would be 1 John 1:9, and if you read 1 John 1:10, you'll get the context:

> *"If we claim <u>we have not sinned</u>, we make him out to be a liar and his word is not in us." (1 John 1:10)*

In this passage, John was speaking to the Gnostics. The Gnostics were a group who thought Jesus did not come in the flesh, that *our* flesh was a bad thing, *and* that they had never sinned a day in their lives. They thought sin wasn't a real thing.

That's why John said, if you claim you have *not* sinned—as in never—you make God out to be a liar. What is the basis of the Christian faith? Being forgiven! Actually admitting you have sins to be forgiven of! So if I say, "I've never sinned," then I don't qualify to be part of God's family because I can't possibly be forgiven.

John knew full well that Christians would sin. As a Jew who understood how to get forgiven—blood—he also knew it wouldn't be through confession, but only through Jesus. Just look at what he said in the following chapter:

> *"My dear children, I write this to you <u>so that you will not sin</u>. But if anybody <u>does sin</u>, we have an advocate with the Father—Jesus Christ, the Righteous One." (1 John 2:1)*

John doesn't want anyone to choose to sin, neither did Paul, neither do I, but sin *is* a real thing. And if we choose to act on sin, Jesus has *already* forgiven us.

"Yeah right, Matt! You're just giving people a license to sin! You're saying we can do whatever we want!"

Friend, we don't need a license to sin. All of us are sinning just fine without one—Christians included. Why would having a license make any difference? It wouldn't. And you say that "we can do whatever we want"? That is true, but we must understand what we truly want as people who are literally possessed by Jesus' Spirit...*we want what God wants.* Why? Because He lives in us!

As a Christian, because your supernatural being is woven together with God, your spirit wants what God's Spirit wants. The parts of your mind which are still unrenewed? Nope. But *you*, you really don't even *want* to sin. It abhors you!

"But you're saying that even our future sins are forgiven! That's just wrong!"

Well how many of your sins were in the future when Jesus died?... Yeah, all of them were. Friend, God is not bound by time, we are—temporarily—but He's not! So when you *first* believed Jesus forgave you, He actually did! That very moment, a literal death of your old spirit occurred and a *new* spirit was born—a spirit given to you by God.

Jesus tried to explain this to Nicodemus in John 3, and he had a hard time with it—Nicodemus, not Jesus. Paul teaches the Romans this same truth, which is our spiritual death and resurrection while still *in* these physical bodies:

> *"For we know that our old self <u>was crucified</u> with him so that the body ruled by sin might be <u>done away with</u>, that we should no longer be slaves to sin—because anyone who <u>has died</u> has been <u>set free from sin</u>." (Romans 6:6-7)*

Do you see it? Our old spirit *was* crucified with Jesus and done away with! Because of that death we have been set free from the power of sin!

"But Matt I still sin! How can you say I'm set free?"

Your *spirit* is set free. Your *spirit* is perfectly clean, holy, and blameless. The real you, the everlasting you, is ready for heaven as we speak! Paul pens his letter to the Colossians, informing them of what has happened to them inside, just like I'm telling you today:

> *"But now he <u>has reconciled you</u> by Christ's physical body <u>through death</u> to present you holy in his sight, without blemish and free from accusation" (Colossians 1:22)*

You died, in spirit! You were raised, in spirit! (See Galatians 2:20). YOU ARE NOW A SAINT! (See 1 Corinthians 1:2). You are no longer made for sin! (Romans 6:2). You've been re-created for heaven! (2 Corinthians 5:17). Can sin enter heaven? NO! That's why you and sin are polar opposites! Oil and water! Peanut-butter and pickles!

So when you choose to act on the power of sin, a conflict *will* happen inside you. However, making the mistake of sinning doesn't change your identity. Instead, it causes you to feel uneasy because you don't have the ability to enjoy sinning any longer. Sure, a flash-in-the-pan thrill might happen for your flesh when you choose to sin, but *you* can't stand it.

"Okay Matt, I think I'm getting it. But what do you mean by *power* of sin? I thought sin was getting drunk, cursing, and whatnot."

Those are fleshly actions of sin that look bad on the outside—typical by the world's view. But there are *good looking* fleshly sins as well, such as mission work and philanthropy. How can those things be sin?...Our attitudes behind them. If we have selfish or arrogant attitudes while acting on anything—even preaching—it's sin.

Sin is a power in this fallen world. It's like gravity. You can't see it, but it impacts absolutely everything. For this reason, you can be driving down the road just fine, nobody is with you, nothing is on the radio, and traffic is smooth—but yet, you get that sinful thought. "Where did *that* come from?" you might think. That thought is the power of sin—*but* that sinful thought is *not* you, *and* it's not coming from your perfect spirit. It's an outside force.

Through Adam, the power of sin entered this world. Through Jesus, the power of sin was defeated. When we believe Christ has forgiven us of our sins committed (even future sins), He comes and lives inside of us *making* us holy after killing off our old sinful spirit (see Romans 5, Romans 6).

As a Christian, sin cannot enter us any longer. It becomes a parasite, a leech, a foreign object in the world and in our physical body—but it's *not* in our spiritual body. Our spiritual body is sealed up forever with perfection until the day we go Home! (See Ephesians 4:30).

But in our physical members—our flesh—sin crawls around and is stirred up by demonic forces and Old Testament Law *tempting* us to *act on* that sin. Do you think what I'm saying is strange? Let's look at Paul's description of sin in his own body, and how Mosaic Law incited such:

> "**But I see <u>in my members</u>** another law waging war against the law of my mind and making me captive to the law of sin that dwells <u>in my members</u>." (Romans 7:23)

In this verse, Paul is not talking about Mosaic Law when he says "law." A more accurate translation is the word "power"—sin is a *force*. And do you see where the sin is powerful? Where it is forceful? In his members! His hands, feet, and mouth! His flesh!

"Okay Matt, but where do you get the right to say that sin is stirred up through Old Testament Law?"

Well, the sin that Paul is explaining here is the sin of being jealous—one of the Ten Commandments *of* the 613 laws and commands Moses gave Israel. Paul says so himself:

> *"But sin, <u>seizing the opportunity afforded by the commandment</u>, produced in me every kind of <u>coveting</u>. For <u>apart from the Law, sin is dead</u>." (Romans 7:8)*

The sin of wanting other people's stuff was aroused in Paul through the commandment of being told, "Thou shalt not covet!" So what was Paul's antidote? GET AWAY FROM THE LAW! He knew that the only way sin would not reign in his members is if he was dead to Law and alive in Christ! He told the Galatians the same thing when they started to go back to the Law of Moses to improve their faith:

> *"For through the Law I died to the Law so that I might live for God." (Galatians 2:19)*

The Law is a ministry of death (see 2 Corinthians 3:7). The Law kills everyone who tries to obey it by showing them how much of a complete failure they truly are (see James 2:10). Attempts at Law observance *causes* sin, it doesn't stop it. Our efforts to obey the Law blows bubbles into the power of sin—it grows fruit of death! (See Romans 7:5).

Paul's solution is to count ourselves dead to sin and alive in Christ, because we truly are in spirit! (See Romans 6:11). Paul's solution is to walk by God's Spirit. We are to let *Him* counsel us—not Moses—and in turn, we won't let the power of sin control us (see Galatians 5:16). Paul's solution was to simply be ourselves as God's kids, and as we do, we won't let sin reign (see Romans 6:12).

He was saying, "*Be* the forgiven person you are. Live it out! Don't go eat from the dumpster because you are seated at God's table!" This truth changes us! This graceful identity produces organic heavenly behavior and Christ-like attitudes! You are going to act like who you think you are! A spade is a spade, so be a spade!

One last thing about sin. Try to remember, sin is an *it* (see Romans 6:12, Genesis 4:7). We can bring that *it* to life through acting on it, but as Christians we are stronger than the sin of this world!

So today, my friends, know this: Jesus has defeated the power of sin through His perfect sacrifice once and for all! (See Hebrews 10:10, 10:14, 1 Peter 3:18). When we choose to act on sin as God's children, we are not being our true perfect selves—we are being fake. Further, it is the power of sin which causes us to *not* believe God and that's what He's wanted all along—for us to believe Him! Had Adam believed God he wouldn't have sinned! Even before the Law of Moses was given, taking God by His word is what He's most desired. The only reason the Law was brought in was so that sin would become much more obvious to us. However, obeying the Law never made a single person righteous. Only believing God can do that! If you'll believe Him, He'll solve your sin problem once and for all through your faith in His Son, Jesus. Believe today and become His child forever! (See Romans 5:20, Galatians 2:16, 3:11, John 1:12, 3:16-17 Ephesians 1:5).

> **A prayer for you:** *Good morning, Heavenly Father. Thanks for waking me up. Yesterday, I heard about a young lady in my neighborhood dying, and it reminded me of how short this trip to planet earth is. Today, I ask that you bring her family comfort, and I also ask for you help these dear readers to understand how temporary our human life is. Please teach them that you want us all to be with you in heaven, and the only way this can happen is if our sin problem has been taken care of. Reveal to them that only faith in Jesus can accomplish this feat! Open*

up their hearts and minds to this truth! Teach them how to not let sin reign, but to overcome that weak power by simply being themselves, children of God. We love you, amen.

Day 22

I Was a Victim of Religious Abuse

*When Jesus heard this, he said to him,
"You still lack one thing . . ."*

See Luke 18:22

Religious abuse is real. How can you recognize it? Simple. You have to point out the anti-gospel actions of the abuser. Here are some red flags to be aware of:

1. The abuser will attempt to make themselves seem "more holy" than you.
2. The abuser cannot stand grace by itself.
3. The abuser is focused on *your* sin.
4. The abuser is *not* focused on their own sin.
5. The abuser only praises you for your good behavior when you do things exactly as they say.
6. The abuser takes Scripture out of context and tries to make you obey Old Testament laws and commandments as they fail miserably at them themselves.

7. The abuser will give you the silent treatment if you don't shape up according to their liking.
8. The abuser will threaten you with hell, as if they have the right to send you there.
9. The abuser will claim God is withholding your blessings because you don't do what *they* say you should.
10. The abuser will claim you are rightfully being punished by God because of your inability to be more like them.

I'll stop at ten, but I could easily go up to 100 examples of the characteristics of religious abusers. If you still aren't catching my drift, allow me to add a narrative. Here are some things they say:

"BACKSLIDER! You call yourself a Christian? You better *beg* God for forgiveness, STOP SINNING, and get your butt in church! If you don't, you *will* be going to hell!"

"How dare you rob God! You refuse to give your tithe to the one who loaned it to you! You will suffer greatly because of that!"

"You didn't *really* repent! You didn't give your *whole* heart to God! You made Him Savior but not Lord! Had you done this, you wouldn't be struggling with that! You are showing everyone that you are *not* saved!"

"The tithe is just the beginning! If you would show your level of faith and give *more*, you'd *finally* be financially blessed by God! It's *your* fault! You gotta give an offering *above* the tithe! Where is your faith?"

"Have you confessed lately? You better! If you don't, you will be in danger of the fires of hell! Pray to Mary for help!"

I'm going to stop there. Just typing that stuff causes my blood pressure to rise a tad. It's no wonder you hear people say, "I don't know what happened to them. They grew up in church, and now they don't want anything to do with God."

Well, I *do* know what happened. They never got to see God from the people who were supposed to be representing Him. All they saw was mean, graceless, conditional-love people. They might be Christians, they might not be. However, I do know that putting a suit on a monkey doesn't make it a man.

What the abused person had witnessed was a quasi-gospel. They experienced denominational spin-offs, and spin-offs are never as good as the original. The abused witnessed a person yelling at them, or attempting to make them feel like dirt. The abused heard false-teaching from people who wouldn't be clear about what our Creator has really done for us through Christ. Instead, religious guilt and manipulation was used to control them. They were taught they weren't good enough, and that they'd never be.

They were taught to believe they were in God's Army and they had to fight the world, when they should have been taught this: *You've been adopted into God's family and the world is thirsty for what you now have.* They were taught, "Hurry up and make those sinners repent! Be radical! Stay hungry! Do more! Be more!" When they should have been taught to relax and simply be themselves as they lived their normal, everyday lives.

So for those who have witnessed a "lifelong Christian" heading for the hills after experiencing religious abuse, be happy for them. They could very well be saved, they've simply had enough religion to last a lifetime. That person is now free from their abusers and God is still with them in full—that is, if they believed Jesus has forgiven them. Congregations and brick and mortar buildings don't keep us saved, Jesus does (see Hebrews 7:25, 1 Corinthians 6:19).

The abused don't want anything to do with their abusers any longer, and I don't blame them.

Growing up, I too experienced some severe religious abuse. And again, even as a grown man, the cliquey-church impacted my faith negatively. I was taught that church—and the pastors in them—were more important than Jesus Himself. Then, I was taught that Christ was the bouncer at church, and the pastor was the owner of the club. "Be gone. You don't belong here any longer."

Rather than being taught how loving and accepting God truly is—because of what Jesus had done for me at the Cross—I was taught the Cross didn't fully count and I had to add to it. Jesus was *not* the focus, grace was *not* the focus, our one-time spiritual perfection was not the focus—my actions were. My obedience to God and the church staff was. Sadly and frustratingly, according to them my actions were never on par. "You ain't livin' right!" they'd say.

I'd soon find out that such rejection creates stress *and* anger. This is a bad combination as well as a deadly formula for a church, leaving them open for retaliation from the shunned. For this reason, Jesus emphasized how important it was to accept all people for who they were.

"Stop sinning! Read your Bible! Don't skip church! Do *exactly* what the preacher says because he is man of God!"

"But I have questions. Why won't he answer me clearly?"

"Who do you think you are, questioning Pastor? He's got a seminary degree and knows what he's talking about! Sit down! Shut up!"

I wasn't really saved! According to them anyway. I was taught that God had favorites and He was a big, mean, angry bully who was ready to thump me when I made a mistake. The church leaders were called by God to enforce His impossible rules, so I better fall in line, or else.

"You are getting what you deserve because of *your* sin! God does *not* put up with sin! You better repent while you still can! If you don't, you will be thrown in the hottest place of hell because you knew better!"

They made it seem as if the punishment Jesus took on the Cross wasn't good enough for my sin, as if it was only a partial punishment and God still wanted to punish me on *top* of Christ's suffering. Because of this mental abuse, I became afraid of everything. I was even afraid to *think*. I thought my *thoughts* were going to revoke my adoption into God's family, that He would be disgusted with me and say, "Ewwwww...gross. I'm *done* with you."

This abuse caused me to believe my salvation was fake. "Boy! You gotta take the *whole* of Scripture—RIGHTFULLY DIVIDE IT! Then you'll see how *wrong* you are!"

Eventually, I shrugged my shoulders and threw my hands up toward this bunch. I was over it. I became extremely aggressive and rebellious against them. Even the ones who had good intentions and understood the gospel, I attacked. I didn't trust *any* of them. I was mad and hurt on a very deep level.

"I can never live up to these people's expectations, so why even try? If God is really like this, then I'll do without!" Thankfully, over time, the Holy Spirit taught me He's nothing like they said. He was actually the opposite.

So how do we know if a person is truly teaching what God wants them to teach? Why not look to Jesus for the answers, crazy idea, right? There are two main characteristics which will organically sprout out from the true teachers of the gospel:

1. Love. Jesus said the world will know we belong to Him by our love (see John 13:35). Love is the heart of God (see 1 John 4:8).
2. Rest. Jesus said we will find rest for *everything that burdens us*, through Him (see Matthew 11:28). The true rest which comes from the gospel is understanding that you're okay with God, and you always will be.

LOVE. REST. These are the two things we should walk away with every Sunday at noon. A sigh of relief is the calling card of Christ—a powerful, loving, restful Person, who wants to live through us.

Why is this so hard for the church to understand? Why has scare tactics, hierarchies, and giving-to-get teaching grasped so many leaders in our congregations? That's a simple answer: *pride*. The very same thing which got the most beautiful angel of all time, Satan, kicked out of heaven, is the very same thing that causes religious abuse.

"Matt, I'm not teaching *only* grace! Grace is just a license to sin!"

No it's not. Grace is what empowers us to live the lives God longs for us to live as His kids. Just look:

> *For <u>the grace of God</u> has appeared that offers salvation to all people. <u>It teaches us</u> to say "No" to ungodliness and worldly passions, and to live self-controlled, upright and godly lives in this present age (Titus 2:11-12)*

Grace *teaches* us to be who we really are! Self-controlled, upright, godly people! I've never witnessed a person who truly understood God's grace fall off the deep-end, as a matter of fact, just the opposite! I've witnessed a person who was struggling with life to the point of near suicide, completely addicted to "trying harder" and "doing better" and he broke free through grace!....ME!

You will only live like you are spiritually perfect when you believe it! You will only believe it when you understand you became spiritually perfect by way of grace! Are we too prideful to understand that? Can we not stand the fact that everyone gets the same reward, which is Christ in us for good, for free?

"But I've gone to school to be able to teach at church! I've done more than anyone else I know!"

Friend, that's pride. Pride pushes God back and says, "I don't completely believe you." Pride says, "There's more to this gospel than grace. I'll prove it."

Pride is what causes some supposed Christians to be cut off at heaven's door and turned away by Jesus:

> *"Not everyone who says to me, 'Lord, Lord,' will enter the kingdom of heaven, but only the one who does the will of my Father who is in heaven. Many will say to me on that day, 'Lord, Lord, did we not prophesy in your name and in your name drive out demons and in your name perform many miracles?' Then I will tell them plainly, 'I never knew you. Away from me, you evildoers!'" (Matthew 7:21-23)*

"See Matt! It says it right there! 'The one who does the *will* of my Father'! I'm not prideful, I'm doing *my* part to do God's will!"

Do you hear how silly that sounds? As if you are assisting the Person who causes this planet to spin? And further, wha*t is* God's will? I can tell you what it's not: us trying to *add* to what He's been handing out to everyone for free since the event of Jesus' resurrection…freedom (see Galatians 5:1).

God's will is to *believe* this truth. His will has always been, "Please, believe me." Before the Law was given, during the Law's time in place, and after the Law, God's will has always been, "Believe." Jesus tells us so:

> *"For my Father's will is that everyone who looks to the Son and believes in him shall have eternal life, and I will raise them up at the last day." (John 6:40)*

"But that can't be right! That's too easy!"

Jesus didn't think so. He knew it would be the hardest thing *ever* for many people. He knew that those with prideful hearts wouldn't be able to *just* believe. He said it's easier for a camel to go through the eye of a needle to a man who wouldn't *just* believe (see Matthew 19:16-23). He said the path of belief in Him alone—with nothing added—is an extremely narrow path. The other path, however, is wide:

> *"Enter through the narrow gate. For wide is the gate and broad is the road that leads to destruction, and many enter through it." (Matthew 7:13)*

Believe. Believe in His love. Believe in His rest. Believe in His forgiveness. Believe in your spiritual perfection. Believe in nothing else added to this. Believe in grace. Paul calls the gospel, "the gospel *of* grace" (see Acts 20:24). Grace leads to the truth of the Father's unconditional love. Grace leads to lush, calm, green pastures of rest. Grace leads to belief. Grace causes pride to fade away like a mist, as Jesus walks *through* that mist, to reveal Himself in full.

A prayer for you: *Dad, thank you for teaching me how to think of my abusers with grace. I made a decision to forgive them—an act of my will—and I have forgiven them. However, you are still helping me with my feelings over this issue, and I'm grateful. Thank you for your patience. The very thing they were against, grace, you are showing me how to give them. Your grace is empowering me to be able to exude my true character of love. Right now, I lift up all who are reading this, directly to you. So many of them have been religiously abused and they are in pain. Help them today. Ease them today. Let them know how much you truly care for them. Teach them the truth of your gospel of grace. Let them know you are not disappointed in them in any way. Reveal in their hearts and minds that you are their Abba Father—Daddy—and you call us to sit on your lap as you embrace us for all we are as your Children. We love you. Heal our pain and counsel us into your wisdom. In Jesus' name, amen.*

Day 23

Don't Listen to the Accuser

"For the accuser of our brothers and sisters, who accuses them before our God day and night, has been hurled down."

See Revelation 12:10

"Matt, what do I do? I just can't seem to forgive myself. I'm such a horrible person and I know it!" Ron, we'll call him, emails me about a struggle he's had his whole life. According to him, no matter what he does or doesn't do, he feels condemned and constantly thinks about "how terrible of a person" he is.

Little does he know, he's *not* a terrible person at all. He is cherished by God Himself. God's opinion of Ron has been drowned out by Satan's opinion, through Ron's thought life. This is why it's so important that we teach people the truth of their *true* identity in Christ. Sure, Paul had behavior passages in which he taught about how to live *out* who we are inside, but He never said our incorrect behaviors would cause God to go back on His promises. As a matter of fact, Paul said the more we mess up, the more God's grace increases:

"But where sin increased, grace increased all the more" (see Romans 5:20)

He never said our mistakes would cause God to leave us—that's Judaism. That's Old Covenant. None of us are qualified to teach Judaism, which is an obsolete faith (see Hebrews 8:13). The only ministry we are all *equally* qualified to teach is the ministry of reconciliation (see 2 Corinthians 5:18, Colossians 1:22).

That's what Paul did. He told everyone they were completely reconciled with God through their faith in Jesus, and the religious people hated him for it. "That's too much grace! You gotta have some law in there so we know what to do!" Sadly, this continues on today with the modern church. Grace infuriates selfish people. It insults their wonderful self-made holiness. I mean, after all, just look at how much they do for God.

But anyway, for Ron, because he had been listening to ministries which taught him how worthless he was because of his incorrect actions and attitudes, he was easy prey for Satan. *Those* ministries—ministries of death (see 2 Corinthians 3:7)—brought him to a place of near suicide.

Friend, the gospel is *not* about our commitment to God, it's about God's commitment to us, through Jesus. You are not a promise keeper, God is. Those words will incite rage in egotistical demons who lie to legalists each day, but I'm not here to lie to you: you are an absolute failure when it comes to your commitment to God—and so am I.

For this reason, Satan loves ministries that teach us to try harder, do better, repent, and be radical; that way, *when* we fail—not if—he can easily pounce. "Just look at you! You suck at being a Christian! Give up!"

On the other hand, he hates ministries that teach Christians about what has truly happened to them inside their spirits...*perfection*. He can see your perfect spirit because he is in the spiritual realm. His theology is that of God's, he knows the truth, and he's here to twist it so *you* don't understand it.

The devil knows we will act like who we *think* we are. If we know and *think* we are heaven-ready saints who sometimes sin—but the temporary insanity of choosing to sin won't change our identity—Satan's demonic forces stand no chance against us. As children of God, the devil and his dummies can't *touch* you, they can't *possess* you, they can't do anything to you *except* accuse you. Just look at what John said:

"for God's Son holds them securely, and <u>the evil one cannot touch them</u>." (See 1 John 5:18)

As a Christian, you are literally possessed by Christ's Spirit (see Colossians 3:3, 1 Corinthians 6:19, John 14:23, Ephesians 4:30). Because of such, His Spirit will not share your body with a demon or the devil. In all of history, no Christian has ever been possessed by Satan or a demon.

Now, they might be around people who *think* such—and even act this fallacy out—but God won't share your spirit with anything from hell. You see people wiggling on the floor in some churches, getting "demons cast out," but this is simply an incorrect act which has been passed down over the generations. It is a *learned* thing, something they'll have to unlearn. Sure, the enemy wants them to think they are possessed—but they're not—that is, if they believe Jesus has forgiven them.

There is not one single recorded event in the Bible where a demon is being cast out of a Christian. Unbelievers? Yeah, quite often. But not someone who has God indwelling them. THEY ARE SECURE!

I wanted to get that out there because understanding this truth will help you realize just *how* weak our accuser is. Honestly, that's all he does to us, *accuse us day and night*. For this reason, John called him, "the accuser of our brothers and sisters" (See Revelation 12:10).

It's very difficult to get over our past if we are believing this moron's lies. In our minds, the devil can convince us that God is angry with us. He wants you to think your salvation didn't stick and your thoughts and choices prove that. Thoughts and choices can't change anyone's identity, so believe me when I say God is not mad at you.

"Matt, that can't be true! He *has* to be mad at me over my sin! He *has* to be punishing me!"

Friend, He's not. What do you think the Cross was for? God's wrath over *all* sin was completely satisfied through Jesus' punishment (see

Romans 5:9). Trust me, you don't want to deal with even a drop of His wrath like those who rejected Him before Jesus—and you never will! Why? Because you are His child! He's not mad at you one bit! He loves you, He counsels you, He disciples you, He wants the best for you, but He is not mad at you!

"Well...fine! Maybe He's not mad, but I know He's disgusted with me!"

Nope. He's not disgusted with you either, you are actually His masterpiece. Masterpieces are set up high for all to see and enjoy! Paul told the Christians in Ephesus this truth:

> *"For we are God's masterpiece. He has created us anew in Christ Jesus . . ." (See Ephesians 2:10)*

So today, my friends, know this: Believe the truth about yourself today! Believe you are God's masterpiece! Believe you are the apple of His eye! Believe you are His cherished child, because that's who you are! When the accuser tries to convince you otherwise because of your mistakes, inform him of your heavenly heritage! Inform him that you know who your Dad is! Inform him that his days are numbered and that you are a saint! And he might say, "Yeah, but you still struggle with _____!" To that, simply reply, "Even more proof of how secure I am in Christ! Loser." That's what he is, a loser, and he can't stand it. You, however, are royalty!

A prayer for you: *Heavenly Father, thank you for teaching me about the spiritual world and how the enemy works. Thanks for revealing how weak he is. All he can do is bark like a stupid, angry, frustrated dog on the other side of a fence who can't get at me. Most of the time I ignore him, but at other times I STOMP at him, and he scampers off like the sissy he is. He can't touch us! All he can do is point out the mistakes of our past, and the temporary failures we have each day. Right now, I lift up all who are reading this, directly to you. For the believers who don't* *truly understand who they are inside, reveal it to them! Let them know their spirits are perfect! Let them know their past, present, and even future sins are forgiven—because you are not bound by time! Teach them how to walk by their spiritual perfection. When they make choices and have attitudes that don't match up with who they really are inside, remind them gently. I know you will. You are a gentle God. Sure, before Jesus was punished on the Cross, your wrath was poured out left and right over the sin of the world, but through the New Covenant you are satisfied with us in full! We love you so much! Thank you! Teach these dear readers how to focus on that love, and to ignore the accuser's lies so they can enjoy their lives so much more. In Jesus' name I pray, amen.*

Day 24

God Wants to Help You with Your Choices

"And I will ask the Father, and He will give you another Counselor to be with you forever." ~Jesus

John 14:16

Here are eight choices anyone can make at any time:

1. "It's no big deal, it's just porn. The house is empty and nobody will know."
2. "It's been a hard day. I think I'll stop by the liquor store and get something to drink so I can relax."
3. "I'm the pastor! They should be respecting me! I've been to seminary! I'll show them how much hard work I've put into studying Scripture by pointing out how terrible *their* sin is in my sermon. They don't need any more grace! They need to obey me *and* God's laws!"
4. "Nope! I am *not* forgiving that toxic person again!"
5. "That's it! I'm unfriending them and making sure everyone hates them on Facebook!"

6. "He works hard for our family. It's not a serious issue that he drinks all the time. The kids will be fine."
7. "God hates me! The pastor said that God hates people just *like* me! I can't change how I am so I'm killing myself! God made a mistake by creating me!"
8. "I'm allowed to sin all I want because all I have to do to get forgiven is just confess it on Sunday. So for now, I'm having fun!"

Decisions, decisions, decisions. We can regret our choices *or* we can allow God to help us *make* them. Here are the same eight choices, the only difference is the Holy Spirit is helping with each of them:

1. "God, thank you so much for helping me not watch that porn. I know that's not how you want me to look at women, so please, help me with these urges I have. You made me like this, so please provide a way that I can have sex how you designed me to. In the meantime, help me. I need relief."
2. "Man, it's been a hard day. I'm tempted to go to the liquor store *but* I don't drink. God, thank you for teaching me how to feel my feelings, bring them to you, and not be controlled by alcohol. I feel so free. Even on my most frustrating and difficult days, I'm free."
3. "Heavenly Father, although I'm the pastor of this church, thank you for teaching me that my identity is not found in this position. Help me to use my gifts to teach my congregation that they and I are on the exact same level with you. We are all saints because of Christ in us—equally. Help me grow into deeper knowledge of your grace so that I can exude the true gospel to everyone I encounter."
4. "God, I'm hurt! I don't feel like forgiving them again! But because you have forgiven me, I am choosing to forgive them yet again. I know I would *stay* forgiven with you even if I never forgave them, that's why I *am* forgiving them. I'm choosing to today!"

Please help me with my feelings, and with this pain! Teach me how to establish healthy boundaries so that I can protect myself from future harm, and bring me comfort, God...please."
5. "Heavenly Father, I've used social media for far too long to hurt those who've hurt me. I don't want to do that anymore. Teach me how to exude the self-control you've given me in Christ, and to honor those who I don't feel like honoring."
6. "My husband works really hard for our family, and I appreciate that. But God, you are going to have to strengthen me in regard to standing up to his over-drinking. It is impacting the kids negatively, and they shouldn't have to see alcohol abuse all the time. Help me, God. I love him, but I need your strength to stand up to this."
7. "God, I'm in pain! I don't want to live any longer and you see that! HELP ME! The pastor keeps telling me that because of my sin you hate me! I know that's not true, so help me with these suicidal feelings! HELP MEEEEEEEEEE! I know I am your child!"
8. "Dad, you are teaching me that confession doesn't forgive me, all it does is allow me to agree with you, and that's what I want to do. I'm tired of taking advantage of your kindness. I'm learning that I actually want what *you* want. I'm also learning that by being my true self, I can have the most fun! Continue to counsel me into your wisdom as I learn more about our loving relationship through Jesus."

My friend, big or small, all of us make many choices which impact our lives as well as the lives of others. When we allow ourselves to be led by the Spirit, those choices can result in wonderful things. And when we don't, the opposite can and will happen, eventually.

The good news is, as Christians, we have help with our choices! God's own Spirit resides in our bodies! He will help us make every choice from big to small *if* we let Him! And when I say every single choice, I mean it! There's no decision too big for our Creator that He can't handle by guiding us in the proper direction. But at the same time, there's no decision too *small* that He doesn't care about it! Everything is small to God!

My Grandma used to pray over the strangest stuff, little things that would make me squint in confusion. Sure, she would pray for people who were struggling with addictions, and for those who were sick or sad, but she would also pray over the family dog or our vacuum.

"Grandma, God doesn't care about that vacuum bag," I'd say sarcastically.

"Oh hush your mouth, sure He does," she'd reply, and then give me a warm smile.

She constantly brought God into the picture of every decision she made—every choice! Why? Because she understood the fact that He *wants* to be involved in every decision, and every choice.

Friend, this happens when we let Him live through us, that is, *through* our choices. Yes, *we* decide, but it is *He* who gives us the nudges *in* our spirits as to what we should do. If we are listening and being our true selves, we will organically allow those choices to come to life. As we do this, little by little, we begin to grow something in our lives called "fruit of the Spirit." Fruit of the Spirit is simply outward results of consistently allowing God to help us make our choices (see Galatians 5:22-23).

For me, at first, this was like trying to cage a wild animal. I had a lot of learning to do from God's Spirit—and even more importantly, I had a lot of *un*learning to do. Graceless, poor teaching from others caused me to believe that God had extremely high expectations of me. Those same lies had me convinced I was constantly letting Him down. That was *so* wrong. God taught me this truth by helping me understand His grace.

"Yeah right, Matt! God gets disappointed in us every day! He has *very* high expectations of us! Liar!"

Friend, I'm sorry but you are wrong. What Jesus did at the Cross—and our faith in that event—has caused us to be completely approved by God in full. Jesus fulfilled all of the high expectations of God—which was perfection—*for* us (see Colossians 1:22, Romans 5:1).

And now, as God's children, sure, He can be grieved by our incorrect attitudes and actions, but He is never disappointed—and He is *never* pushy. He is patient and kind. He understands us on a deeper level than even we understand ourselves. Our Father simply wants us to *be* ourselves as we live out our everyday lives while including Him in all of our choices.

So today, my friends, know this: Let God help you. While you take the kids to school, to your attitude toward your boss, with your husband or wife, and even with your congregation...involve Him. It doesn't matter if it's a big choice or a small one, God simply wants to be thought of and loved! He *gives* you choices. He lets *you* pick. No matter what you decide, He's with you and won't go away. So begin to let Him help you with all of your choices, today.

A prayer for you: *Dad, thank you for being so kind to me. It took me so long to finally understand your kindness, and I know that even when I enter into eternity, I'll still be learning about it forever. Thank you for helping me with all of my choices each day. Keep doing it. Right now, I lift up all who are reading this, directly to you. For those who think you are an overbearing, angry Father, help them realize you're not. You simply want us all to be forgiven, and Jesus gives us that choice to make. After we do, we can then enjoy a deep relationship with you as sin-free saints in our spirits. You come to live with us, teaching us, correcting us, encouraging us, and loving us unconditionally. We are grateful! Teach us how to go deeper into this wonderful relationship with you as we make our choices today! Amen!*

Day 25

How Can I Get Over My Past?

"Forgetting what lies behind and reaching forward to what lies ahead"

SEE PHILIPPIANS 3:13

It's so easy to be ashamed of our past, especially when certain people hold our past against us. It could be a spouse whom you've cheated on, physically or emotionally, and they bring it up all the time. It could be a pastor or church leader who knows about your prior drug, alcohol, or sex addiction, and they passive-aggressively blackmail you to do things for them at the church.

You could even *be* a pastor, one who used to teach Old Testament Law rather than the true gospel of grace. This false teaching ruined the lives of many people as they tried to please you. Now, a lot of them resent you because the Law requires perfection, yet, you kept telling them to live up to the standards of it. You exacerbated your congregation with threats of hell and less rewards in heaven, as you, yourself, failed to follow all 613 laws which is the requirement should a person choose to live by it (see Matthew 5:48, John 8:11, Galatians 3:10, James 2:10). Satan had you fooled about your status with God because of where you physically stood each Sunday morning.

However, through your legalistic burn-out, God has opened up the eyes of your heart to what Jesus has really done at the Cross, and you're very sorry about teaching Law. You've changed your entire message, but still, many people remember how you were, and what your angry teaching did to their families and lives.

My friend, whoever it is that tries to throw up your previous poor choices in your face, I want you to know something: THEY DON'T DEFINE YOU IN ANY WAY, GOD DOES.

Your loving Heavenly Father knew you were going to make some serious mistakes in life even before you made them. Because of this, He provided a way to *change* your life by giving you a *new* life! First, on the inside, and second, through your actions and attitudes!

You may have been saved for years, and then again, you may have just recently believed Jesus forgave you of your sins; either way, it takes time for us to learn and grow into what has really happen inside of us. Do you *know* what's happened? Oh, it's good stuff! *Understanding* what's happened will be the most important thing you understand—ever!

Christian, do you know who you really are? Because when you do... HA! Oh my gosh I get excited just typing about this subject! YOU ARE HEAVEN-READY INSIDE THAT BODY! YEP!

Paul tells the people in Corinth what Jesus did inside of him—and try to understand Paul's past, he was a legalist *and* a bounty hunter of Christians! He was a racist, he loved the Mosaic Law (all 613), and he hated Christians! (See Philippians 3:4-7). How's that match up to *your* past? No matter, just look at how he describes himself after placing his faith in Jesus:

> *"Therefore, if anyone is <u>in Christ</u>, the new creation <u>has come</u>: The old <u>has gone</u>, the new <u>is here</u>!" (2 Corinthians 5:17)*

Each time Paul described what Jesus has done inside of us he uses past tense verbs. All throughout his letters, he wanted the audience to know what Jesus *has* done to our spirits: GIVEN US A NEW ONE! Not when we die, but *now*, right now! Our spirits will not become new in heaven, only our bodies will! (See 1 Corinthians 15:35-58). In the supernatural realm, we are *already* seated with Christ in heaven! (See Ephesians 2:6). That is, our spirits!

Every believer in Christ *has* allowed the Holy Spirit to kill off their old spirit and give them their new spirit! (See Romans 6:6-7). When this happened, you might not have felt anything, and then again you might have, but either way, when you *first* believed Jesus was your Savior, your old self died and you got a new *perfect* self! Your self is your spirit! Your spirit is the part of you that will never die! That *new* spirit is now interwoven with Jesus' Spirit like strands of thread in a single piece of cloth! You and Christ are one! Here's another description from Paul:

> "I *have been* crucified with Christ and *I no longer live*, but Christ lives in me . . ." (See Galatians 2:20)

Again, past tense. He's describing his old self. Do you see that? Paul wasn't saying we are waiting to *be* crucified with Christ in heaven. He's referring to the spiritual realm here, not the afterlife, and obviously not physically, right now. Paul was not speaking in hyperbole, he was being very literal! He was talking about your spirit!

So supernaturally, *after* we are crucified with Christ—by grace through faith (see Ephesians 2:8-9)—God's Spirit comes and lives with us, making His home in *our* spirits (see John 14:23, Colossians 3:3, 1 Corinthians 6:19). It's not "all of Him and none of me"—heck no! IT'S BOTH OF US TOGETHER! Paul says so in the same verse:

> "The life *I now live in the body*, I live by faith in the Son of God, who loved me and gave himself for me." (See Galatians 2:20)

C'MON PEOPLE, THIS IS AWESOME! The first half of Galatians 2:20 is referring to our old selves (which Paul also talked about in 2 Corinthians 5:17); and then the second half of this verse is referring to our *new* spiritually perfect selves, who still live temporarily in this body-shell! God has made you new! Your identity has changed! Even if your choices and thought-life hasn't, *you* have! You *were* a caterpillar, and now you are a butterfly! YOU DON'T HAVE THE OPTION OF GOING BACK! Even if you want to *act* like a caterpillar *as* a butterfly, this won't change the fact that you now have wings! FLY! YOU CAN FLY! GET UP AND FLY HIGH! GET OFF THE GROUND AND BE WHO YOU REALLY ARE!

This is the revelation you need in order to get over your past. The opinions of others are *so* weak when you know the truth of who you are. You are not the same person as you once were, even if you acted like it in your past—and even if you *still* act like it. Behavior will never change identity. Crawl around all you want, you've been remade to fly and your life will never make sense until you do.

"I hear you, Matt. I was already saved and I messed up real bad, and sometimes I still do."

Me too. Friend, welcome to humanity. We *all* mess up real bad, all the time, but those mess-ups don't define us in any way, God does. Listen, we are all learning and growing in the knowledge of who we are, that takes time. Our poor choices don't shock God, He's seen it trillions of times before. So please, stop focusing on veering off the road, just be glad that Jesus is in the passenger seat. Even if you do trek off into the wilderness, He'll *always* gently guide you back onto the truth of who you really are. It's up to us to listen to Him, but make no mistake, He'll never bail on us—ever.

The Bible says we are to be transformed by the renewing of our minds, this is a process (see Romans 12:2). It also says that He who began a good work in you will carry it on to completion. When is that completion going to take place? When Jesus returns or your body finally wears out (see Philippians 1:6). So please be easy on yourself. God knows you aren't used to having those wings, and He understands that you're not sure how they work. And yes, they *are* intimidating, but they really *do* belong to you!

Don't be hard on *you* because even God isn't hard on you. Religious people are, the devil is, even our old caterpillar thinking is, but God is not. He is gentle, humble in heart, and patient. He looks at you with kind eyes, especially when you fall down, so don't be afraid of Him. He'll help you back up as many times as it takes, and He'll keep encouraging you with the truth of who He's made you to be!

So today, my friends, know this: Don't believe the lies of others when they say you've not changed, God would beg to differ. You are learning more and more each day from His Spirit inside you. The life you now live you live by faith, not by the past—even yesterday. Let *yesterday* go... even last hour, let it go. Sometimes we feel like wobbly-kneed babies as we reach out for Daddy to help us walk, and He just smiles. "Look at you! You are standing up! I'm proud of you!" You are His cherished child, infinitely loved forever!

A prayer for you: *Dad, thank you for pointing out the life of Paul to me, I know he had it rough. On one side of him he had the legalistic Jews holding his past against him, and on the other side, he had the Christians who didn't fully trust him. But that didn't matter to Paul because he knew who he was inside. He knew what you had done! In 1 Corinthians 4:3, when others judged him over his past, he said he didn't care about their opinion of him because he no longer even judged himself. He wasn't focused on what he did or didn't do, but instead, he kept his mind set on who you had made him in spirit. What confidence! Paul is such an inspiration! Right now, I lift up all who are reading this, directly to you. For those who are believing the lies of the devil, and of the people who like throwing up their past in their face, strengthen them. Help them to realize what you've truly done to their spirits, which is recreate them as perfect! As they learn more and more about this fact, empower these dear readers to live out that perfection!*

Even though it's not completely possible on this side of heaven, we trust that you will reveal more about who we are! Thank you, Father. Amen.

Day 26

What's the Difference Between Spirit, Soul, and Body?

"Do you not know that your bodies are temples of the Holy Spirit, who is in you, whom you have received from God? You are not your own"

1 Corinthians 6:19

If I were to ask you, "What three forms can water come in?" you would more than likely be quick to answer with, "Liquid, solid, and gas." Three different forms, but all *three* are equally water. Just because water is in a different form, that does not change the fact it's still completely water.

This is a great way to describe who we are as humans, as well as God, the Trinity, three in one. For us, we *are* a spirit, we *have* a soul, and we *live* in a body. As Christians, all three are equal, blameless, and describe us as a *person* (see 1 Thessalonians 5:23). I'll get to us in a minute, but for our Creator, if we look for the word *Trinity* in the Bible, it's not there. However, if we put one and one and one together, it's easy to understand that God is three parts. Jesus mentions it, so does Paul, as does John (see Matthew 28:19, 2 Corinthians 13:14, 1 John 5:7).

Even from the opening book of the Bible—the opening *chapter* even—God is mentioned in plural form (see Genesis 1:1-2,26). So God is: Father, Son, and Holy Spirit. Three Persons, one God. The Son is not the Father, the Father is not the Spirit, and the Spirit is not the Son—nor any slicing of it. However, they are all three in perfect harmony as one God.

I wanted to set that up because we too are three-part beings: spirit, soul, and body. When we understand the separation of the three—how different each part of our being is—things will start to make a lot more sense. Mainly, you will stop mistaking one for the other, which will give you confidence and peace. Also, the devil will look like the idiot he is, because his lies will be even more blatant to you.

First of all, all Christians are perfect, *spiritually*. At our core, in the everlasting part of us, our spirits, we've literally been crucified with Christ, buried, and raised back to life as new spiritual beings. When this happened, *once*, by believing Jesus has forgiven you, your spirit was made brand new! (See Romans 6:6-7, Colossians 1:22, 1 John 3:9, Hebrews 10:10).

There are Bible passages which mention the destruction of an unbeliever's spirit, as in annihilation. But there's still a biblical possibility that a rejecter of Christ, their spirit, will *not* be destroyed and will be punished forever. Either way, our faith in receiving God's Spirit *right now* will always keep us safe with Him. Jesus explains:

> "And so I tell you, every kind of sin and slander
> can be forgiven, but blasphemy against the Spirit
> will not be forgiven." (Matthew 12:31)

For this verse, Jesus is *not* talking about saying the Lord's name in vain. The grace-confused Christians want you to think that so they can control you with fear. Just imagine if God left us for good because we said a swear word? What a stupid idea. Jesus is talking about *rejecting* His Spirit into yours. Blaspheme means "to speak evil of." If you speak evil of God's Spirit, you obviously will not be accepting Him into *your* spirit.

Further, we accept Him into our spirit by grace through faith; by simply believing He is our Savior (see Ephesians 2:8-9, John 1:12, 6:29). Once we *do* believe that Jesus has forgiven us, He makes His home inside of our bodies and spirits (see Colossians 3:3, 1 Corinthians 6:19).

Next, I want you to know you do *not* have a sinful nature. For so long, even I thought I had a sinful nature. This was because I was reading a NIV Bible that had not been updated. In order to be more readable the publishers changed *the flesh* to *sinful nature* in the 1984 version of their NIV Bible. Since then, they've changed it back to *the flesh*.

Why is this important? Because the words *sinful nature* are not in the Bible. The original Greek word is *sarx* which means *the flesh*. Sarx doesn't mean *sin* and it doesn't mean *nature*—it means *the flesh*. So each time you read the words sinful nature in the older version of the NIV, you can scratch through it and write "the flesh"—literally.

This matters because your body is your flesh, one of the three parts of you. Your flesh is not *the* flesh. Your flesh doesn't have a sinful nature nor is it sinful. In fact, it's holy (See 1 Thessalonians 5:23). There's nothing wrong with anyone's flesh. It is a suit to wear. God likes our flesh, it was His idea. So any sinful desire you have comes from the power of sin *through* your flesh, equalling *the* flesh. The flesh even offers sinful thoughts through our brain.

From the opening book of the Bible, God has warned us about the power of sin—the *force* of sin:

> "*sin is crouching at your door; <u>it desires</u> to have you,*
> *but you must rule over it.*" (See Genesis 4:7)

Do you see that *it* desires? This power of sin—not us acting on it, which is called "committing sins"—but sin by itself, it is a separate entity from us and has nothing to *do* with us as Christians. It is a tumor, so to speak. It's in us, but it's *not* us. Christ, who now lives in you, He has defeated the power sin had *over* your spirit! He did so by killing off your old spirit and giving you a new, perfect spirit which is already seated in heaven with Him! (See Romans 6:6-7, Colossians 1:22, Ephesians 2:6).

Therefore, Christian, you are not at battle with yourself. Yourself is good! Yourself is holy! Yourself is settled up with God forever because of Christ making His home in you! (See Hebrews 7:25, 10:10, John 14:23). So, the *power* of sin—which is everywhere on this planet like gravity—*it* tries to influence your flesh each day (see Romans 7, Galatians 5). But as we walk by our true selves—perfect spirits—we overcome sin as it takes a back seat. We now know we've been remade to not *act on* sin's influence in our flesh. Paul explains this to the Romans:

> *"Don't <u>let</u> sin reign in your <u>mortal body</u> so that you obey <u>its</u> desires" (Romans 6:12).*

Do you see that it is *us* who *allows* sin to go to work in our lives? To reign? And do you see where that happens? In our mortal bodies, our flesh! And lastly, do you see once again that sin is an "it"? This is very important to understand because as a Christian sin is *not* you! You are not sinful! YOU'RE NOT A SINNER! You are holy, blameless, and free from all accusation from God! YOU ARE A PERFECT SPIRIT! You are completely reconciled with your Creator in the part of you that lives forever! Your spirit! (See Colossians 1:22, Romans 5:1).

As for our flesh, it is but a tool. Tools do what the person holding it decides. A hammer can't hammer itself. As heaven-ready people, we have God's desires written on our spirits which is now supposed to guide our flesh (see Hebrews 10:16). We want what God wants, we really do! So we live that out *through* our bodies!

Because of our God-given freedom, we can allow our flesh to be led by the Spirit of God in us, or we can allow our flesh to be led by sin. Which, ultimately, will result in us acting *out* sin, therefore bringing it to life (see Galatians 5, 1 Corinthians 6). We can also allow our flesh to be influenced by the lies and temptations of the enemy and his demonic spiritual forces. This began in the Garden with Adam and Eve and it continues on today.

Your flesh *can* still act on sin if you let it because sin is still *in* it as a parasite (see Romans 6:11-14, 7:17). But *you* are not of the realm of *the* flesh! You've been transferred into the realm of God's presence by allowing the Holy Spirit to possess you! (See Romans 8:9).

However! *We*, perfect spirits, children of God, are still responsible for walking according to our true, holy selves. At any point in time we can choose to walk by a manner that does not match up with our identity in Christ—but, we cannot out-sin our perfect identity! (See Romans 5:20). Because of Jesus already taking on the full punishment of our sin at the Cross, even when we *do* sin, our spiritual perfection stays sealed up forever! (See Ephesians 4:30, 1 John 2:1).

So this begs the question, "Then why not go ahead and call up Guinness to record our new sinning record? After all, choosing to act on sin won't change my identity in Christ." Paul knew the Romans would ask something on the lines as this. So he made clear that our perfect spirits weren't *made* to sin, as in, sin will never match up or feel right permanently no matter how much we do it! Just look:

> *"What shall we say, then? Shall we go on sinning so that grace may increase? By no means! We are those who have died to sin; how can we live in it any longer?" (Romans 6:1-2)*

Again, this is another passage that is used by the self-centered Christians to try to make others think we will never sin. And again, a moronic idea in the fullest. God does not grade us on a curve. We must be perfect, and that can only come by way of being reborn in the spiritual realm (see John 3:7).

Paul is saying, "Listen, *you* are now an eagle! I know you were born a chicken, but you are *not* a chicken any longer! Why would you want to sit in that barnyard with those other chickens, pecking around on the ground? You were made for more! You are regal! Stop acting like someone you're not! You weren't made for KFC buckets, you were made to soar!"

Now, *can* an eagle stare at the ground and act like a flightless bird? Sure. But just because an eagle chooses to do something so stupid, that will never change its DNA structure. It's an eagle. Period. Forever. Same with us as reborn children of God! We are heavenly spirits! We are saints! Not by what we do, but by birth!

Friend, once we shed this flesh-shell and are removed from this fallen planet—which still has the power of sin floating around—only *then* will we be completed *in our bodies* because we will get new bodies! We will get a body like Jesus had after He rose again! Poppin' out of thin air, walking through walls, and floating up into the sky and stuff! It'll be awesome! (See 1 Corinthians 15:35-58). But for now, this is the tool God has given to us to use *for* Him. We do this by simply being ourselves! (See Romans 6:13).

So lastly, what is the soul? It's our mind, free will, and emotions. Another way to look at our soul is this: it's our thinker, our chooser, and our feeler. Plainly stated, your soul is what expresses you at any point in time. Your soul gives off a flavor of you at any particular moment, but that taste does not change your substance. Happy, sad, mad, glad, indifferent—you are *still* a child of God!

Never mix up your *who* with your *do* because they are not the same. Incorrect attitudes and actions are not coming from your perfect spirit, but from unrenewed, immature thoughts. Once we understand this, the gospel begins to make a lot more sense because we can comprehend what Jesus has done inside of us permanently.

So today, my friends, know this: God gave you your flesh so that you can be a part of this physical world. He gave you your soul so that you can enjoy this world and make your own choices. One of those choices He longs for you to make is to believe Jesus has forgiven you. As for your spirit, God *made* you a spirit so that you can live on forever in heaven with Him. But not just that, He also made you a spirit so that He can come and live with you, right now, today.

A prayer for you: *Heavenly Father, thank you for teaching me the truth of my own trinity, my body, soul, and spirit. With this knowledge, I understand so much more about myself and your grace. I ask that you continue to teach me more so that I can go deeper into your wisdom. Thank you. Right now, I lift up all who are reading this, directly to you. So many of them have been taught that their poor choices define them, and they do not. I ask that you open up their minds to the truth of their spiritual perfection! Teach them that as believers, you now live in them, and they've been completely remade for good! Now that they know this truth, help them to live it out as they simply be themselves in Christ! In Jesus' name I pray, amen.*

Day 27

How to Confront Others in a Healthy Way

"Finally, be strong in the Lord and in his mighty power."

Ephesians 6:10

Healthy confrontations do not come natural for those of us who have struggled with codependency. You might be wondering, "What is codependency?" Like alcoholism, codependency is something that I am *also* in recovery for.

Now, you might be thinking that you don't *have* a codependency issue, and that could be correct. I'm not here to head-shrink you. However, through my testimony, you might be able to look within *my* codependency recovery as a way to help you with relationship issues in your own life. As a former codependent I have to constantly be aware of the actions and attitudes of others, as well as myself, that can land me right back to where I was, miserable.

Codependency is a handful of things, it wasn't even a term until the 1980s, but now it's widely used. If I had to describe codependency in a statement, it would be: "I can't be okay unless you are okay."

If I had to describe codependency in a sentence or two, it would be: allowing unacceptable behavior and treatment from others in order to keep them in your life; being addicted to a toxic relationship and you don't know how to fix it or leave it.

And honestly, I hate that term *toxic relationship;* it annoys me, to tell you the truth. It's a cop out, most of the time, for a selfish person to not look within themselves to heal a relationship—on an even level—with the other person. It's having a mindset of, "I never do anything wrong, and you never do anything right. You make me this way." The term *toxic relationship* gets thrown around quite a bit, but this will be the only time you'll see me use it, which is in this paragraph. Codependent people are addicted to the nastiness of a toxic relationship. That toxicity is their drug. The high they get which comes from trying to change or fix another person is what they live for each day. We are usually self-made martyrs who are afraid to be alone, and we will go to any lengths to prevent that from happening.

With my maternal abandonment issues from when I was a child, as well as being ripped away from my close friends all the time because I was in the foster system, I became addicted to bad relationships as an adult. I was the best people-pleaser I knew. I'd be sure you liked me whether you decided to or not! Because of this incorrect mindset, I began to allow lots of unacceptable things to happen in my life that I shouldn't have. Religion only made it worse, as codependency is rampant in our churches.

"Submit to your leaders!" I'd hear, as those leaders took advantage of men, women, and children.

"Forgive or you won't be forgiven!" Another often-used, taken-out-of-context verse, as Jesus was teaching the legalists they can't forgive their way to heaven. Yet, the modern-day Pharisees preach this fallacy with no regard to what it will do to the abused person who can't break free.

"Cover it up with the blood! No matter what they do to you!" A preacher will yell at a battered wife, or the husband who has been cheated on countless times.

Garbage, all garbage. It's no wonder there's so much abuse happening in the religious world. Many churches *breed* codependent, frustrated sheep. They have no clue about the true heart of God. I'll move on from that subject.

Anyway, not just in church, but in all of my relationships, I had no backbone. What I should have been doing all along is standing up to the mistreatment of others how *God* wanted me to. But I hadn't allowed Him to renew my mind in this area...yet. Soon enough, He'd teach me how to stand up for myself how I was designed to in my spirit. As a result, I stopped trying to please people who were impossible to please. What a relief!

I kept asking God to teach me how to have healthy relationships and He has done just that! First, I had to diagnose what the issue was. My issue was that I struggled with codependent people-pleasing, period. Therefore, I had an inability to establish boundaries in my life. Boundaries are very important because they are clear markers of where *you* end and where *you* begin. Boundaries create a middle road, not a wall, but a road, in a relationship. You are on one side, they are on the other, and you both share this road evenly down the middle. Boundaries are like gates, they let people in, keep people out, as well as allow you to open up and get rid of some of your own junk.

When a codependent enabler learns about boundaries, they can crawl out of their dark pit of despair. Jesus was not an enabler. He didn't go around helping those who didn't want help. And a lot of the time, He had something for a person to *do*, who *wanted* His help—uncomfortable things. If you think about it, even as Christians, in order for us to first *become* a Christian, God required us to believe Jesus has forgiven us. Belief in Christ is a boundary our Creator has set up with humanity. Boundaries are a good thing, for both sides.

Boundaries teach you how to say, "No," and mean it. Boundaries teach you how to feel the pain of the worst possible situation—no longer having that relationship—and still being okay. Boundaries teach you how to look people in the eye, let them know how you feel, and then enforce the changes you would like to happen *without* having a come-apart. Boundaries create consequences for those who refuse to honor them.

Boundaries teach you how to show true love and respect, not just to the other person, but to yourself. Boundaries help you say:

"Not this time. I'm busy."
"No, that's not good for me."
"I told you that if you did that again, this would happen. So these consequences are a result of your choices, not mine."
"I love you, but I will no longer accept this as normal."

Codependency and boundaries go hand in hand. Codependency is the *worst* relationship diagnosis, and boundaries is the best cure. So if your addiction is another person, I highly recommend that you educate yourself on both. God did not create you to be addicted to anything or anyone. He created you to enjoy your life as a heaven-ready saint while still here on planet earth. God has boundaries for *us*, so we should have boundaries for people. To do so, we must get used to confronting others.

Those who struggle with codependency issues *hate* confrontations, and they hate them for a couple reasons:

1. **We struggle to find that fine-line of not overreacting, and not under-reacting.** So instead of confronting, we hide what is bothering us, and then blow up when it has become too much for us to bear. Rather than confront, we usually turn those issues inward, therefore incorrectly relieving our stress with an addiction or sinful choices.
2. **Because confronting those who use us *rarely* results in a favorable manner, we just keep quiet.** Our needs are hardly ever looked upon with love and compassion from our user, so we begin to think that our needs are not important—which is a lie from hell.

WE MUST CONFRONT! Confrontations are necessary to enter into recovery from codependency! Confrontations create boundaries!

When we first begin to confront, it usually comes across as anger... this will pass. You have legitimate reasons to be angry, but you don't want to stay in a state of anger. You want to move past that into controlling yourself *while* you confront.

Typically, the user in a codependent relationship will turn confrontations back around on the codependent person by using guilt, belittlement, the silent treatment, and rage. Who is the user? The user is the person *opposite* of the codependent. However, the codependent can also have user qualities. Users will rarely take the codependent person's requests seriously or permanently. Instead, they want to shut the codependent person up so they can go back to doing what they were doing.

But still, this should not stop the codependent from confronting them. Even if you are stammering, stuttering, shaking, or sweating—CONFRONT! That stuff will go away, you'll see. Confrontations are normal and healthy in *all* good relationships. They don't have to be the end of the world, they can even be...peaceful. This will take time, but first, you have to begin confronting regularly. Don't shy away, don't clam up, push *through* your feelings and confront consistently.

Before you confront, pray. Ask God to help you say the right things and to give you wisdom—He will. Next, never plan your confrontation with the hope of changing the user's mindset or unacceptable choices. Instead, plan to say what you have to say while not worrying about the end results. You've got no control over that, right? And we don't worry about things we can't control, right? Right. Simply let them know how they are affecting your life negatively, don't ramble, and don't get mad. Here's the order:

1. Confront them respectfully at a decent time, not while you, or they, are emotional or tired. You can do this face to face, by phone call, email, text, whatever, but confront.
2. Don't worry about their attacks, don't *reply* to their attacks, simply confront! They will want to shift this back on you, but stay

focused and confront! I'm not saying be aggressive and disrespectful, I'm saying express yourself rather than *defend* yourself.
3. Tell them what choices of theirs are impacting your life negatively, tell them *why* those choices are impacting your life negatively, and then let them know what the consequences will be if they choose to continue with those choices.
4. Don't be afraid, just finish, then drop it. You love them but a change has to happen. Be clear about that.
5. You're done. Move on and keep your peace. This is one confrontation of many which will move you forward into recovery. Be proud of yourself for confronting them calmly and expressing your feelings. If you got mad, so what. Don't let them use that against you. Forgive yourself, and next time don't get mad. Rinse. Repeat.

My friend, your goal is *not* to change the other person, and it's *not* to alter their opinion of your feelings. Your goal is to simply continue to confront them in a healthy manner, and then let God work it out. Don't worry about getting an immediate change, they are used to how your relationship currently is. Over time, as they see that you are serious, they will get serious too. Seriously gone, or seriously in-tune with your boundaries. A change *will* happen—in you! If they change, great! That's just a bonus! But the goal here is to be sure that *you* are okay, even if *they* are not okay *with* you. You love them, you respect them, but you also love and respect yourself! You are worth this change! Begin to confront others today in a healthy way. God is with you!

A prayer for you: *Father, thank you for teaching me how valuable I am to you. The enemy and religious people wanted me to believe that I'm not valuable, and that I should put up with crap from others just because I'm a Christian. You've taught me that's wrong! Sure, you want me to love others and help people, but you don't want me to be taken advantage of, used, or treated like a dog. My life is so important* *that you gave your Son for me. Thank you for teaching me this truth! Right now, I lift up all who are reading this, directly to you. So many of these dear readers are struggling with unhealthy relationships, and so many are addicted to people. God, today I'm asking that you break them free from this strangling mindset. Begin to reveal to them just how important they are to you! Teach them how to establish healthy boundaries, and how to feel the pain that comes from doing so. It's that pain they are afraid of, but you've taught me that it's better to feel the pain of being lonely or rejected than it is to continue being treated poorly. Give them wisdom God, for all of their relationships. Show them how to confront people properly, and guide them in love as they do so. In Jesus' name I pray, amen.*

Day 28

Why We No Longer Need Altars in Church

"If we deliberately keep on sinning after we have received the knowledge of the truth, no sacrifice for sins is left"

Hebrews 10:26

The church is dimly lit. The worship team sings softly, "Oh come to...the altar...the Father's arms are open wide." One by one, people begin to walk to the front, near the stage, to a place called "the altar." What is an altar? According to the Jews, it was a flat table where animal sacrifices were made to God. Why were animal sacrifices made? To remind the Jews of their sins committed.

When an animal was killed on the altar—and it had to be their best animal, a spotless one without flaw—the blood covered up, paid for, or "atoned for" that person's sins for an entire year (see Leviticus 23:27, Hebrews 9:22).

Unlike the twisting of today's gospel, where some believe we only get forgiven if we ask for it or confess it to a man in a small room, the *Jews* got an entire year of forgiveness at the Day of Atonement. Because of religious pride, the selfishness of church hierarchies, and taking Scripture out of context, many churches teach a neurotic Christianity of "I gotta ask for forgiveness daily!" or "I gotta confess all my sins weekly!"

This is silly because even the Jews knew that asking and confessing never forgave anyone. Only blood brought forgiveness and that forgiveness was good to go for an entire year (see Ephesians 1:7, Matthew 26:28).

There's not a single verse in any New Testament epistle which states, "Ask for forgiveness." Further, there is only *one* that says, "If we confess our sins He will forgive us" (see 1 John 1:9), and John was writing this verse to the Gnostics. Those who were *not* believers, but instead thought that sin was not a real thing—that they had *never* sinned a day in their life. All you have to do is read the following verse to realize this:

> *"If we claim we have not sinned, we make him out to be a liar and his word is not in us." (1 John 1:10)*

Need more proof? In the same book, John says this:

> *"If anybody does sin, we have an advocate with the Father— Jesus Christ, the Righteous One." (See 1 John 2:1)*

It's funny how context of Scripture clears up the devil's lies and sets us free from fear.

So what does all of this have to do with us taking the altars out of our churches? Because it was *on* those altars where the Jewish animal sacrifices were made, and *we* don't live according to Jewish ceremonial law. For us, we weren't even invited to any altars, Jesus was the final sacrifice, and the Cross was our *only* altar.

Why does that matter? Well, according to Jewish ceremonial law, animal blood never *removed* any sins, but instead, covered them up—paid them off. Blood bought a year's worth of forgiveness, but still, the blood didn't get *rid* of the actual mistakes. The writer of Hebrews explains:

> *"It is impossible for the blood of bulls and goats to take away sins." (Hebrews 10:4)*

That blood did not take away their sins, but instead, put them back in the black with God due *to* their sins committed, for a year. Jesus, on the other hand, *took away* our sins, once and for all so that no more animal sacrifices were needed. Therefore, no altars are needed.

John the Baptist was still teaching Mosaic legalism as he had a message of behavior and attitude repentance, "Stop breaking the Law!" But Jesus had a new message of grace. Jesus had a new message of repenting of *one* thing...unbelief in Him alone. Just look at what John said when he first laid eyes on the Messiah:

> *The next day John saw Jesus coming toward him and said, "Look, the Lamb of God, <u>who takes away</u> the sin of the world!" (John 1:29)*

Do you see that? John was looking forward to the Messiah whom the Prophet Isaiah talked about in Scripture! The one who would not just cover up our sins but actually take them away for good through His own body! (See Isaiah 53:5). And how did He take them away for good? By becoming the final sacrifice for sin! By volunteering to be *the* "Spotless Lamb" killed for all of humanity's failures! This is why John said, "Look, the *Lamb* of God!"

So when people are asked to come down to the front of the church to the altar, I wouldn't go so far as to say it is an insult to Christ, but I would say that if you knew the truth about that wooden platform you'd see it's not needed. The Cross was the last altar! As a matter of fact, it was the *only* altar for us Gentiles! Jesus finished everything at that location outside the city in regard to *our* forgiveness of sin—as well as the Jews'! (See John 19:30).

Again, I want to emphasize that Jesus took *away* the sin of the world for good—ONCE! AS IN, ONE TIME! Past, present, and future sins!

He is not bound by time, we are. We are time creatures, He isn't. God saw all of the sins we'd ever commit and forgave them at Calvary! All we have to do is believe we needed such forgiveness, and we *have* such forgiveness. He didn't cover our sins like the animals, but banished them as far as the east is from the west! Because of Jesus' final sacrifice, the Father chooses to not remember our sins any longer! Look at these promises:

> *"so Christ was sacrificed <u>once to take away the sins of many</u>; and he will appear a second time, not to bear sin, but to bring salvation to those who are waiting for him." (Hebrews 9:28)*

> *"For I will forgive their wickedness and <u>I will remember their sins no more</u>." (Hebrews 8:12)*

> *"And by that will, we <u>have been</u> made holy through the sacrifice of the body of Jesus Christ <u>once for all</u>." (Hebrews 10:10)*

Even the Jews, whom the author of Hebrews wrote, they couldn't fathom this once for all forgiveness. After hearing about the Messiah from the best teachers around—those who walked with Jesus—they still refused to believe He was the final sacrifice for sin. This is why the author told them:

> *"If we deliberately keep on sinning after we have received the knowledge of the truth, <u>no sacrifice for sins is left</u>" (Hebrews 10:26)*

This verse, which was written to the unbelieving Jews—not Christians—has been used for centuries to incite fear in the children of God when all along it was not for us. *We* are not going back to the temple to kill animals for forgiveness at the altar, they were. This is why the writer said, "You've heard the truth of Jesus, so you have no excuse to be making animal sacrifices any longer for your sins."

"But Matt, I got saved at the altar! I enjoy going to the altar and getting rid of my sins!"

Friend, you got saved when you believed Jesus forgave you. Before you even walked to the front of the church *to* that altar…you believed. It is belief that saves. It is hearing the gospel with faith, *not* moving your physical body to the front of a geographical location (see Galatians 3:2, John 1:12).

"But I felt something unlike I've ever felt before!"

That's great! God is not against good feelings! I'm glad your body, soul, and spirit were all clicking together that day with the realization of God's unconditional love for you, but your walking *to* that altar did not save you. There was nothing wrong with going to the altar, but you were saved before you took that step into the aisle.

"Matt, I enjoy going to the altar and leaving my sins behind each week."

So did the Jews who heard about Jesus, only they did it annually. My friend, you have knowledge of the truth, your trip to the front of the church will not bring you any more forgiveness than you already have at this very point. If you want to walk to the front, go ahead, but know that going to the front of a building constructed by man isn't removing any sin. Your faith did that, *one* time. Jesus did that, *one* time.

So today, my friends, know this: The Cross of Jesus Christ was the final altar. It was the last bloody place in which we got forgiveness from our Creator. I'm willing to be misunderstood and even hated in order to get this point across to the believers reading this. Altars are not needed in our churches. The Cross of Christ was the last one. If anything, build an empty tomb and go to that, but not an altar—I say jokingly, of course.

So sure, go to church, enjoy other Christians, fellowship, and worship. You can even go to the front and pray, or do it in your seat, there is no law in prayer. You can *even* confess to God in *agreement* over your sins—not for forgiveness—but simply because you agree with Him in all things! That is, if you are a believer. If you're not, confess you need forgiveness once, and you got it. But why not agree with Him that Jesus was the final sacrifice? Why not agree that the Cross was the last altar the world would ever need? It's the truth, my friends. It really is.

A prayer for you: *Heavenly Father, thank you for the Cross. It was at that Cross my sins were removed by way of perfect blood—for good. I believe that. I know I will stay saved and forgiven forever because Jesus will never die again! Thank you! Right now, I lift up all who are reading this, directly to you. First of all, if there are any praise and worship leaders reading this, or any Christian music makers, help them begin to infuse into their songs, the New Covenant. Teach them they don't have to say things like, "We are calling down your Spirit!" or "God come fill this place." Reveal that your Spirit is in every believer in full! Let them know you will never go away! Open their spiritual eyes to the fact that buildings aren't the places you indwell, as you did in the Old Covenant, but now, we are your temples! And Father, for everyone who goes to a church with an altar, help them to realize it's not an end-all be-all issue to keep it or remove it. Let them know it is simply a wooden table built by a man—it means nothing. If someone's faith is weak and they think they need it, just leave it be for now. It's not a big deal. You'll teach them the truth over time, so teach us how to show grace in this trivial matter. After all, we know that the Cross, held up high with Jesus on it, was the final sacrifice for sin! We know it was the last true altar on planet earth! Thank you, Jesus. Amen.*

Day 29

Dinner with a Former Drunk

"Always be prepared to give an answer for the hope that you have. But do so with gentleness and respect"

See 1 Peter 3:15

A good friend of mine who I grew up with was in town a while back. When he was here, he texted me, and invited me out for dinner. It's always good to see him and catch up on each other's lives in person. Social media is great, but there's nothing quite like having dinner face-to-face with a friend.

As we sat down to order our drinks, I told the server, "I'll have a Diet Coke," and my friend hesitated. After eyeing the long list of beers on tap, he asked me, "Do you care if I drink?"

"Of course not."

"Okay, I'll have a Boulevard," which was one of my old favorite beers.

The server came back with our drinks, and he started to ask me some questions about my sobriety.

"Are you sure you don't care if I drink?" He paused, as he slowly brought the tall beer to his mouth.

"Why would I care?"

"You know . . ." he hesitated once again, as if he wanted to say, "Because you write books on alcohol abuse."

"Mike, why would I want to stop you from enjoying a couple beers?" He looked at me strangely as he sat the beer back down after taking a sip. I continued, "If I was allergic to shellfish, do you think I should get upset with you for enjoying a nice bowl of shrimp fettuccine?"

"Well, no."

"So why should I get upset with you for drinking beer?"

"Ah, okay. I see what you're saying."

"Truth be told, in Jesus' first recorded miracle, He *created* alcohol. So obviously alcohol is not the problem. It's the person's thinking who turns alcohol into an obsession."

By the look on his face, I could see the cogs start to pick up steam in his head.

"So does Jennifer still drink? That wouldn't be very fair to you if she did."

I replied with a smile, "Why wouldn't it be fair? She doesn't struggle with alcoholism."

"Oh yeah. I guess you're right. So you don't get mad at her when she does drink?"

"Why would I get mad at someone for drinking? First of all, I have no control over that, plus, she doesn't drink like I did. She has a glass or two of wine, maybe once a week—if that. When I drank, I drank *bottles* of wine, multiple times a week, usually hers! Heck, I'd drink anything I could get my hands on!"

"Yeah ya did! I remember that!" he exclaimed.

"Exactly! That's why I don't do it now!" We both laughed pretty hard, as we *both* knew how much of a lush I acted like.

"So how long have you been sober now?"

"Over three years, and it feels great. I actually *enjoy* not drinking. It's so much better for me."

"That's awesome bud," he said to me proudly.

I finished up the conversation about drinking, "Mike, there is nothing wrong with alcohol, at all. But there *is* something wrong with *me* drinking it. I can't. When I enjoy it, I can't control it. And when I control it, I can't enjoy it. So I just don't drink."

"I got you, Matt. That's cool," and we moved on.

After the awkwardness of the alcohol issue was over, we had a nice dinner, catching up and talking about old times.

A prayer for you: *Heavenly Father, thank you for my sobriety. If I had known how much better life would be by me NOT being controlled by a liquid, I would have given it up a long time ago. But even still, you were extremely patient with me as you taught me that getting drunk all the time would never match up with my spirit. Thank you for your grace, thank you for your unconditional love, and thank you for never giving up on me. You stayed committed to me, and I'm so grateful. Right now, I lift up all who are reading this, directly to you. For those who are battling an addiction today—any addiction—help them. Help them to realize that as a believer, you have ALREADY set them free from everything that controls them. All they have to do is live that freedom out! They think they are a prisoner to this thing, but they're not! That's a lie from Satan himself! The prison doors are wide open! They are sitting in that cell, and yet, a warm breeze is right outside that doorway! THEY'RE FREE! All they have to do is step out! IT'S OPEN!...Just...step out. They might not KNOW that you've freed them, but you have. Reveal this truth to them. Teach them about their freedom, today. In Jesus' name, amen.*

Day 30

Why Christians Should Not Be Afraid of Hell

"The one who is victorious will, like them, be dressed in white. I will never blot out the name of that person from the book of life, but will acknowledge that name before my Father and his angels."

REVELATION 3:5

The fear of hell has been used to control and manipulate people for a *long* time. I can remember my grandfather on my mom's side using hell fire in his sermons. He was a person whom I've molded my ministry to *not* be like. I can remember feeling panic each time he spoke, or even walked into the room. Panic, however, does not come from God—it comes from the deepest, darkest, *hottest* places of hell.

Hell is a supernatural place of torment that no Christian will ever have to experience. For those who reject Jesus' free forgiveness by grace through faith?...Unfortunately, yes. But not us.

Jesus talked about hell more than He did heaven. In Luke 16, He told a story of a man who died and went to hell. While there, he called out to Abraham in heaven asking him to warn his family about this place of torment. He longed to have a single drop of water to cool his tongue (see Luke 16:24).

But Abraham replied, "Between us and you a great chasm has been set in place, so that those who want to go from here to you cannot, nor can anyone cross over from there to us" (see Luke 16:26). Abraham then tells the man that if his family won't listen to what is written in Scripture, they won't even be convinced if someone rises from the dead (see Luke 16:31).

Friend, hell is a real place, and it is *bad*. The reason why it's so bad is because it's complete separation from God. Many people think we are separated from Him now, on earth, but He *is* here. In hell, He's not—but here, He is!

Simply believe Jesus has forgiven you of your sins and you will not go there! (See John 1:12, Ephesians 2:8-9). If you *do* believe Jesus has forgiven you, you are secure! The punishment of sin, which is death that *leads* to hell, was taken care of at the Cross! Just look at what Peter said:

> *"For Christ also died for sins once for all, <u>the just for the unjust</u>, so that he might bring us to God, having been put to death in the flesh, but made alive in the spirit"* (1 Peter 3:18)

"The just for the unjust"? Who is unjust? We are! Or I should say, we *were*. That is, before we believed we were forgiven by Him who *is* just, Jesus. Now we are justified completely! It says it *right* there! And what were we justified from? Sin! What does sin do? It separates us from God! Jesus took away our sin for good at the Cross!

Christian, your spirit is now sinless! It's perfect! A perfect spirit is what God requires to enter heaven; a perfect spirit is what He requires to come and live inside of you right now (see 1 Corinthians 6:19). This is why you don't need to be afraid of hell: God already lives in you and He'll never go away!

"Matt, that's a lie! Every *true* believer knows that God blots out Christians' names from the book of life all the time!"

Friend, I'm sorry you believe that, but He does not. That verse, Revelation 3:5, is actually a comforting verse for Christians, not a scary one. Just look:

> *"The one who is victorious will, like them, be dressed in white. I will <u>never</u> blot out the name of that person from the book of life, but <u>will acknowledge that name</u> before my Father and his angels." (Revelation 3:5)*

John is telling us that our names will *never* be blotted out, and that Jesus *will* acknowledge us! This isn't scary! This is really good news! Do you see it? This passage, which was supposed to bring peace to us as God's children, has been used to incite terror by the quasi-grace Christians! That is unacceptable! We are not of those who shrink back to this garbage, but of those who stand firm in the truth! (See Hebrews 10:39).

This reassuring verse has been twisted by self-centered people in order to get others to do what *they* say, "NOW! OR ELSE TO HELL WITH YOU!"...as if they are God.

Friends, God doesn't work like that. Legalism does, but not God. His Spirit who lives in us will never stir up fear, but instead, ignite confidence. When young Timothy was struggling with fear, Paul encouraged him with the truth:

> **"For God did not give us a spirit of fear but of power, love, and a sound mind." (2 Timothy 1:7)**

As you can see, fear doesn't come from God. It comes from the accuser and our old, unrenewed thinking (see Revelation 12:10, Romans 12:2). Thankfully, God retrains our conscience to know *when* we should be afraid of *what*. Hell is not one of those things. Getting drunk and speeding is, but hell isn't. Therefore, as God's kids, when we *feel* fear about hell, a red flag should pop up in our souls warning us it's not coming from Him.

"Yeah right, Matt! *Real* Christians know we can lose our salvation! That's something to be *very* afraid of!"

Is God a liar? Was He naive about making His home in us for good? Is He constantly changing His mind about us being saved or not saved?... No. The answer is no. He wasn't temporarily stupid when He decided to make us spiritually perfect for free based on belief and grace. He hadn't lost His mind when He saw that we'd still struggle with our actions and attitudes. He's very smart. He knew the only way we could become heaven-ready is if He accomplished this feat *for* us. So He did. If you think you can lose your salvation you sure do think highly of yourself—as if you are actually maintaining it. Whew, that's a lot of pressure.

Friend, the reason why we will stay saved is two main reasons, and neither have anything to do with us:

1. **The New Covenant is based on a promise between the Father and the Son, not us.** We are simply the beneficiaries to their bloody contract. We didn't create this agreement, and we can't sustain it. Instead, we just open up our hands and say, "Thank you." In Hebrews 6, the Bible says God swore by Himself—that is, the Father to the Son, and vice versa—two unchangeable things. *This* is the anchor of our salvation, which is their promise to one another at the Cross.
2. **The only way we can lose our salvation is if Jesus dies again, and that ain't happening!** Hebrews 7:25 states, "Therefore he is able to save completely those who come to God through him, because he always lives to intercede for them."

In 1 John 4, John writes to the early church about how we have nothing to be afraid of any longer. According to him, the reason why we shouldn't be afraid is because, "God's love for us is perfect" and "fear has to do with punishment." In his gospel he notes *we* won't be punished for anything! (See John 3:17-18). If we are to be punished, the Cross wasn't all it was cracked up to be! John was saying if you are still afraid of God it's because you still don't understand His love! (See 1 John 4:18). A love so great He'd never send you to hell!

So today, my friends, know this: Your old spirit has died and your new spirit will never experience hell! (See Galatians 2:20, 2 Corinthians 5:17, John 3:16). From the moment you first heard the gospel with faith, your old spirit was crucified *with* Jesus, it was buried with Jesus, and then resurrected with Him in the spiritual realm! (See Romans 6:6, 10:17). YOU ARE NEW! Perfectly new! That new spirit inside your body is sinless and will never experience torment in hell! (See Colossians 3:3, 1:22, John 10:28). You have been sealed up *with* Christ until the day of redemption! (See Ephesians 1:13, 2 Corinthians 1:22). CHRISTIAN, YOU ARE NOT GOING TO HELL, SO DON'T BE AFRAID! God already lives inside you, so be confident in this truth!

A prayer for you: *Heavenly Father, thank you for teaching me about your perfect love, which casts out all fear. Oh my goodness, I had so much fear to unlearn. Thank you for teaching me the truth of what you've done in me. Right now, I lift up all who are reading this, directly to you. So many of them are having a difficult time believing what I've just wrote, and I can relate. They've been incorrectly taught—by way of fear—that they are actually doing something to maintain their salvation, but they're not. It was free in the beginning, and it's still free. We didn't "get" our salvation, we received it as a free gift. Please ease their minds today. Let them know that anything which begins with "I do" or "I don't do," in order to keep their spot in our Family is incorrect. We keep our heavenly heritage because of what Jesus has done, and nothing more. We are grateful for this hope which anchors our souls! Your promise to Jesus, and His to you, was a wonderful, loving idea! Help us to grow in the knowledge of such grace and become confident in who we are in you! Amen.*

Month 2

"All this is from God, who reconciled us to himself through Christ and gave us the ministry of reconciliation"

2 Corinthians 5:18

Day 31

How to Change the World as a Christian

"And whatever you do, whether in word or deed, do it all in the name of the Lord Jesus..."

SEE COLOSSIANS 3:17

Have you ever felt pressured as a Christian? Maybe you've been taught to "Be radical!" or to "Make disciples of disciples!" but you're not sure how to do such things. Maybe you've trembled in your seat as the preacher yelled, "Get out there and change the world! If you don't, the world's blood will be on *your* hands!"

My friend, that's a big, hot crock of you know what. If you are feeling pressure, that's not coming from God. It's coming from religious people who find their identity in what they do, it's coming from old, stinking thinking, and it's coming from hell. Please understand this: God does *not* pressure you. He counsels you, He's patient, kind, and loving. He wants you to stop worrying so much and enjoy Him! (See Luke 10:41-42, 12:25, Matthew 6:27).

Further, as a Christian, nobody's blood will be on your hands for anything. That's an Old Testament verse from Ezekiel being pulled out of context to try to motivate you with fear. The grace-confused Christians use this passage to generate stress and anxiety. They think such a method is the only way to motivate people, but panic is the worst kind of motivation out there.

The Law-loving person might yell at me, "Yeah right, Matt! God has called us to witness! If we don't, we will be held accountable!"

Nope. Christians won't be held accountable for anything. What in the *world* do you think the Cross was for? We Christians will *enjoy* meeting our Maker, we won't have to tuck our tail and say, "Did I do alright?" The Bible says we can have confidence on the day of judgment because God's love has been made complete in us (see 1 John 4:17). It's just *sick* that people twist the gospel into something that it's not—as if Jesus' sacrifice didn't fully work.

But the religious folk are dying to have their ears tickled by pastors who brag on all of their wonderful evangelism. It's really sad. Listen, friend, Jesus came to put your mind at ease, not to cause you to freak out about letting people know about Him. Look at what He said:

> *"Come to me, all you who are weary and burdened, <u>and I will give you rest</u>." (Matthew 11:28)*

REST! Jesus came so that we can rest! Today's fake Promise Keepers, like the Pharisees of old, think that their amazing religious works are earning them status with God. The truth is, Jesus wants us *all* to just chill out.

"Matt! How can you say that? If we don't get out there each day and let the world know about Him, we *will* be liable!"

Liable for *what*? The salvation of the world? Sounds demonic to me! Again, what do you think Jesus died for? Was it so we can witness until our witnesser falls off? Did He die so we can live a stressed out life, trying to be sure we feel good about ourselves as we become religious weirdos? NO! *We* are not responsible for the salvation of the world, Jesus is!

"So are you saying that we shouldn't do anything at all?"

No, that's not what I'm saying. I'm saying…relax. Rest. Take a deep breath and be still. Only in a state of resting and *knowing* that you are secure in Christ, will you begin to live out your witnessing, organically.

Friend, we are simply created beings, we are not God. We get saved by grace, we live by grace, and we witness by grace. We change the *world* by grace. Grace equals zero pressure, ever. There is *no* stress or strain on us, all of the pressure is on Jesus. He can handle it just fine. Pressure is a red flag. Pressure is anti-gospel. God did not make His home in us so we can be exacerbated each day, He simply wants us to be ourselves as heaven-ready saints.

Believe it or not, you're not responsible for a single person making it to heaven—God is. You are a branch, you are not the vine. The gospel *will* be spread, somehow, someway. Even if we no longer have the ability to let others know about Jesus, the rocks will cry out! (Luke 19:40). Nothing will stop this message.

Over time, planet earth will be infected by the love of Jesus, God promises (see Mark 16:15). For this reason, we don't need to wake up each day and feel as if we *must* do something or else God's gonna get us—because He's not. He understands your life and He empathizes with all of your circumstances. He is with you from the time you have your coffee, until the time you lay your head down at night. He's working *through* you, mundane moment by mundane moment. He doesn't just show up when you talk about Him, He's with you all the time! (See Philippians 2:13).

"Okay, Matt. I think I see what you are saying. So what do we do?"

Be yourself. You are complete in Christ, and you're a good person inside (see Colossians 1:22). If you believe Jesus is your Savior, His Spirit lives in you in full (see 1 Corinthians 6:19). He will guide you every second of the day. Not only that, but you, *your* spirit, wants to do the same things *His* Spirit does! It's a beautiful relationship! You're not at battle with yourself *or* God—THAT'S BAD TEACHING! You actually want what God wants! (See Galatians 2:20, Romans 6:6-7, 2 Corinthians 5:17, Hebrews 10:16, Romans 6:17).

So as you simply *be* yourself in your everyday life—and you are relaxed—you will do *more* for God than you've ever done before! So relax.

"But what about the people overseas? What about mission work, church work, and evangelism?"

All of that stuff will happen organically. Trust me. I don't talk about it much, but I've been on both ends of this spectrum. For a time, the devil had me convinced that I had to "Get the world to believe, and fast!" As a result, I just about drove myself crazy "trying" to spread the love of Jesus, when all along, all I *had* to do was stop trying, chill out, and *start* trusting! It's an indescribable paradox, you'll see.

The author of Hebrews attempts to put it in words:

> *"Let us, therefore, make every effort to
> enter that rest"* (see Hebrews 4:11)

The strangest thing happened to me once I began to strive to enter God's rest. I began to be more evangelistic than ever before—because I knew I didn't have to be. Peter wrote to the early Church, letting them know the secret formula which I finally found:

> *"Always be prepared to give an answer to everyone who
> asks you to give the reason for the hope that you have. But
> do this with gentleness and respect"* (see 1 Peter 3:15)

Be ready. Be prepared. Be yourself. If you want to go to Africa, go. If you don't, don't. God is with you either way and He lets you pick. Good dads give their kids choices. He's proud of you no matter what, and you're in His Family for good! (See John 1:12, Ephesians 2:19). It's impossible to be out of the will of God, once you place your faith in Jesus. If that sentence upsets you, then you still don't understand what Jesus has truly done for you.

So today, my friends, know this: To change the world as a Christian, relax. Sure, at first, this freedom will be strange, you'll be using it to figure things out. It will take time to recalibrate *how* you talk to others about God. But eventually, you will come to understand that God is in you and He lives through you, so your *life* speaks for itself every single day! You are a light for the world! You're a light while you do laundry, you're a light while you sit in your cubicle, you're a light in the mission field, and you're a light while you smile at people during your child's ball game. You *are* changing the world for the better! Keep being yourself! God is very proud to call you His own!

A prayer for you: *Father, thank you for the understanding you've given me about how I'm supposed to change the world. I was taught all wrong for so many years. I was taught that if I wasn't constantly rushing, you'd be mad at me, and people would be going to hell BECAUSE of me. Thank you for teaching me those were lies. Your Word says in 1 Corinthians 13, that you keep no record of my wrongs. It also says that you protect me, trust me, and that you always have hope in me. Thank you for revealing these truths! Right now, I lift up all who are reading this, directly to you. For those who have been incorrectly taught that the salvation of the world is on their shoulders, give them rest today. Reveal to them that such a pressure was only put on Jesus, and He handled it perfectly. Teach them how to simply wake up each day and be themselves, and that by doing so, they will naturally alter the course of humanity, for the better! In Jesus' name I pray, amen.*

Day 32

The Truth About Tithing

"Each of you should give what you have decided in your heart to give, not reluctantly or under compulsion, for God loves a cheerful giver."

2 Corinthians 9:7

In the book of Acts, there is an account of a man trying to buy God's Spirit—literally (see Acts 8:18-19). His name was Simon. He thought that by giving his money he'd have the ability to do what the apostles were doing. Peter gave him a firm tongue-lashing about how incorrect his thinking was. Had Simon known the truth—that he could receive the Holy Spirit for free—he wouldn't have offered money. Of course, now he knows.

Sometimes we have to have cold water thrown in our faces for us to be able to understand certain things—to "snap out of it." The truth about tithing is no different. Like Simon, we can incorrectly believe that God's favor and protection can be bought through our legalistic giving. "You gotta rebuke the devour!" they'll say. Now, I already know that I will get a lot of kick-back on this subject, so I'm going to present every rebuttal I can possibly think of, beginning with what I just stated above: "Matt! How can you say that tithing is legalistic? That's just wrong!"

Friend, the word tithe literally means *ten percent*. That is a law in itself—a mathematical law. So let's define the word "law."

1. Webster's Dictionary claims a law is: *a rule or order that it is obligatory to observe*. Obligatory means you are obligated. "You *have* to do this, or *not* do this—or else."
2. According to the Old Testament, a law was something you physically did, or *refused* to physically do, in order to gain God's approval—or to be sure you didn't *lose* His approval.

Anything we physically do is a "work." For example: *I* do this, so that *I* get that. I *don't* do this, so that I *don't* get that. Paul makes clear to the Romans how wrong this is according to the gospel because the gospel is based solely on grace. What is grace? Grace is absolutely free, unearnable favor. If you can earn it or lose it, it was never based on grace. Here's Paul's proof:

> *"And if by grace, then it cannot be based on works; if it were, grace would no longer be grace." (Romans 11:6)*

This can apply to anything in the Christian life, not just tithing. Say, for example, a Christian believes that attending a Bible college or seminary will earn them favor with God. *That* is a work—something in which they are physically doing. Therefore, if earning righteousness—or *keeping* righteousness—is the motivating factor behind their studies, their academia is dung, it's total crap. Paul said this, not me, after listing off all of the "amazing feats" *he* had accomplished (see Philippians 3:3-8).

This is why pastors need to stop lying about tithing. Some pastors just don't know any better, but some do. The ones who aren't telling the truth about tithing are too fearful of the church not getting the funds they need. So, they manipulate their people with the pressure of *not* being blessed by God *if* they don't tithe.

"Matt, you're a false teacher! Read your Bible! You are wrong! God Himself will make you *suffer* for saying we aren't supposed to give any money to the churches!"

Relax. Take a deep breath and count to ten...it's gonna be okay. You might burst a blood vessel if you don't. Friend, listen, I'm not saying *don't* give, I'm saying change *why* you give. The same way you got saved should be the same way you give: *with grace*.

You didn't abide by any law to *get* saved, but instead, you died to the Law so that you could live for God! (See Galatians 2:19). You were saved by grace, not by Law observance. Therefore, there shouldn't be any law *percentage* in your giving either. A percentage is a law. Instead, you should give gracefully from the core of your being, as a heaven-ready saint (see Colossians 1:22, Romans 5:1).

Give whatever you want, whenever you want, to *whomever* you want—without a numerical equation. Numerical equations are laws. So is any type of physical effort to achieve anything with God. This is why Jesus did so many physical acts in front of the Pharisees when He wasn't supposed to be—acts which went *against* their Law (see Mark 2:23-24, 3:1-6). Further, Jesus only refers to tithing when He is pointing out the hypocrisy of those who were focused on their tithe *rather* than on important matters of the heart (see Matthew 23:23).

There is not one single verse in any New Testament epistle which states a New Covenant believer must give ten percent of their money to anyone. Paul, Peter, James, John—none of them wrote anything in any of their letters about tithing. Don't you think if tithing was a part of the gospel they'd say so? This is why we should completely remove the word *tithe* from our vocabulary and replace it with a different word: *giving*.

Rather than hound the Christians in Corinth about forking over a tenth of their earnings, Paul educated them about giving—not tithing—when he said:

> *"Each of you should give what you have decided in your heart to give, not reluctantly or under compulsion, for God loves a cheerful giver." (2 Corinthians 9:7)*

Notice that Paul tells them to give freely and *not* under compulsion. Calculating ten percent can easily be compulsive, "Is that before or after taxes? What about my tips? What if I give someone a loan? Do I tithe on my birthday money? Oh God, please be easy on me if I'm wrong!"

Another version of this verse says "don't give under pressure." Any action of a Christian which is done under pressure is *not* coming from God. Remember, we are branches who produce spiritual fruit, and Christ is the vine (see John 15:5). To grow fruit, branches are never pressured by the vine. Instead, they simply rest and be themselves. This is why frantic, pressure-filled, or even emotional giving, should always be a red flag for us to pause, pray, *then* proceed.

We are to be doing everything from a state of rest (see Hebrews 4:11). Sure, we are at war, spiritually, but even the armor we put on is Christ *in* us coming *out* of us—this can only be done by resting gracefully in Him (see Ephesians 6). By way of an attitude of rest, we can naturally allow Christ to live through us to produce the good things He wants us to produce (see Galatians 5:22-23). This includes our giving.

"Matt, you think you're soooooooo smart. Are you saying that we don't have to give anything at all? Are you saying we can just relax?"

Yes, that's exactly what I'm saying. We are free. God has set things up this way because He knows that love cannot exist or thrive without freedom. Without freedom, everything we do and *don't* do is a duty. No intimate relationship is based on duty. The Galatians couldn't get this in their thick, legalistic heads. They were trying to earn *more* of God's favor through physical acts. Paul corrected them:

> *"It is for freedom that Christ has set us free. Stand firm, then, and do not let yourselves be burdened again by a yoke of slavery." (Galatians 5:1)*

Slavery is forcing people to do things—or to not do things—because we legally say so. With slavery, we don't even *earn* anything. That's exactly what the Law did, it created religious slaves. It caused its observers to be slaves because even when they did what it said for them to do, they *still* didn't earn anything from God. God has always been concerned with our hearts and faith in Him—*not* in Law observance (see Genesis 15:6, Romans 4:3). Any jerk can obey laws, but to understand our Creator, love and belief in Him must be present. This is why Jesus died! So we could be free from the *whole* Law and enjoy uninterrupted fellowship, right now! (See Romans 8:2).

So why is it we will agree that Christ has set us free from the slavery of Law *except* for giving away a tenth of our money?...Simple: *Bad teaching*. Bad teaching that *attempts* to combine Law with grace—a self-destructing, double-talk mix of the Old and New. *Confusion* would be a great way to describe it.

Many pastors have incorrectly taught their congregations that in order to be blessed by God they *must* give a tenth of their money to their church. Some even falsely claim that the tithe is only the beginning! They say that if a person gives an offering *above* the tithe, they will become extremely wealthy. "The tithe is just to be sure you get to keep what you got! An offering will get you more!" This is a lie. Honestly, it's not just a lie, it's an anti-gospel Ponzi scheme—especially when they say an offering above the tithe will generate great wealth.

If this were the truth, then why doesn't *that* pastor simply give away all of their church's money to *another* church, and then sit back and rake in the dough? After all, wouldn't that be even *more* holy? Wouldn't that cause God to open up the floodgates of heaven even wider? It's garbage, it's slavery, it makes no sense for a reason: it's not the gospel.

Further, tithing has never made anyone wealthy except for the pastors who preach this falsity. Saying that God promises "a return on your monetary investment" is a lie from Satan himself. You can't *buy* God's favor, He's your Dad! What kind of good parent would do such a terrible thing to their kids? Who would force their kids to give *them* money, so they will give their kids back even *more* money? No parent in their right mind would do this! This stupidity would be called *mental abuse*, and *that's* what the lie of tithing is doing to God's children! It is damaging the minds of many!

Just imagine if you told *your* child, "Here, take this twenty dollars and go have a good time at the mall. But if you don't bring me back *two* dollars, you can forget about eating dinner tonight. And, if you bring me back *five* dollars, because you gave above the ten percent, I'll give you dessert! But don't you dare rob me of at least my ten percent! It's mine and I want it back!"

This trash teaching has to stop! If I wanted to, I could give my child a $100 bill! I don't expect her to give *any* of it back to me! I don't *give* to my daughter so she will give any amount back, but because I love her! This is how God sees *you*! And let's be clear about the verse in question; the Scripture which has been used to create the tithing law is Malachi 3:10:

> *"'Bring the whole tithe into the storehouse, that there may be food in my house. Test me in this,' says the Lord Almighty, 'and see if I will not throw open the floodgates of heaven and pour out so much blessing that there will not be room enough to store it.'"*

From the get-go, we've established the foundation of tithing incorrectly. Tithing had nothing to do with money whatsoever. Malachi is talking about...drumroll...*grain*! A "storehouse" stores grain! This is about food! God is not talking about a physical church building or cash, but about a grain silo and groceries!

This verse has nothing to do with Christianity *or* churches, but instead, the *Jews* and being able to *feed the priests*. Malachi was written hundreds of years *before* Jesus, and the first church *building* wasn't even officially erected until 200 years *after* Jesus! So how are we going to take *that* verse and squeeze it into what we have on *this* side of the Cross?...By taking it out of context. We can make up a lot of stupid stuff by copying and pasting Scripture to complete our own agenda—tithing included.

The fact of the matter is that the Jews had to tithe their grain in order to feed the Levitical priesthood who weren't *allowed* to earn a living because they were too busy doing priestly stuff. The grain tithe was so they could eat! How dare us for taking this particular verse and then retrofitting it into the gospel. What a deception! What a shame!

Another big zit on the face of Christian tithing is unless you are a Jew, you weren't even *invited* to obey the tithing law. But more, even if you *are* a Jew, the Old Covenant is now obsolete anyway because a New Covenant has replaced it. The author of Hebrews tells us this. He, or she, claims Jesus' death and resurrection created a new agreement between God and humanity:

> *"By calling this covenant 'new,' he has made the first one obsolete" (Hebrews 8:13)*

It's the *same* God of the Jews, but a *new* Covenant for everyone! The first Covenant—which included tithing—is put aside because it is worthless. Obsolete means worthless! There is a reason you don't use a pay-phone any longer, and there is a reason you don't live by the Old Covenant any longer—THERE IS SOMETHING BETTER! CELL PHONES AND JESUS!

Of course, I'm sure I'll hear, "So Matt, do you think we should just rip out Malachi and throw it away? How dare you! Jesus said not one jot or tittle will be removed from the Law!"

Friend, I'm on the same page as you. I agree that not one part of the Law will ever go away, Jesus was not lying when He said that. However, the Law was completed *in* Christ, and now we are living under a different system of belief *not* Law. Only unbelievers are under Law, and the only thing the Law will ever do for them is increase their realization of their need for a graceful Savior:

> *"For Christ has already accomplished the purpose for which the Law was given. As a result, all who believe in him are made right with God." (Romans 10:4)*

So sure, leave Malachi exactly where it is—don't rip it out. It belongs in the canonized history book of our Savior's lineage. But we *Christians* are not under a law from Malachi, or from any law in any book. Period. We are under a New Covenant based on faith in Jesus' finished work (see John 19:30, Hebrews 10:10). When we mix in a drop of the Old Covenant with the New Covenant, it is no longer the New Covenant, but instead reverts back to the Old.

Paul was trying to get the Christians in Galatia to stop mixing in Old Covenant rituals with the New Covenant of grace. He called them *fools* for doing so (see Galatians 3:3). Their incorrect mindset was, "If grace is good, it would be even better if we mixed in some law with it"—NOPE! Paul put and end to this false teaching:

> *"A little yeast works through the whole batch of dough." (Galatians 5:9)*

Paul was telling them, "*One* law—just one—mixed in with grace, would be the same as one drop of arsenic mixed in with your Gatorade. Why would you do such a foolish thing?" Jesus also warned us against combining the Old Covenant with the New. He said it's like putting new wine into old wineskins—the wineskin will burst! (See Matthew 9:17). This would include tithing.

Let's do another counterclaim to what I'm teaching here, let's talk about Melchizedek. Now, some legalistic Bible scholars who don't understand grace, will cherry-pick an event from the Old Testament about Abraham tithing to a mystery man named Melchizedek (see Genesis 14). A couple things they will use for their stance of tithing as New Covenant believers is:

1. Abraham tithed Melchizedek—which was before the Law was given by Moses.
2. In Hebrews, a *New* Testament epistle, the author refers to tithing Melchizedek.

Both stances crumble pretty quickly when you dive into Scripture for yourself. For number one, Abraham didn't tithe Melchizedek grain, but spoils of war. How can a Christian tithe their booty to their local church if they aren't confiscating plunder from war? So this theology is just straw-grasping.

How do I know it was spoils of war and not grain or cash? Because Abraham had just won a battle, and afterwards, he met up with Melchizedek to hand over the loot. This had nothing to do with tithing to a church, so this argument falls flat on its face.

For number two, Hebrews 7 goes into great length explaining the relationship between Abraham and Melchizedek. Some scholars claim that Melchizedek was Jesus appearing in the Old Testament *before* He came as a baby. Just read Hebrews 7:3:

> *"Without father or mother, without genealogy, without beginning of days or end of life, resembling the Son of God, he remains a priest forever."*

Sounds like Jesus to me, or at least a foreshadowing of Him. But let's not get off track here. The author of Hebrews goes on to tell how important Melchizedek was, so much so, that he deserved a tenth of Abraham's plunder (see Hebrews 7:4). But *then* he says how much *more* important Jesus is! The author claims, "Jesus has become the guarantor of a *better* covenant" (Hebrews 7:22, my emphasis added). Here's more proof:

> *"The former regulation is set aside because it was weak and useless (for the Law made nothing perfect), and a better hope is introduced, by which we draw near to God." (Hebrews 7:18-19)*

So if the former regulation, the Law, was weak and useless—and tithing is a matter of the Law—then how much better is our *giving* based on grace?! How much more authentic and loving is our giving when it's done from the heart? Immensely!

Many Christians won't even give two or three percent because they think it won't count! And some give *more* than ten percent because they think by doing so, they are forcing God to buy them that new car! These types get great satisfaction by putting their money envelope in the basket with the amount written real big *just* so the person next to them can see them doing it! We gotta *stop* counting numbers, and *start* being branches! Branches have it so easy!

Friend, God does not bless us because we give Him a percentage of our money as if He's our Heavenly Broker demanding His cut before He continues to work. No, He blesses us because we are His children, just the same as *any* loving parent would do.

Your Dad can't be bought. He gives to you because He cares for you. Truth be told, with Christ living in you, you are *already* blessed with every possible blessing! (See Ephesians 1:3). Should we give? Absolutely! But we need to give whatever we want to give, because we want to give it. As a New Covenant believer, you can give 10%, 2%, 89%—or even 0%—there is no law in giving. You can't legislate love *or* God's blessings through any particular number. You are free.

So today, my friends, know this: We don't give to get. We don't give to keep what we got. We give because we are natural givers at heart. We give because God lives in us and *He* is the greatest giver of all time (see John 3:16). So let's all begin to give, but *give* with the right motives. Let's give because we are not under any pressure *to* give, but because we *are* cheerful givers!

A prayer for you: *Heavenly Father, today I want to thank you for the revelation of your grace giving. I can remember the days I'd feel terrible about myself because I "tithed" but I wasn't sure if I tithed to the exact percentage. You know full well how I lived in fear and condemnation over my tithing—eventually giving up altogether. The torment Satan created in my mind through this law was terrible. Thank you for setting me free! Right now, I lift up all of the pastors who are reading this,* *directly to you. Begin to reveal to them that you know how much their bills are, and you know what they need. You know their goals, ambitions, and plans, and you want the gospel to spread just like they do. However, you want the gospel to spread based on the truth of tithing being a law which we are free from. Take the pressure off of them this very moment, so they can take the pressure off of their congregations. Give them peace knowing you will take care of their financial situations, organically, with the truth. And for everyone else who is not a pastor, help them understand that their giving should be based on their love for you. Like a hand-made, uneven, clay coffee-cup that says "Daddy," you take our gift with a warm smile and a hug. We are your children and you are our Dad. Help us all to understand this amazing truth on the deepest level possible. Amen.*

Day 33

God Does Not Care About Your Outfit

"Woe to you, teachers of the law and Pharisees, you hypocrites! You are like whitewashed tombs, which look beautiful on the outside but on the inside are full of the bones of the dead and everything unclean." ~Jesus

Matthew 23:27

"Tuck your shirttail in boy! And you better get back in that bathroom and part your hair! Ain't no grandchild of mine going to the house of the Lord looking like a heathen."

And so it began. From the time I was just a child, religion was already being beat into my innocent head with a hammer. Grandpa was a preacher, "So I better listen." I would never talk back, a couple backhands to the face stopped that idea even before I learned how to write my name. Not only that, but when I *didn't* listen, I knew I'd have to go somewhere and hide because his hand was like a rock. He even bragged on how hard it was.

I always dreamed of running away, and one time I even did. Which, my quest for freedom didn't last long because I got hungry and didn't know what to do with my time. Hiding behind the bushes at school and walking through the neighborhood only lasted for so long. Mom and Grandpa didn't even notice that I *had* run away, thankfully.

This was the mid-1980s, when Grandpa still had his thumb on every part of my mom's life. She was young herself, in her early 20s. Mom hadn't yet fallen off the deep end with her addictions, so she had full custody of us. We lived with my grandpa while Mom and Dad battled it out in the court system to see who would be awarded five kids. I hated living with Grandpa, and I missed my dad severely. This angry old man was stiff, cold, and a royal you-know-what. The beatings that came by way of a "godly man," my own grandfather, was something I always felt the rest of the day. It was wrong what he did to us.

As time went on, my defense mechanisms to overbearing religious people grew in aggression. Through this man, Satan had warped my mind in regard to just how loving my Heavenly Father really is. I had a lot to unlearn. When I was little, if I showed up at Grandpa's church with something wrong with my outfit, I'd be quickly grabbed by the ear and pulled into the back hallway for a fast butt-beating.

"I *told* you to change that shirt! C'mere! Don't pull away from me or you'll get it worse!"

I hated church. I hated religion. I hated everything that had to do with Sunday and dressing up. I was experiencing severe religious abuse, and my feelings were justified. The devil loved what my grandfather was doing to me. Lucifer and his demons got a sick thrill from the misrepresentation of God *through* this abusive preacher-man. The enemy starts out in our lives at a young age—some of us, even in the womb. His goals are to steal, kill, and destroy (see John 10:10). That includes the confidence of children and their idea of God.

Unfortunately, this happens to countless people all throughout the world, every single day. It's no wonder Christians have such a bad rap, it's because of those who are supposed to be representing God's unconditional love—yet, they don't. Instead, they represent legalism, bitterness, conservatism, and fear-mongering. God couldn't care less about what you wear on *any* day, He's concerned with your heart! Does He live there or doesn't He? Does He have the green light to live *through* you, or doesn't He?

"Yeah right, Matt! We are supposed to represent God in His house! We are supposed to look nice!"

Really? This facade of "looking right" on the outside began a long, long time ago. So long, even Jesus addressed it. Let's see what He had to say about getting all cleaned up, on the outside:

> "*Woe to you, teachers of the law and Pharisees, you hypocrites! You are like whitewashed tombs, which look beautiful on the outside but on the inside are full of the bones of the dead and everything unclean.*" (Matthew 23:27)

That's a burn if I ever heard one. "You're beautiful on the outside but on the inside you're dead." Wow.

Friend, I'm not saying that we *shouldn't* dress nice. If you want to put on a 3-piece suit or a pretty dress, go right ahead. I'm sure God thinks you look great! I'm sure *I'd* think you look great. But what about the inside? Is it beautiful in there too? Is it handsome in there too?...This is what matters most to our Creator. Does the inside match up with the outside, and vise versa?

On the flip side, if you have God living in you and you want to wear a wrinkled shirt and have messy hair, *you* are beautiful and handsome too! God likes your style! So when old Betty Blue Hair makes a rude comment about your get-up, don't go off on her and then call her an old goat. That will never match up with who you are inside. *You* are patient, kind, and loving. You are not quick to get angry (see 1 Corinthians 13, James 1:19).

The wise thing to do would be to *kindly* confront this Pharisee woman. Look her in the eye, be confident, and say, "Listen, I want you to know that when you make crude comments about my clothes and hairstyle it makes me resent you. I don't want to do that because I'm not a resentful person. Further, I *like* how I look, so please keep your comments to yourself, okay? Thank you." and then walk away. Easy, peasy, lemon squeezy. You didn't let that stuff bottle up, and you didn't have a come-apart. You confronted a person in a healthy way. Bravo! This type of thing makes God proud!

And do you see how the Holy Spirit worked *through* you? You didn't flip out and then have to go back and apologize, but instead, you got your point across in a firm way. This is the *good* plan God has set for us in all of our difficult relationships—which is simply showing love and respect for people *and* for ourselves!

So today, my friends, know this: God is concerned about your heart, not your outfit. God is concerned about you growing spiritual fruit, not your blouse. God would rather you wear a black garbage bag for the rest of your life bag—and He live in you—than He would you *only* wear Armani suits, and He doesn't. There is nothing wrong with a suit! There is nothing wrong with a nice dress! Wear whatever you want! But while doing so, begin to realize that you are *already* dressed up perfectly, because you are already wearing Jesus Christ!

A prayer for you: *Heavenly Father, thank you for teaching me that I am the House of the Lord, and that I can wear whatever threads I please. For so long I believed that what I wore made me holy, but that's 100% incorrect. We can dress up a team of monkeys in little mini-suits and dresses and sit them on the front row at church, that still wouldn't make them holy. Only faith in Christ can do this! Right now, I lift up all who are reading this, directly to you. So many of them have been hurt by whitewashed tomb people. The self-centered legalists have misrepresented you so drastically, these dear readers think you're mad at them because of their style. Please reveal the truth! You're not! You're not even disappointed! All of our disappointments to you were taken care of at the Cross! YOU ARE PROUD OF US! WE ARE YOUR MASTERPIECES! And Dad, please help these brothers and sisters of mine to forgive those who've hurt them. Help me too. Yes, I've made the decision TO forgive, and Grandpa is dead, but I still have hurt feelings.*

Help me with my feelings. Please, strengthen all of us with your grace as we choose to forgive those who don't deserve it—just like Jesus did for us. In His name I pray, amen.

Day 34

God Wants to Help You with Your Attitude

*"Have this attitude in yourselves which
was also in Christ Jesus"*

Philippians 2:5

Here are eight thoughts in which we need help from God with our attitudes:

1. "Just my luck! Nothing good ever happens to me, why even try?"
2. "That was the last straw, I'm never forgiving them again."
3. "I *hate* that man."
4. "What a gold-digging phony. The only reason she's with him is for his money. She doesn't care about him at all. Just look at what she posts on Facebook."
5. "What does he know? I went to seminary and he didn't! He has no idea what he's talking about, and *I* do! I'll show him."
6. "God wouldn't care if I watched this porn. He sees how my wife withholds sex, what else am I supposed to do?"
7. "Look at how big that church is! All that pastor cares about is ripping people off and taking their money!"

8. "Look at how small that church is! If they *really* knew the gospel more people would go there!"

Now, here are the same eight thoughts, the only difference is, God is helping us with our attitudes *about* these thoughts:

1. "I feel very let down, but I know God is still in control. I trust Him, and I still have hope."
2. "This time, I'm choosing to forgive, but I'm standing firm on the consequences of the boundaries they keep crossing. God, strengthen me to be able to pull this off how you see fit."
3. "I really don't like that person at *all*. God, you see how they rub me wrong. Please help me with these feelings of resentment. I don't want to feel this way, so help me to not act these feelings out."
4. "God, I've witnessed this woman do some pretty bad things in regard to her marriage on social media. I'm not her judge, so please help me to think of her with goodness. Also, help her to come to know you deeply so that she will honor her husband, as well as you, and to keep private matters private."
5. "Father, this person seems to really know you. I understand that my degree from seminary doesn't make me more important to you, so please help me to see this person in the same light that you do. We are brothers."
6. "I need relief. God you created my body to want sex, and you see that's not possible right now. Please, help me to not become addicted to fantasizing. I know these thoughts are normal, so help me to keep them under control, and help me with these urges. I really want to have sex, but I also want to honor you and my wife."
7. "Wow, that's a big church. God, I'm grateful that you use all of your churches to somehow, someway, change lives and spread the gospel. We might not all agree on everything, but as long

as Jesus is preached, you'll take care of the unimportant stuff. Thank you for that church."
8. "Wow, that's a small church. God, I'm grateful that you use all of your churches to somehow, someway, change lives and spread the gospel. We might not all agree on everything, but as long as Jesus is preached, you'll take care of the unimportant stuff. Thank you for that church."

Do you recognize the main differences in allowing God to help us with our attitudes? Man, I sure do! Those differences are: peace, hope, love, confidence, and contentment!

God's design to live through you will help you to be *who* you really are inside! Christian, YOU HAVE A GREAT ATTITUDE! The attitude of your perfect spirit matches up with the attitude of God, seamlessly!

The top eight attitudes are the attitudes of unbelievers *or* believers who just don't know who they are! Do you not see it? Believer in Jesus, do you not know who you are? HEY! KNOCK KNOCK! Take your mask off and look in the mirror at your glory! YES! YOU HAVE GLORY! Jesus said so:

> *"I have given them the glory you gave me, so they may be one as we are one." (John 17:22)*

But you can only see your glory—a heaven-ready saint with a wonderful attitude—when you remove the veil from your face! How do you do this? By believing the truth of what God's Spirit is saying about you! Paul explains:

> *"And we all, with unveiled face, beholding the glory of the Lord, are being transformed into the same image from one degree of glory to another. For this comes from the Lord who is the Spirit." (2 Corinthians 3:18)*

We go from glory to glory as we learn who we are inside! DO YOU SEE IT? Unveil your face! Take off your mask of a bad attitude! It doesn't belong on you! You and God are not battling with one another *over* your attitude! He's not trying to help you with your attitude to *change* you, He's trying to help you with your attitude to *teach* you that this is who you really are!

When we do this we are revealing who the Sons and Daughters of God are to *all* of the world, right now! They are waiting for us to be our true selves! Look!

> *"For the creation waits in eager expectation for the children of God to be revealed." (Romans 8:19)*

Friend, stop focusing on your incorrect actions and attitudes and simply reveal who you are inside! Creation is impatiently waiting for you to be you!

Please begin to realize that you're not trying to "get closer" to God to *fix* your attitude, YOU ARE AS CLOSE AS YOU CAN POSSIBLY GET—INSIDE HIM! (See Colossians 3:3). Further, you're not "following" Jesus to learn from Him—HE'S *IN* YOU, TEACHING YOU YOUR IDENTITY! (See 1 Corinthians 6:19, Romans 12:2, Philippians 1:6). The apostles physically followed Him, but we have something so much better on this side of the Cross! WE HAVE ONENESS WITH HIM FOR GOOD! (Ephesians 1:13).

So today, my friends, know this: You *have* the same attitude of Christ—you're not trying to achieve it. His Spirit bears witness of this truth to *your* spirit, at all times. What will it take for you to believe Him? Please, I say this with all love and respect, but wake *up* and realize that you and God are one. Your old spirit died and you got a new, perfect spirit which is connected to Him (see Romans 6:6-7, Galatians 2:20). Stop trying to work for or "get" what you already have! BE YOURSELF AND LIVE HIM OUT! You are not a conduit, you're a person. You and

God work *together*. It's not "all of Him and none of you," no, it's both of you, equally. You want what He wants, and He wants what you want! Your minds are one! When you believe this truth about who you really are inside, a wonderful attitude will sprout up and out of you, organically. Have a great day, you holy saint!

> **A prayer for you:** *Father, thank you for another day of life! For so long, I didn't like my life, and that's because I had an attitude which was not authentic. Now that you've revealed who I am inside, I'm starting to get it! I was re-created in spirit to have the same mind of Christ—and I actually do! Awesome! Right now, I lift up all who are reading this, directly to you. So many of them struggle with their attitudes, and that struggle is happening for a reason. Bad attitudes are not legitimate for heaven-ready people, and that's who we are. When we have poor attitudes, it doesn't feel right because it's not right. WE have great attitudes! We don't have fake attitudes, but REAL attitudes. All day long, you give us the ability to acknowledge difficult situations, people, and thoughts, and then you gently counsel us into the truth of who we really are. Keep doing it! We trust you! In Christ's name I pray, amen.*

Day 35

How Suffering Can Be a Good Thing

"In all this you greatly rejoice, though now for a little while you may have had to suffer grief in all kinds of trials. These have come so that the proven genuineness of your faith—of greater worth than gold, which perishes even though refined by fire—may result in praise, glory and honor when Jesus Christ is revealed."

1 Peter 1:6-7

Suffering sucks. I'm not going to lie. I used to be a rah-rah guy, but as I've grown in the truth of how this Christian thing works, God has taught me it's much more important to be real. It's much more important to feel our sad feelings and express them, than it is to act like they don't exist.

Today, I want to talk to those of you who are in deep pain. I want to reach out to my friends who are suffering. Deep suffering can lead you to thoughts of suicide, addiction, martyrdom, and codependency—that is, if you look at suffering on its own. This is Satan's plan for your life, so please recognize that. He does not want you focused on God, he wants you focused on the pain.

God is not bringing this suffering on you. This fallen world is, demonic forces are, the poor choices of people are, and many other players in the game of life. God, however, is *for* you *in* this fallen place. He is not against you (see 1 John 4:4). If you believe that Jesus is the Savior of your sin, God does not bring suffering into your life. He might *allow* suffering—for a greater good—but He is not *causing* your suffering. He's a good Dad, not a cruel one. Good dads don't exacerbate their children.

This will sound strange, but please understand something: the results of your suffering can be extremely beneficial to you, to others, and for eternity. Don't believe me? Just look to the Cross. The darkest day in history turned out to be the most beautiful.

Suffering is a good thing because it draws you into deeper relationship with God. If I had to highlight one sentence from everything I write today, that would be it. Suffering is *not* a good thing because of how it makes us look, or the attention it can bring—especially when we have the tendency to want to play the victim. We are not victims! We are overcomers, children of God, saints!

Suffering is a good thing because it refines our thought life. Suffering allows us to place our complete dependence on our Creator because we have no other choice. You do *not* make decisions like you once did, and this causes you enormous pain! You are not your own and you know that! So you "gladly" suffer! (See 1 Corinthians 6:19-20).

I put quotation marks around the word *gladly* to emphasize sarcasm because being glad about suffering is a crock. Was Jesus glad in His actions and attitudes as He carried that Cross? No. So neither should we be. BE REAL! Express yourself! Jesus was glad about Sunday, not Friday. He wasn't "faking it until He made it," smiling for the crowd to see—HE CRIED OUT IN PAIN! (See Matthew 27:46).

Friend, suffering allows you to learn more about who lives inside you, and why He lives inside you. Suffering draws out God's character *from* you (see Galatians 5:22-23, 1 Corinthians 13). In our deepest agonies, He reassures us He's there.

Suffering refines us! It doesn't destroy us! It shows us that we *can* make the choices God wants us to make, no matter how badly it hurts! When we suffer in our health, in our relationships, in our finances, and even in our confidence—GOD IS STILL THERE! GOD IS STILL WORKING ALL THINGS TOGETHER FOR AN ETERNAL GOOD!

...So we trust Him. Suffering builds trust with God. It was in Jesus' suffering that trust with the Father was built. As He pleaded for another way *other* than the Cross, He grew in trust through pain (see Luke 22:42). As we continue to be who we are in our spirits, we start to see the benefits of trusting God through our own pain and suffering. We start to notice the byproducts. James explains:

> *"Consider it pure joy, my brothers and sisters, whenever you face trials of many kinds, because you know that the testing of your faith produces perseverance. Let perseverance finish its work so that you may be mature and complete, not lacking anything." (James 1:2-4)*

So today, my friends, like James says, consider your suffering pure joy. Your suffering is testing your faith. The testing of your faith is producing perseverance. Please, be patient as that perseverance finishes its work so that you may be mature, complete, and not lacking anything. This life is short, eternity is forever. Keep suffering for good things, so that heaven will be more densely populated. Your suffering is *not* being wasted! It's being used in heaven! God notices what you're doing! Keep going! He's with you! Sunday is closer than you think!

A prayer for you: *Dad, I know you love us, and I know you are with us. But so many of these dear readers are in deep pain today. They are suffering. Like Christ, we know that suffering will ultimately result in wonderful things, but we still don't like it. Paul said in Romans 8, "I consider that our present sufferings are not worth comparing with the* *glory that will be revealed in us," and we believe that. But still, today, I'm asking for an extra portion of your grace. We need to feel your strength! Help us! We trust you, we count all our suffering as joy, but we still want you to hurry up and get us out of this storm. Please. In Jesus' name I pray, amen.*

Day 36

How's Your Relationship with Yourself?

"I care very little if I am judged by you or by any human court; indeed, I do not even judge myself."

1 Corinthians 4:3

For so long I didn't like myself. I had a very bad relationship with myself. The lies of people and the devil had me convinced I was a person whom I was not. God was telling me one thing, yet, hateful people and demonic forces were telling me something completely different. Oh, but it didn't end there!

To compound my self-loathing, my unrenewed mind caused me to speak ill of myself *about* myself *to* myself. I believed a huge lie: I'M MY OWN WORST ENEMY.

Positive self-talks did not come from any part of my mind. My old, stinking thinking—which was trained by way of cruel people and dark forces—caused me to believe I was worthless. In turn, my relationship with myself suffered greatly.

I thought that getting married would fix this. Nope. Not even close. Having my daughter? No, that didn't fix my incorrect opinion about myself either. Maybe working harder than anyone else I knew? If I could just become successful financially *then* my evaluation of myself would be positive!...Nah. Another dead end.

"What's it going to take for me to like being around myself? I know, church! I'll start going to church, and *then* I'll like me!"

Yeah freaking right. What I got there was *not* what I needed—not at that church anyway. I was being taught how bad of a person I was. I was being taught, "Repent! Respect the House of God! Don't you *dare* question Pastor!"

I was looking for some unconditional love and relief, but instead I was told, "You ain't livin' right! A godly man would get his house in order!"

"I'm trying! That's why I'm here!...Forget this. I don't need this crap." Little did I know, God didn't want me to try, He wanted me to rest. He wanted me to learn who I really was inside, and then enjoy living my life according to this truth.

I tried another church, and all they did there was brag on how big their church was and how I *had* to give them money if I wanted God to truly take care of me. "You gotta give back to God what He has loaned you, that's a minimum! Stay hungry and give *above* the tithe in order to be blessed beyond your wildest dreams!" We even chanted parts of this.

They made my loving Heavenly Father out to be a loan shark. That place preached *church*, not Jesus. Jesus was just a little add-on now and again, especially around the holidays. They constantly boasted on how "influential" their church was rather than on what Jesus had done for me. I was being taught *church*. I was being taught "praise the pastors," rather than praise Christ's finished work.

Striving to enjoy my relationship with myself eventually drove me to numb my feelings *about* myself. Drinking, many different hobbies, and even getting in good shape was all out of balance as I grasped for straws. Each day, I woke up not looking forward to being around...me.

"GOD! WHY DO I HAVE SUCH A BAD OPINION OF MYSELF?"

He replied, "Because you don't know the truth about yourself. Matthew, you are going to have to understand *my* opinion of you, only then will you see how valuable you are."

"But I still mess up so much!"

"I know, but you are *not* messed up. Your choices and thoughts might be off, but you're not. I live in you and you are my masterpiece. Your spirit is perfect, just like me."

...Crickets. You could hear crickets. "Wha...?" I said with a squint. "How's that possible? The pastor of that church said if I'm still sinning, I'm not really saved. So how can you say I'm spiritually perfect?"

"I'll show you. Be patient and trust what I say about you."

This was going to take some serious convincing on God's part. However, as I grew deeper into the knowledge of His grace, our relationship began to flourish! The Holy Spirit of God started to reveal who I truly was inside! At first, I didn't believe Him.

"Father, how can I be so infinitely loved and cherished by you when my actions and attitudes are so terrible?"

"Me." Jesus cut in and said. "What I did for you is your answer. I'm the *how*, and I'm the *why*."

Jesus began to expunge the thoughts I had about His sacrifice not being good enough! He started to delete, one by one, the ideas in my mind about how I must earn my spot with God—and worse, *sustain* my spot with God!

"Yep! I took care of that sin for you too!" Jesus continued, "Yeah, that one as well. Stop focusing on sin. Focus on your true self. Matt, remember who I've made you to be, *perfect* in your spirit. You can't change this so stop worrying about it. Just be yourself."

"Just be myself? How can you say that?"

"Because I know who you are. You are good, like me."

"But that sounds like some sort of blasphemy mumbo-jumbo! How can I say I'm good like you?"

"Because I live in you, because I've given you a brand new spirit, and because I've joined you *in* your spirit. It will take time, but I'll teach you more about this as we live together. I'm giving you eternity to understand who you are. Just believe me."

Day by day, Jesus' Spirit was educating me on what He's done *for* me and *in* me. My opinion about myself was slowly changing. The chess match between Satan and me was over. "Checkmate." I NOW KNEW WHO I WAS—and he knew that I knew. Hell was officially in a lot of trouble.

Even when people tried to un-convince me of who I was inside, it didn't work. I believed God. Try all they liked, even *I* couldn't convince myself that I was a bad person any longer—Jesus wouldn't let me! I was being trained by the Spirit of God! IT WAS AMAZING! IT STILL *IS* AMAZING!

I was learning how to separate my *who* from my *do*! I finally understood that my behavior—good, bad, or indifferent—could not change my identity!

Was God being naive with this plan? No way! God is pretty smart! He knew that we are going to act like who we think we are—the devil knows this too! That's why God decided to make us spiritually perfect for good, for free, forever! All we have to do is believe He's forgiven us *through* Jesus—and we are! THAT'S THE GOSPEL! THAT'S YOUR IDENTITY! Christian, you are a spiritually spotless, heaven-ready saint!

Through the revelation of this truth, the tide had changed in my relationship with myself. I began to *like* myself—a lot. Not in an arrogant way, but in a way which reflects the fact that if *God* says I'm infinitely loved and valuable, then who am I to say I'm not? I finally learned how to take a compliment. I stopped insulting myself to look better. False humility was out the door. I knew the truth of who I was, and now my mission was to gracefully convince others that God had done the same in them—or that He *will*, for free, if you want Him to.

So today, my friends, know this: God wants you to have an enjoyable relationship with yourself. Everywhere you go, you are there, so you may as well get along with you. If you are harder on yourself than even your Creator is, stop that. You don't deserve that. Be nice to you, forgive you, and love you. You are learning and growing each day into the familiarity of *who* you really are! God only has good things to say about you, so why not agree with Him? Why not say good things about yourself? After all, it's the truth! The Father, Son, and Holy Spirit would all three agree!

A prayer for you: *Heavenly Father, I want to thank you for opening my eyes to the truth of my identity. For so long, I focused on my mistakes, but you wanted me to focus on my true self! Paul said, in 1 Corinthians 4:3, that he wasn't even worried about PEOPLE judging him because he didn't even judge himself! HOW AWESOME IS THAT? He was so fixated on his spiritual perfection that when he made a mistake, he brushed it off like a fly on his arm. Teach us how to do the same! Right now, I lift up all who are reading this, directly to you. So many of them don't like themselves, and I know exactly how they feel. They've believed the lies of people and the devil, and their minds need to be renewed to the truth. Help them begin to do this today! Reveal who they are! Reveal that they are perfectly loved Sons and Daughters of God! In Jesus' name I pray, amen.*

Day 37

How to Endure Like Jesus

"For the joy set before him he endured the cross, scorning its shame, and sat down at the right hand of the throne of God."

See Hebrews 12:2

There are three sides to life: difficult times, mundane times, and good times. Like us, Jesus experienced all three. However, it was in the difficult times that our Savior stood out as a shining beacon. The trust in His relationship with the Father, as He faced every type of temptation and trouble you and I face, was remarkable.

Jesus knows exactly what we are going through because He went through it too! He doesn't feel sorry for us, He empathizes! He can relate! The author of Hebrews tells us how Christ identifies with His created beings:

> *"For we do not have a high priest who is unable to empathize with our weaknesses, but we have one who has been tempted in every way, just as we are—yet he did not sin." (Hebrews 4:15)*

Unlike the fake priests of Catholicism, Jesus was a real one—*the* real one. He faced countless trials and temptations, yet He never made a wrong choice. Therefore, He has set the example for us to do the same, and His Spirit within us, guides us!

He has made our spirits perfect, that way our actions and attitudes can match up a lot more often; but even still, when our choices and thoughts fall *short* of perfection, our holiness stays the same (see Hebrews 7:25, 10:10, 1 John 2:1).

In order for this rigged system to be possible, Jesus endured the Cross! Sure, He had the power to stop what the Romans were about to do to Him, but instead He decided to stay focused on what the pain would produce: spiritual perfection for all who would believe!

Through His endurance, Christ gave us the opportunity to have free righteousness. In the same way that Jesus did not deserve pain and death, because He never sinned, *we* would receive honor and praise, no matter how many times we've sinned—or *will* sin. His commitment to endure has made us perfect forever! Not perfect in what we do, but perfect in who we are! Don't believe me? Just look:

> *"For by one offering he has perfected for all time those who are sanctified." (Hebrews 10:14)*

One offering, that's Jesus Christ on the Cross! Perfection for all time, that's our spirits! Those who are sanctified, that's all who will believe! Sanctified simply means "holy." Holy means, "set apart." What are we set apart from? The unbelievers. The rejectors of Christ's forgiveness. The goats. We are the sheep! We are set apart! Jesus explains what will happen to the sheep and goats when He returns:

> *"When the Son of Man comes in his glory, and all the angels with him, he will sit on his glorious throne. All the nations will be gathered before him, and he will separate*

the people one from another as a shepherd separates the sheep from the goats. He will put the sheep on his right and the goats on his left." (Matthew 25:31-33)

Just imagine it, you are the Son of God and you know it. Yet, you also know that your mission is to take on the sin of the world *in your body* (see 2 Corinthians 5:21)—you know full well what that involves! TREMENDOUS TORTURE, PAIN, AND DEATH! Yet you *still* plan on enduring this because you want to be sure humanity has the chance to enjoy heaven with you! What love is that? AN EVERLASTING LOVE! AN UNCONDITIONAL LOVE! AN ENDURING LOVE!

This love for us caused Jesus to trust the Father during those difficult times. He was willing to do whatever it took to give everyone the opportunity to become righteous, freely. He was looking ahead, *past* the pain! We are called to do the same! We are called to endure! We have the same Spirit of Christ living in us, empowering us to be *able* to do the same! (See Luke 10:19).

So today, my friends, know this: Don't give up on what God's Spirit is leading you to do! You are outlasting the enemy! You are steadfast in His love! And most of all, you are being yourself. By simply being who God has made you to be in spirit, *His* Spirit will continue to empower you forever. You *are* enduring! Keep going!

A prayer for you: *Heavenly Father, thank you for teaching me how to endure. Through your Spirit, you've taught me many things, but endurance is near the top. You've taught me the art of doing nothing—simply being still and waiting—this takes severe endurance. You've also taught me how to shake the ground like an earthquake, rattling trees and knocking over buildings—enduring, as I've finally stood my ground against unacceptable treatment and behavior. Thank you for revealing the power I have inside, which is Jesus! Right now, I lift up all who are reading this, directly to you. So many of them feel like they can't endure any longer, God, they need relief! Let them know you are* *with them, strengthening them at this very moment! Let them know your power is made perfect in their weakness! Reveal the fact that your grace is sufficient and you are working all things together for good! THEY DO HAVE THE ABILITY TO ENDURE LIKE CHRIST! Give them wisdom in their decisions and help them stay focused on who they are inside! Every believer is a strong, loving, heaven-ready saint! We are overcomers who endure all things! In Christ's powerful name I pray, amen.*

Day 38

How do I Know if I'm Going to Heaven?

"This is how love is made complete among us so that we will have confidence on the day of judgment: In this world we are like Jesus."

1 John 4:17

It's the middle of the day at work and I glance up at the video surveillance monitor in my office after hearing someone walk in the front door. Sitting at my desk, I can see the patron stroll through the lobby of my store, so I get up to walk out and greet him.

"Hello, how are you doing today?"

"Oh, I'm fine," the man says to me.

"Mr. Black! I didn't know that was you!" I've changed his name for this story, but Mr. Black is a long time customer of mine. He's had my security system in his home for years. So I ask him, "What's going on? Do you need me to set you up a service call for your system? Is there anything you need help with?"

"No, no, nothing like that. Everything is working fine," he replies, as he hovers over by my stack of books. If you walk into Alarm Security, all of the books I've written are sitting on a section of the front counter with a sign next to them which reads: Free! Take one!

Wondering why Mr. Black is standing by my books, I ask, "So what's up? You want one of those books? Didn't you take Volume 1 last time? Here's Volume 2, you can have it, and while you're at it, here's the first book I wrote a couple years ago, True Purpose in Jesus Christ. It's a short read."

"Well thank you. Thank you so much," the elderly man tells me with a mannerism of gratitude.

"So did you finish 60 Days for Jesus, Volume 1?"

"Yeah, I sure did, and I gotta tell you, I really like it."

"Well good! Here, take these, and have a great day. Let me know if you need anything else."

"Thanks, Matt."

"No problem."

Strangely, Mr. Black doesn't leave, he just stands there quietly, looking down at the books.

"Are you okay?" I asked. By this time, one of my employees had come out into the lobby and was working on the computer.

Mr. Black softly replies, "No. I don't think so. I don't think I am okay. Can I talk to you outside?"

After pausing for a second, because I wasn't expecting him to say that, I said, "Sure."

I followed him out the front door, and it closed behind us. He had been looking toward the ground nearly the entire time we spoke, and now that we were outside, he was still looking down. All of a sudden he looks up at me, and has tears in his eyes.

"Matt, I just want you to know I appreciate you, and I'm praying for you."

Taken back, I put my hand on his shoulder and say, "Thank you."

He continues, "You just don't know what your book has done for me."

I still couldn't quite read Mr. Black. Was he about to set me straight after buttering me up with some kind words? He lives far off, so was his trip to my store his journey to tell me that my theology was all wrong? Was he going to say I needed to repent before it's too late? What was going on here?

Most elderly people have their idea of God set in stone, so I was expecting him to say, "Your book is great—*but*—your book is *this* and your book is *that*." However, that did not happen...the opposite happened.

"Matt, please, tell me, how do you *know* that you're saved? How do you know you're going to heaven? How can you be so confident in the things you write? I've done a lot of bad things in my lifetime, and I've gone to church, and I've tried to make up for that stuff by doing good things. But I'm still not sure if I'll make it."

I was immediately hit with a feeling of deep compassion for this old man. Empathy flashed across my face, as I could tell he was in turmoil over his salvation. He knew his time was short, and he wanted reassurance.

"Jim, I know that I'm saved, because I know that I'm saved," I said with a warm smile, hoping that he would understand he is saved by a knowing as well.

"Yeah, but that's too easy. How can you say that, and yet, my pastor says something so opposite of you?"

I exhaled, "Perfect love casts out all fear. God's love for you is perfect, so you have nothing to be afraid of. Fear has to do with punishment, and because of Jesus dying on the Cross and taking *on* your punishment, you don't have to be afraid."

He began to tear up heavily, and slightly tremble, "But how do you *know*? How?"

"Grace."

"Grace?"

"Yeah. Our God is a God who is full of grace. Let me ask you, has there ever been a time in your life when you believed Jesus has forgiven you of your sin?"

"Oh yeah, long time ago."

"Then you've experienced God's grace. God lives in you right *now*, and you have nothing to worry about. He promises that He will never leave you. He won't leave you now, and He won't leave you when your body passes away. Jim, don't be afraid, be confident. He loves you."

Mr. Black remained silent for 20 or 30 seconds. I didn't say anything else because I wanted him to reply, but he didn't. He just stood there nodding his head while staring forward. Then he looks over at me, gets closer, maybe 18 inches from my face and says, "I hope you're right."

He hugs me very tightly and then shuffles off toward his vehicle. Unbeknownst to me, his wife had been sitting in the driver's seat of their SUV the whole time, watching us. I have a feeling that Mr. Black felt a sense of relief that day, and I'm glad I got to be a part of it.

A prayer for you: *Heavenly Father, thank you for the relief you've given me by way of understanding your unconditional love. Like Mr. Black, you and I both know the torment I used to feel when I thought about meeting you. However, as I've grown deeper into the knowledge of your grace, you've revealed to me just how perfect your love is. I cannot express my gratitude in typed words, but you know how thankful I am. Right now, I lift up all who are reading this, directly to you. So many of them have been taught to be petrified of you, and that's not what you want. Many of them compare you to their earthly fathers and you're nothing like that—you're so much better. Even if they had a great dad, that great dad STILL cannot come close to who you truly are. You have no desire for us to be afraid of you, instead, you want us to be afraid of a life without you. You are gentle, patient, and kind. You care for us deeper than we can even fathom. Please remove any fear from these dear readers in regard to you. Renew their minds to the truth of your grace. Any incorrect idea they've been taught, wipe that slate clean, as you reveal just how unconditional your love is. It's so unconditional that we don't even have to wait to experience heaven. Instead, heaven is in us right now. In Jesus' name I pray, amen.*

Day 39

Do You Worship the Bible or God?

"You study the Scriptures diligently because you think that in them you have eternal life. These are the very Scriptures that testify about me, yet you refuse to come to me to have life." ~Jesus

JOHN 5:39-40

Not too long ago there was a pastor in Florida who was going to have a Quran burning. He announced it, set a date, and began collecting boxes of the Muslim holy book. However, once the word of this spread, many people reached out to him to voice how deadly such an act would be.

Unbeknownst to him, Muslims see the Quran on the same level as Christians see Jesus. The actual *book* is extremely holy to them. Sure, we Christians like our Bibles, but most of us know it's just a book with pages and ink. Muslims, however, will kill you if you defile or destroy the Quran. That is, the Muslims who are strictly abiding by the authentic teachings and commands of Mohammad.

"This will get you killed and your church will be destroyed," one person told the pastor. Another, "I wouldn't do that if I were you. That's a death sentence." After much consideration and counsel, he backed out of the planned blaze of books. Wise choice.

Besides, what a terrible way to show Muslims the love of Jesus. If anything, sit down and discuss the writings *in* the Quran over a cup of coffee. Burning their holy book (it's holy to *them* and we should respect them) would create conflict rather than offer up love, compassion, and friendship. And people wonder why we Christians have such a bad reputation. It's because of stupid stuff like that.

But misrepresenting God is not the point of my devotional today. Today, I want to talk about the mistake of viewing your Bible as more holy than the Spirit of God Himself.

First, please know that I love my Bible. I'm all *for* the Bible. Everything written in it is just, holy, right, perfect, and from front to back, it *is* the actual inspired words of God. I'm not here to bash the Bible, I'm here to help you understand there is something more *important* than the Bible: a relationship with God.

Knowledge of the Bible means nothing if you don't know the Author behind it—especially if you don't *care* for the Author behind it. Satan even has all of Scripture memorized (see Luke 4:1-13). Jesus was the first to point this out to the religious people who had the entire Old Testament down pat:

> *"You study the Scriptures diligently because you think that in them you have eternal life. These are the very Scriptures that testify about me, yet you refuse to come to me to have life." (John 5:39-40)*

Of course it wasn't called the Old Testament back then, but the point He was making is the same. It was Scripture. Written words that were inspired by the Spirit of God *through* man. The Pharisees could correct non-scripturally-educated people down to the jot and tittle. But still, they refused to see Jesus as the one those very Scriptures were referencing.

There is a very well-known person on the radio who has the Bible memorized nearly verbatim. Like a human search engine, he can pull up any chapter and verse almost instantly from his memory banks. However, I've heard this man say many things that go *against* the grace of God, while at the same time, being uber-critical of other Bible teachers. He regularly rips into them with no mercy.

Often I've thought, "Why did he even memorize the Bible? Was it so he can use it as a weapon to hurt others and look righteous?" I don't listen to him any longer, but before I stopped, I found myself tuning in to his program just to see if his tone would ever change into a loving tone—a *graceful* tone. It did not. Thankfully, the Spirit of God in me pointed out that his style of teaching was off. But at the same time, the Spirit of God also revealed that I must think of that man with the same grace I do everyone else. His faith is weak, and that's why he is so rude and pompous (see Romans 14:1).

Friend, have you ever encountered a Christian who used the Bible as a way to attack you? They quoted Scripture all the time, attempting to manipulate and control you? Their goal was to instill tremendous fear, anxiety, and guilt by way of listing off Bible verses?

This is one of the main reasons why so many people stop going to church. They're saved, they still love Jesus, but they've had enough of the hateful, religious people to last a lifetime. They want nothing to do with them, and I don't blame them.

If that's you, and you've been hurt, let me tell you something. Your salvation is still secure. Don't let the enemy cause chaos in your mind because you don't go to a geographical location for an hour each week. If you believe Jesus is your Savior, *you* are the church! On this side of the Cross, no building can ever house God! (See 1 Corinthians 6:19). Go if you want to go. Don't go if you don't want to go. You are free! (See Galatians 5:1).

In regard to the Bible, some Christians refuse to rightfully divide God's Word between Old Covenant and New Covenant. They mix the two together, creating a poisonous quasi-gospel, when the Old Covenant is completely obsolete! It is a ministry of death! (See Hebrews 8:13, 2 Corinthians 3:7-10). It's only useful for unbelievers, and even then, all it does is funnel them into God's grace! (See 1 Timothy 1:8, Matthew 7:13-14, Galatians 3:13).

Just so I'm clear, *all* of the Bible is perfect and valid, but we—all of humanity—only have the *one* option of living by the Spirit of God, according to the New Covenant. The New Covenant is the only Covenant available! Therefore, we do *not* live by words on a page! Not a *single* word, on *any* page!

"So Matt, if we don't live by any words on any page, then how do we know what to do?"

God's Spirit. Friend, believe it or not, His Spirit *in* you will guide you into all truth. You don't even need the Bible—keep reading, I'll explain.

Jesus said this very thing, and so did Paul. The gist of what the gospel truly is can be explained very simply—*so* simply, even a child can understand it: By believing Jesus has forgiven you of your sin, God lives in you, *with* you, guiding you, and He'll never leave you despite your behaviors or attitudes (see Matthew 18:3, John 14:6, Galatians 5, 2 Timothy 2:13, Hebrews 10:14, John 3:16, Colossians 3:3). Jesus tells us more:

> *"But when he, the Spirit of truth, comes, he will guide you into all the truth. He will not speak on his own; he will speak only what he hears, and he will tell you what is yet to come." (John 16:13)*

The Spirit of truth *is* God. God lives *in* you. So you know the truth.

As you can see I'm using the Bible for everything I'm referencing. I LOVE THE BIBLE. It is a compilation of love letters from God to us. When you feel pressured to read the Bible, don't. Your Good Father does not pressure you to read anything He's written to you through man. Instead, He gently guides you toward these letters, but He is not guilting you to read anything.

He loves you, even if you *can't* read. Even if you don't have eyes to see it or ears to hear Scripture, you are still infinitely loved as God's own child. Your belief in Jesus solidifies this truth (see John 1:12). Make no mistake, if you never read a word of the Bible, God's Spirit will still live in you in full, and He will guide you just as much as a Christian who knows the whole Bible by heart. Believe you need Jesus and this happens (see Hebrews 8:11, 10:16).

I can already hear an angry rebuttal from a person who knows lots of Scripture, "This is wrong, Matt! Without knowing the Bible, we can't know God! We gotta have His Word *in* us! We gotta *know* His Word so that we know how to live our lives! You are just a Bible basher!"

I'm not a Bible basher. Have you read my books? They are riddled with Scripture like bullet holes. And as for us *not* being able to know God without knowing the Bible, tell me this:

1. How did Adam, Eve, Noah, Abraham, Isaac, Jacob, Moses, Rahab, Malachi, Jeremiah, Ezekiel, Samson, Daniel, David, Solomon, and every human being *in* the Bible know Him before it was written?
2. How did the early Christians know God when the Bible wasn't even completed until 400+ years after Jesus ascended? How did they know what to do and what not to do?

Friend, the answer is simple. The answer will grab the ego of a legalist, slap it on the back of the neck, and say, "Get outta here!"...The answer is...God's Spirit. God's Spirit is how everyone has always known Him! God's Spirit is how we *still* know Him! Not from words on a page, not by tablets of stone, but by His Spirit we know our Creator!

So today, my friends, know this: We are so blessed to have the divinely inspired words of God in a nice, neat, organized book. But even if we didn't have a Bible like the people before us didn't, God would still make Himself known to us. God's Spirit doesn't speak in King James English, He speaks to our *hearts* in whatever way we can understand

Him. We are *so* fortunate to live in the epoch we live in, this time period allows us to do so much and to know so much! This time period has been gifted by God *with* the Bible! However, God's Spirit in us can teach us so much more than words on a page! You, Christian, already know more than any book can ever teach you because God is in you! Use the book! God will back up what you already know *through* the book! That book is alive and active through God's own Spirit! But without being led *by* His Spirit as you read it...it means nothing. So invite God into your spirit first, and then afterwards, read His love letters. They are awesome.

A prayer for you: *Heavenly Father, today I want to thank you for your Spirit AND for the Bible. When both are combined together amazing things can happen! For so long, I felt obligated to read my Bible. I even had a checklist I used each day. Sure, I read a lot, but I was reading for the wrong reasons. If I missed a day I felt guilty and anxious, and you didn't want that for me. You wanted me to relax and just get to know you even better. There was never any pressure on me! What a relief to understand that you are an easy-going, compassionate Dad who only wants the best for me! Right now, I lift up all who are reading this, directly to you. So many of them have been hurt by grace-confused Christians who've acted like they were more holy than them. These hurtful people, who've memorized more Scripture, have used that head-knowledge as a weapon against less-biblically-educated people. That's just wrong, and these readers have been victims of such. Please reveal the truth today! Reveal that it doesn't matter how much of the Bible they know, what matters is that they know you! Once they know you, you will always guide them into truth! You will always guide them into unconditional love and grace! Let them know that if the Bible never existed you would have STILL made a way to reveal yourself to them through Jesus! This fact alone is what draws us toward the Bible, because we want to know more and more about this great love! Take us deeper! Amen.*

Day 40

I am the Righteousness of God?

"God made him who had no sin to be sin for us, so that in him we might become the righteousness of God."

2 Corinthians 5:21

Your righteousness is perhaps the most important truth you can possibly understand as God's child. Sure, knowing you are loved unconditionally is crucial, and realizing your spirit is perfect is significant. Believing the truth, "where sin abounds, grace abounds much more," that too, is paramount in our faith.

Among these certainties, God making His home in our spirits for good—where we go He goes—this epiphany will also change how we view ourselves. But knowing we are righteous?...Forget about it, this changes everything.

When we find out that because of what Jesus did at the Cross, *we* are just as righteous as He is, our idea of ourselves makes a hard left. The trajectory of our lives and mindsets branch off into a previously unknown area, actually *knowing* that we are the righteousness of God!

"I am the righteousness of God."

"I am the righteousness of God."

"I *am* the righteousness of God!"

Repeating this to myself was a regular thing for me. It's hard to believe. It even sounds arrogant, but it's not—it's the truth!

"How in the *world* is this possible?" I'd chuckle, smile, and shake my head. I already knew the answer, but it was still fun to ask myself such a powerful, rhetorical question. It was Jesus! *Jesus* had caused me to become the righteousness of God! It wasn't because of a single righteous thing I had ever done, or ever will do! IT WAS A GIFT! OUR RIGHTEOUSNESS IS A GIFT FROM GOD THROUGH OUR FAITH IN JESUS!

What does righteousness even mean? It means *right standing*, it means *justified*, it means there's nothing wrong with you! NOTHING! Your identity is right! Accepting this truth, that your spiritual identity is right with the Creator of the universe? My goodness, talk about a shot in the arm!

Now, to be clear, I'm not talking about faking it'til you make it. I'm not talking about the notion of "I'll be righteous with God when I get to heaven." NO WAY! I'm talking about now! Right *now*, I *am* the righteous of God! And so are you, if you believe you are, through Christ.

When a self-centered person hears such a claim, they will immediately think of my sins, "How can you say such a thing? You *better* be careful, Matt, lest you eat your words and sin! You're not perfect in word or deed!"

Exactly! Even more proof of just how powerful the Cross actually is! Even more proof of the infinite magnitude of God's grace! I can't out-sin my righteousness! WOOT! (See Romans 5:20, Romans 7:25, 10:14). No wonder the gospel means GOOD NEWS!

Even when we make mistakes we are still the righteousness of God! Yep! What in the Sam Hill do you think Jesus died for? OUR HELP? No flippin' way! He doesn't need our help! He didn't need it back then and He doesn't need it now! He did a stand up job making us right with God on His own!

I'll tell you what arrogance truly is: thinking we can possibly cause ourselves to become righteous. Thinking that what we do and don't do tips the scales in our favor to *stay* righteous, or to get *more* righteous. How dare we do such a thing! This vain mindset *spits* on the face of Christ on the Cross, and says, "It's not good enough! I'll make it good enough!"

It's idiotic. It's demonic. It's selfish. It's *un*righteous...What Jesus did *was* good enough. *He* made us righteous, right now, and He doesn't need our help. He gives us this righteousness for free at our choosing—not our taking, but our *choosing*. We choose to receive a gift, we don't take it. We simply open up our hands and say, "Thank you so much."

So today, my friends, know this: If you believe that Jesus Christ is the Savior of your sins you are the righteousness of God! I know it feels weird to say, but this is the truth that will skyrocket your confidence in who you really are! YOU ARE RIGHT WITH GOD! Stop focusing on what's wrong, and focus on what's right! YOU! Say it with me, "I am the righteousness of God!" and believe it because this is the absolute truth!

A prayer for you: *Father, thank you for teaching me who I really am. Through your Spirit, I've learned just how amazing a feat Calvary actually was—Jesus accomplishing my righteousness! I am forever grateful! I didn't deserve it, but now that I have it, I will embrace it! Keep teaching me how to get rid of my false humility as I speak the truth of what you've done. Right now, I lift up all who are reading this, directly to you. Dad, so many of them have been incorrectly taught that they are dirty, wicked people. But if they believe Jesus has saved them, they are none of those things. They are completely righteous with you! Please begin to transform their minds with this truth as they live their righteousness out! Teach them just how AWESOME they really are because of their faith in Jesus! REVEAL THEIR RIGHTEOUSNESS! Teach them more and more about who they are in Christ! In His name, amen.*

Day 41

The Truth About Speaking in Tongues

"We hear them declaring the wonders of God in our own tongues!"

SEE ACTS 2:11

Right from the get-go, I want to be very clear about something: speaking in tongues has not gone away. *None* of the spiritual gifts have gone away. Who are we to put God in a box? The problem is, just like in the early church, the spiritual gifts have been misconstrued, misinterpreted, and even lied about.

God can do anything He wants, any *time* He wants—including using the gift of tongues in 2017. However, misinformation and misguidance, along with massive amounts of incorrect church tradition, pride, ego, and hierarchies, have turned this amazing evangelistic gift into a repellent for unbelievers and believers alike.

In regard to the gift of tongues, there are only two places in the Bible where it's explained in detail: Acts 2 and 1 Corinthians 12-14. Acts 2 is the account of the first human beings actually being *indwelt* by the Holy Spirit—this had never happened before! *Before* this first-time event, the

Spirit of God would be *with* people and *on* people, but never *in* people! (See Joshua 1:9, John 20:22).

Prior to Acts 2, God was never inside of any man or any woman because all of humanity had sinful spirits. Unbelievers still do to this day. God cannot be connected to sin in any way, this is why He could never be *in* our spirits *with* our spirits, or in our physical bodies.

But because of what Jesus did at the Cross—which is *removed* our body of sin, our spirits, by killing them off and giving us new, sinless spirits—the apostles' spirits were *also* crucified, buried, and resurrected with Jesus as new, perfect spirits! Therefore, God's Spirit could finally make His home in them, as well as in all who would believe! (See Romans 6:6-7, Galatians 2:20, Ezekiel 36:26, John 1:12, 3:16, 14:23, 2 Corinthians 5:17, 1 Corinthians 6:19).

When this happened—God literally possessing the apostles—they began to speak in tongues. They didn't speak in tongues to *get* His Spirit, they spoke in tongues *after* the Holy Spirit conjoined with them. If you read all of Acts 2 in context, you'll see. They didn't speak in tongues to *achieve* the Spirit, or even because they had *received* the Spirit. Instead, they began to speak in tongues because of the audience around them... foreign language speakers.

There were people from many alien nations and areas in their midst—*this* is the proper context of the apostles speaking in tongues! They began to speak in peoples' *native* languages! The different tongues of different dialects were allowing the unbelievers around them to be *able* to hear the good news of Jesus! They had miraculously started to talk in the language of all of these different people groups:

> *"Parthians, Medes and Elamites; residents of Mesopotamia,*
> *Judea and Cappadocia, Pontus and Asia, Phrygia*
> *and Pamphylia, Egypt and the parts of Libya near*
> *Cyrene; visitors from Rome (both Jews and converts*
> *to Judaism); Cretans and Arabs"* (Acts 2:9-11)

The apostles were not speaking in angel talk—I'll get to that misnomer shortly—they were speaking in the local language of each person! Don't believe me? Just look!

> *"When they heard this sound, a crowd came together in bewilderment, because each one <u>heard their own language being spoken</u>." (Acts 2:6)*

Let's repeat: they heard their own language being spoken! Why is this important? Because it is a sign to that person whom you are speaking to in their own tongue that *what* you are saying is legit! THE GOSPEL! THIS IS WHY THE CROWD WAS AMAZED AND PERPLEXED! (See Acts 2:12).

Just think of it, if I'm Tai, Russian, or Vietnamese, and I know for a fact that you cannot speak my language—yet you do, fluently—don't you think that *what* you are saying about Jesus, I'll probably believe as true?... Um, *yeah*!

This is what was happening on the day of Pentecost! This is what was happening during *all* expressions of the gift of tongues! This is how the gospel spread so quickly! CHRISTIANS WERE GIFTED TO SPEAK DIFFERENT LANGUAGES!

I'm sure tongues still happens today, but not as often because most nations know about Jesus. However, God will do whatever it takes to get our attention. Why do you think Jesus performed so many miracles? IT WAS FOR THOSE AROUND HIM TO BELIEVE.

Friend, we don't speak in tongues to receive God's Spirit. Some people don't even have a tongue. Will God not make His home in them? Will they not receive God in full? The enemy came up with this idea of twisting the truth about this amazing gift. He placed this incorrect notion of *having* to speak in tongues to receive God's Spirit in the mind of man as a distraction, and it worked. Satan wants us to feel like second-class Christians if we don't speak in tongues and that's just wrong. He's caused us to take a beautiful evangelistic tool and turn it into a modern-day church law.

"Yeah, you might be saved, but you still need to receive God's Spirit! You gotta be slain with a second baptism of the Holy Ghost or else you're missing out!"

This is ludicrous. Being saved *is* receiving God's Spirit. We don't need a second dose. Being saved doesn't mean we lose our self-control and wiggle around on the floor as proof of our salvation—or "better" salvation. Matter of fact, just the opposite should happen. We should be exuding self-control (see Galatians 5:22-23). The enemy has handed off the baton of acting insane in church, we've taken it, and then sprinted away with all fury!

Please understand, we receive God's Spirit by hearing with faith and nothing else (Romans 10:17, Galatians 3:2). We don't need a "second blessing" or a second portion of the Holy Spirit. We get Him in full from the moment we first believe Jesus has forgiven us. Paul said that we can't even *say*, "Jesus is the Lord" without His Spirit being in us (see 1 Corinthians 12:3). He said that if we *don't* have the Spirit of God in us then we don't even belong to God (see Romans 8:9). So being knocked over or hootin' and hollerin' to *get* God's Spirit is way off base. The Spirit doesn't bring on craziness, but instead, order, peace, and relaxation (see 2 Timothy 1:7).

We must refocus. We must refocus on the freedom found in Christ. We must stop convoluting spiritual gifts into spiritual requirements. It's demonic and we are being blinded by this dog-and-pony show. It's bad advertising for the real gospel.

I'm not saying stand around stiff as a board, no way! Enjoy yourself! Clap, sing, have a good time! I'll be the first to bump the guy next to me with my worship! But at the same time *know* that every Christian has all they need for life and godliness—tongue speaking is not required (see 2 Peter 1:3).

In 1 Corinthians 12-14, Paul explains the spiritual gifts and how to handle them properly. Speaking in tongues is one of them and he makes clear that *he* speaks in tongues more than anyone else. Why? Because he was traveling the most. Paul was not an apostle to the Jews, he was an apostle to the non-Jews, the Gentiles. Therefore, if he is traveling to many different foreign locations, he would have to speak in many different foreign languages.

He taught the church very important matters about tongues. Keep in mind when you read this, Paul is speaking to a group of believers, *not* foreign people who needed to hear the gospel in their native language:

> *"I would like every one of you to speak in tongues, but I would rather have you prophesy. The one who prophesies is greater than the one who speaks in tongues, unless someone interprets, so that the church may be edified." (1 Corinthians 14:5)*

Now, for the person who finds their identity in speaking in tongues, they will immediately bark at me, "See Matt! Paul wants everyone to speak in tongues!"

But to this rebuttal I'd have to say, "Hold on to your hanky for a minute." First of all, he just said prophesying is greater, so why aren't you telling people they need to prophesy as evidence of the Spirit rather than speak in tongues?

Second, if we are keeping the gift of tongues in context, why would Paul say this to people who all spoke the same language? I'll tell you: Because the evangelistic gift of tongues is amazing! If each one of them were traveling to different areas, spreading the gospel by way of tongues, "That's awesome!" Paul is saying. "Tongues is great!"

But Paul is *not* making a law out of tongues, he's simply saying it is a very good thing. I mean, after all, just look at what happened in Acts 2! Lots of different nations heard the gospel! But for this letter to the Corinthians, because it's a *corporate* setting of Christians who all spoke the same language, Paul said the gift of prophesying is greater. Why would he say such a thing? Well, if we have the gift of prophesying twisted like we do tongues, this can confuse us in even greater ways.

New Covenant prophesying is not future-telling. It's not someone standing up on stage, scanning the crowd, pointing to someone then saying, "In six years, you'll have four kids, live in Vermont, and have a homeless shelter ministry." No way.

On this side of the Cross, because God's Spirit lives in us He speaks to us directly. We don't need a self-proclaimed, or a momma-proclaimed prophet "reading" our future. How off course can we possibly get? No wonder people think we are weirdos! New Covenant prophesying is about edification, which is building people up. That's why Paul said prophesying is greater "so that the church may be edified" (see 1 Corinthians 14:5).

Edify means encourage, counsel, guide, instruct, and exhort! It means to spur one another on toward love and good deeds! (See Hebrews 10:24). Like some of today's churches, even back then, the gift of tongues was being abused to make the speaker look better than others—more "holy."

> *"Anyone who speaks in a tongue edifies themselves, but the one who prophesies edifies the church." (1 Corinthians 14:4)*

Do you see it? Friends, this is *so* simple. Sure, a person's ego will be furious about this truth, but we don't *need* our egos anyway. Paul is saying that a person who speaks in tongues without foreign people in their midst, nor an interpreter to interpret that foreign language, they are just trying to look good. They are just trying to edify themselves.

Paul's answer to put a rein on the latest episode of *Tongues Gone Wild* was to prophesy. "Recenter the focus on edifying the body of believers around you so they can grow in the knowledge of God's grace."

If you really think about it, what happens when we speak in tongues and nobody who speaks that *language* is there to interpret it? Or even worse, what happens when we all do this at once? People think we're crazy!

What do even *other* Christians say about churches who speak in tongues together as a group? "Those people need to be committed! I'm outta here!" It's those *around* us who witness this incomprehensible nonsense as a repellent to the truth of God's unconditional love—that is, when it's not done properly.

The judging of tongue-speakers as nuts is not a new thing, it started from the beginning. When the apostles spoke in tongues in the book of Acts, many of the hearers thought they were drunk! Peter quickly corrected them and said, "It ain't 5 o'clock yet! This is legit!" (See Acts 2:12-15). Paul even warns us about visitors thinking we're mad:

> *"So if the whole church comes together and everyone speaks in tongues, and inquirers or unbelievers come in, will they not say that you are out of your mind?" (1 Corinthians 14:23)*

Believers, we must refocus. We must stop acting as if a spiritual gift is something that everyone *must* do. Believe it or not, there are even some people out there who think tongues can be taught! *No* gift can be taught! That's why it's a gift! There are actual schools that "teach" how to speak in tongues. Image that?

The enemy has us so hung up on a particular gift that *schools* have been created *for* the gift! I bet that moron just laughs his butt off each time someone attempts to teach it! I mean, seriously, what happens when you can't pull off speaking in tongues organically? When you absolutely *can't* speak a foreign language *from* God's Spirit within you, you only have two choices:

1. Fake it.
2. Give up and consider yourself a second-class Christian, or not a Christian at all.

Speaking in tongues is a gift! IT'S SOMETHING YOU *RECEIVE* FROM GOD! You can't study to get a gift! You can't *work* to get a gift! If you could then it would no longer be a gift! It would be something you deserve! It would be something you've earned! Gifts and grace are not earnable!

Some people are even attempting to "kick start" others into tongues. They'll start the person out, holding their hands, "Okay, now repeat after me, 'Shamalamalama...now you keep it going . . .'" You believe this crap? C'mon people! REFOCUS!

An angry person might say to me, "But we gotta have signs! Without receiving confirmation through signs and wonders how will we know if our salvation is real? Or if anything is real?"

...Believe. Friend, you don't *need* signs. You don't need confirmations. Just look at what Jesus said:

> *"Unless you people see signs and wonders,*
> *you will never believe." (John 4:47)*

Can't you feel His attitude toward this mindset? I can just picture Jesus shaking His head as He spoke that sentence. And then look at what He tells Thomas, a man who doubted everything unless he got confirmation:

> *"Blessed are those who have not seen and*
> *yet have believed" (John 20:29)*

Yes, Jesus was talking about Himself, but the same point remains, *believe without seeing.*

A grace-confused person might yell at me, "Matt, you've gone too far! I've always liked what you've had to say, but in regard to tongues, you have no idea what you're talking about! Tongues is an angel language! This is how we pray and how *He* prays for us!"

Friend, I'm so sorry, but that's wrong. First of all, there is not a single Bible verse that says tongues is used in private prayer. The reason for this is because tongues is a sign to the unbeliever, not the believer (see 1 Corinthians 14:22). We already know what we mean, so we don't need to speak in tongues to ourselves. Further, God knows what you mean too, so He doesn't need it either.

As for the Holy Spirit praying for us? Yes, He absolutely does, but that's not happening in foreign languages. It's happening in godly groans we cannot even fathom as finite human beings. Romans 8:26 says the Spirit prays *for* us, because we don't know what to pray for. It says nothing about speaking in tongues. Have you ever had times in your life when you didn't know what to pray?...I sure have. The good news is during those difficult seasons the Holy Spirit *knows* we don't know what to pray for, so He steps in and prays on our behalf. This has nothing to do with tongues and everything to do with His great love for us.

And when you say "angel languages," that too falls flat for a couple reasons. First of all, a lot of times tongues is not even coming from the mouths of people by way of the Spirit. It's being forced. So it's not even tongues at all. Instead, it's someone forcing strange noises out of their mouth because of feelings they are having, as well as what they are being incorrectly taught or coerced to do. It's phony tongues.

There was a linguistic study which analyzed many different churches who claimed to speak in tongues. What that study revealed was the syllables and sounds coming from a lot of the tongue-speakers was *never* a syllable or sound that did not already exist in their native language. Now don't you think that if a person was speaking in an angel language—a dialect from heaven—that person would have a much larger variety of sounds coming from them? Of course they would.

When Paul talked about angel languages, he was saying *"even if" we speak in the tongues of angels, but don't have love, we are only a clanging cymbal* (see 1 Corinthians 13:1). In context, you can see he is speaking in hyperbole. Paul isn't referencing the gift of tongues here, he's talking about actual angel language. But even if he was, just look at what our tongues would be without love...annoying sounds.

I say he is speaking in hyperbole because Paul also says *"even if" I can move mountains but I don't have love, I am nothing* (see 1 Corinthians 13:2). I haven't seen anyone causing mountains to float around, so again, this is exaggeration for Paul to prove what is most important! Love!

THE POINT IS LOVE! THE POINT OF THE GOSPEL IS LOVE! Not speaking in tongues, not moving mountains—not any gift or angel language—but love!

There will be many people who meet Jesus on the day of their death, as well as when He returns, and they'll point to their gifts and achievements to try to get into heaven:

"Lord, Lord, did we not prophesy in your name? In your name, did we not drive out demons? In your name, did we not perform many miracles? Did we not speak in tongues ? LOOK AT EVERYTHING I'VE DONE FOR YOU!"

Sadly, Jesus will reply:

"I never knew you." (See Matthew 7:23)

So today, my friends, know this: God would rather you speak five words in love, that you can understand, than He would 10,000 words *without* love, that you cannot (see 1 Corinthians 14:19). Refocus. Refocus on love, and refocus on what Jesus has done for you. This is what He wants *from* you, much more than any gift He's given *to* you.

A prayer for you: *Heavenly Father, thank you so much for spiritual gifts! Although there are many listed in the Bible, I know that the gifts you've given us are countless! We Christians are all gifted with your Spirit—evenly! And it is in that Spirit, combined with OUR spirit, our gifts soar! THANK YOU! Right now, I lift up all who are reading this, directly to you. So many of them don't know what their gifts are, and some do. For those who do, help them to stay focused on the most important aspect of their gift, LOVE! And for those who are wondering what their gift is, let them know it will be revealed to them in a peaceful, easy, non-pressure-filled way. Sure, that gift may skyrocket in the midst of the greatest trials of their life, but even still, expressing that gift will always feel nice and natural. Let these dear readers know that because of their faith in Jesus, they are already gifted with EVERY spiritual blessing! In His name, I pray. Amen.*

DAY 42

DO YOU FEEL SORRY FOR YOURSELF?

*Then Jesus said to him, "Get up! Pick
up your mat and walk."*

JOHN 5:8

I used to struggle with self-pity...*a lot*. If you only knew the battles I faced in my mind about how unfair certain situations were, and how I was being mistreated, it would shock you. The enemy, along with my learned stinking thinking, had me convinced that "poor old Matt" never got the good things he deserved.

Before I continue talking about how off-balance my thought life was in regard to feeling sorry for myself, I do need to say there were definitely legitimate reasons for me to lean toward self-pity—and there still are to this day. All of us have difficult situations we face, and all of us deal with people who are just not fair to us. This is part of living life on planet earth.

My problem was, my thinking about such things was off-center, especially how I considered my "luck." I put luck in quotation marks because there's no such thing. The enemy wants us focused on that word so we will stay in a state of panic, blame, and sadness. After we have our minds set on our "bad luck," he then wants us to constantly speak it out into existence, post it, and tweet it, so that it comes to life.

Sure, there are random chances that happen, but luck is an abused word by those of us who stock up on self-loathing and refuse to look within ourselves for what we truly need. If Christ lives in us, we already have everything we need! We just have to tap into it!

"Figures! Just my luck! I always get treated this way!" That statement could regularly be put in a bubble above my head. It's exactly how I thought. God's Spirit in me wanted to change that, but first, some growing pains had to happen.

The growing pains I'm referring to is in my mind—in my *thinking* (see Romans 12:2, Philippians 4:8, 2 Corinthians 10:5). Learning how to have our thoughts match up with what God says about us is extremely painful, but soon enough we start to believe the truth! One of those main truths you'll learn is this: self-pity is worthless, absolutely worthless.

When we begin to allow the Holy Spirit to point out triggers that bring on self-pity—and even extreme, over-the-top sadness—*then* we can recover. He will always guide us in our thinking, that is, toward what *He* says about us. But we have to pay attention. After we let Him start to counsel us, the cold, dark, uber-sad moments of feeling sorry for ourselves become few and far between!

Friend, I'm not saying *don't* feel your feelings—FEEL THEM. But bring them to God. Don't be controlled by them, and *don't* let them ruin your day. Feelings pass, but the consequences of incorrect choices based on those feelings do not. So look to your Creator within you and He'll comfort you, strengthen you, and He'll put things in perspective based on His promises.

Jesus indwells all believers on the exact same level and He'll never go away. Nothing you do or don't do will change this fact (see 2 Timothy 2:13, Colossians 3:3, 1 Corinthians 6:19, Ephesians 2:8-9). But even still, He is constantly teaching us new things each day. If we are allowing Him to live through us the lessons will happen organically and we'll grow in wisdom and grace. If we're not, then the enemy will have a field day, every day.

That dingleberry will hit you with a non-stop barrage of trying to get you to focus on everything and every*one* you can't control. Not only that, but his goal is to continually bring up the mistakes of your past—not just from years ago, but from yesterday, from this *morning*. The accusations will come flying at you like flaming arrows! They will pierce your mind *if* you let it happen...*if*.

This is your choice. *You* have a say-so. *You* can put on your shield of faith!

It's all about your focus. If you will keep your focus on Christ in you—not people, not circumstances—you'll begin to see major changes! Changes in what? In people and circumstances? NOPE! IN YOU! In *your* reactions! People and circumstances *might* change, but that isn't what you're worried about any longer because you have no power over that and you know it!

To be fair to you, in regard to this subject, think about it this way: How long has it taken for people and circumstances to get where they're at in your life? Probably a long time. Therefore, you should give Christ a long time to get things in order. Be patient and trust God. React as *He* guides you. Sure, you'll fail, but so what. Forgive yourself and refocus.

Do *your* part and stop worrying about people. Do *your* part and stop living a life of anxiety over the circumstances you never had any control over to begin with! As you do, the things you *can* control, you absolutely will.

Jesus once had an encounter with a man who had been living in self-pity and blame for a long time. At nearly forty years old, he still thought everyone around him was at fault—and I'm sure some of them were. But what did Jesus say to him? Did He say, "Oh, you poor baby, let me take care of that for you."? No way! Jesus said, "Get up!" (See John 5:8).

There are times in our lives when God says the same to each of us. When we've taken our eyes off of who we truly are inside—perfect, holy saints (see Colossians 1:22, 2 Corinthians 5:21)—as well as who God is,

He'll jolt us with the truth! He's not mad at us, He's not disappointed, but He's saying, "C'mon, get up! Please listen to me. You're better than this. I've got *better* things planned for you, but you're going to have to refocus. Refocus on me, and refocus on who *you* are."

So today, my friends, know this: God knows what you're going through and He cares. He knows about every situation, He sees how you're being treated, and He knows about all the unfair stuff. But He *still* wants you to get up! You weren't *made* to stay down! You are an overcomer! THERE'S MORE FOR YOU! God wants to *use* you! He has a plan and a purpose for your pain! BUT YOU GOTTA *GIVE* HIM THE PAIN! Cry! Scream if you have to! LET IT ALL OUT! He can handle it! He wants you to understand your value and He wants you to bear good fruit! You can't do that when you're not focused on the truth! *REFOCUS!* If you believe in Jesus as your Savior, you have all you could possibly ever need, right now! Let's gooooooo! Get up! Get up! GET UUUUUUUUP!

A prayer for you: *Dad, thank you so much for teaching me how to pay attention to my thoughts. Just yesterday I started to listen to a sad song and I could immediately feel myself start to get sad. I know that listening to sad songs are not a bad thing, and I know that I should feel my sad feelings when I have them, but you pointed out that it was the song that CHANGED my feelings. Thank you for teaching me how to pay attention to the things around me that can trigger self-pity. I will guard my heart against that stuff, with your help of course. Keep teaching me more as I go deeper into the knowledge of who I truly am inside. I feel like I'm swimming in the ocean of your grace, and I'm grateful! Right now, I lift up all who are reading this, directly to you. So many of them are in severe pain, and rightfully so. Many unfair situations have come their way and even things they might deserve. Father, help them to realize you're with them during all of it, and that you are a God of infinite mercy. You don't hold their sins against them, and when trouble happens, you will guide them into the proper choices. Self-pity is* *not one of them—that's from the enemy. Let them know it's okay to be sad—healthy even. But please begin to change their thinking ABOUT being sad. Lead them toward thoughts of strength, confidence, love, and peace! These things come from you IN them! When the enemy temporarily knocks them down, you always help them up! They have to want your help up, but when they do, you gladly stretch out your hand and lift them. In Jesus' name I pray, amen.*

Day 43

It's Impossible to Get More of God

*"For you died, and your life is now
hidden with Christ in God."*

Colossians 3:3

It's Sunday morning and the worship leader is deep into his third song, "God, we need more of you! Please! Fill this place with your Spirit! Come *down* and let us know you're here! We want to feel your presence!"

At first glance, there doesn't seem to be anything wrong with what he's just said. But if you understand the New Covenant, it's wrong all the way through. With this type of speech, he's no different than someone dancing around a campfire, begging a god for rain or to join their people group.

According to the New Covenant, we don't need to call down God to join us or to make His presence known. Instead, our spirits are *in* God, and God's Spirit is *in* us—in full—and even better, nothing can alter this! Paul uses the example of being joined with a prostitute:

> *Do you not know that he who unites himself with a prostitute is one with her in body? For it is said, "The two will become one flesh." But whoever is united with the Lord is one with him in spirit. (1 Corinthians 6:16-17)*

Paul's example of conjoining with God's Spirit is good, but it still doesn't describe it perfectly. Not to be too graphic here, but when sexual intercourse happens, a man is inside of a woman. The woman, however, is not inside of the man. This would be the difference in how we and God are one. We believers are in God and God is in us! (See Colossians 3:3, 1 Corinthians 6:19).

Here's another example: Our oneness with God's Spirit would be the same as taking food coloring and pouring it in a cup of water. Afterwards, there is no distinction between the food coloring and the H2O, they have become one. Yet, at the same time, they are still separate on a molecular level. This is what happens with our spirit and God's Spirit from the first moment we believe Jesus saved us from our sins! God is poured into us and we become one!

When this happened, you might have felt something, and then again, you might not have. Salvation isn't based on our feelings but on a fact of faith. Yes, a *fact* of faith. You read that correctly. Our salvation is based on a knowing, and this knowing happens one time (see Hebrews 10:10, 10:14).

Therefore, we don't need to keep asking God to "come down into this place" or "join us" or "show up!" like they did in the Old Testament. If you are in church, He's there! He's inside of you! If you are in the grocery store, He's there! He's inside of you! If you are putting on your pants after having an affair at the Holiday Inn, He's there! HE'S INSIDE OF YOU!

"Matt! How can you say that last part? He won't go with you into a hotel to cheat on your spouse!"

Well what does He do? Wait outside? Friend, no...He goes in there with us. He *never* leaves us nor forsakes us, ever! (See Hebrews 13:5). No matter how terrible our actions and attitudes may be, He stays committed to us!

HOW IS THIS POSSIBLE?...The New Covenant. The Old Covenant, which was based on God coming and going according to how well a person followed the Mosaic Law, it's now obsolete. Look:

> *By calling this covenant "new," he has made*
> *the first one obsolete (see Hebrews 8:13)*

Jesus' blood created a new contract between God and mankind—a covenant is a contract. What happens when a new contract is written up? The old contract is no longer valid. So now, the Old Covenant is only enforceable against non-believers in Christ.

We, Christians, are dead to the Law and alive in Christ! We've died to the Law *so that* we can *be* alive in Christ! You can't have a mixture of both! (See Mark 2:22, Romans 7:4-6, Galatians 2:19, 5:19).

All of the Jews who attempted to live by the Old Covenant failed miserably. ALL OF THEM. The only ones who thought they were doing well were the liars and hypocrites. That's why the rich man went away sad, and that's why the Pharisees and teachers of the Law killed Jesus. He stepped on their toes, to say the least. Their identity was in their behavior—not in faith—not in their complete reliance on God's grace. This continues today with many churches.

Even before the New Covenant was put in place by Jesus, righteousness with God was *still* based on faith alone *not* by way of Law observance. So the New Covenant is older than the Old Covenant. Don't believe me? Here, just look:

> *Clearly no one who relies on the Law is justified before God, because "the righteous will live by faith." (Galatians 3:11)*

And another:

> *For all who rely on the works of the Law are under a curse, as it is written: "Cursed is everyone who does not <u>continue to do everything</u> written in the Book of the Law." (Galatians 3:10)*

Continue to do everything? Wow! There's not just 10 rules in the Law, but 613! Are we starting to understand how impossible it is to behave our way into right standing with God? It's *absolutely* impossible! The Law is an all or nothing proposition. If you fail at one, you fail at all of them. James, the brother of Jesus, explains how it works:

*"For whoever keeps the whole Law and yet stumbles at just
one point is guilty of breaking all of it." (James 2:10)*

The only reason the Law was brought in by Moses was to point out sin in even greater ways. It was meant to be a mirror showing us the dirt on our faces but it never had the ability to clean us up! Humanity already knew what sin was, right and wrong is written on our consciences (see Romans 2:15). All the Law did was literally spell sin out and then make it impossible for anyone to live a perfect life!

The Law was supposed to reveal our desperate need for a Savior. It was meant to corral us through a narrow gate of grace (see Matthew 7:13-14). Paul told the Romans exactly what the Law is useful for:

*"The Law was given so that all people could see how sinful
they were. But as people sinned more and more, God's
wonderful grace became more abundant." (See Romans 5:20)*

SO! According to the New Covenant—a will which was brought in by way of Jesus' perfect blood (see Hebrews 7:22, 9:22)—God doesn't look at the believer's sin as a gauge of whether or not He'll stick around. He stays with us no matter how many sins we commit. Why do you think the gospel means *good news*? But at the same time, *because* He never leaves us, His Spirit always points us away from sin (see Romans 2:4).

We can still choose to sin but it will never feel right permanently because we have God living in us and our new spirits don't even like to sin. We might get a quick, flash-in-the-pan fleshy thrill from sin, but afterwards, we *know* we weren't made for it (see 1 John 3:9, Romans 6:1-2,11). That's why God doesn't want us to sin in the first place! And honestly, why *we* don't want to sin either! You don't like sin! You are a heaven-ready, completely forgiven, holy saint! (See Colossians 1:22).

So today, my friends, know this: As Christians, we have God in full! This New Covenant is based on a promise between God and God, that is, the Father and the Son! They could not swear by anyone greater so they swore by themselves! (See Hebrews 6:13-20). Our promise to them means nothing! Our promise to them is a joke! The true gospel is about *their* promise to us *through* each other! We are simply the beneficiaries to this new contract! We didn't create it, we can't sustain, and we can't make it better! EVERYTHING WAS FINALIZED AT THE CROSS! (John 19:30). Our only job is to receive it and say, "Thank you!"...So rather than beg God for more of Him, or ask Him to come back—or worse, work hard to get Him to come back—just keep thanking Him for being in you in full. Soon enough, you'll begin to live Him out, organically, but only after you realize He'll never go away.

A prayer for you: *Heavenly Father, thank you for teaching me the truth of the New Covenant, that you and Jesus came to an agreement for all of humanity at the Cross. It took me a long time of trying harder and harder to earn your approval to finally realize what happened at Calvary actually worked! THANK YOU! Right now, I lift up all who are reading this, directly to you. So many of them have been taught that you come and go based on what they do and don't do. Let them know that's called Judaism, and that faith went away when Jesus died and was resurrected! Reveal your commitment to THEM, rather than their commitment to YOU! The enemy wants them focused on what all they do for you so that you'll stay with them, yet, the New Covenant doesn't work that way—it's the opposite! It's YOUR goodness and commitment to us that leads us away from bad choices, NOT your wrath. Your wrath was satisfied in full, in Christ's murdered body. LET THEM KNOW HOW SECURE THEY ARE IN HIM! Let them know they can always EXPRESS you more, but they can't possibly get any more of you! You've made your home in them forever and nothing can change this! Not even THEY can change this, once it's happened! Your Word says so in 2 Timothy 2:13 and Hebrews 7:25! REVEAL THE TRUTH OF WHAT JESUS HAS DONE FOR THEM! In His name I pray, amen.*

Day 44

How to Fight Like a Christian

*"The weapons we fight with are not the weapons
of the world. On the contrary, they have
divine power to demolish strongholds."*

2 Corinthians 10:4

It's okay for Christians to fight, we simply need to learn how to fight in the right way! First of all, the war has already been won! The Cross brought victory to all of humanity! If you so choose to believe Jesus is the Son of God who saved you from your sins, you are *already* enjoying the spoils of war! Not when you get to heaven, but *now*! CHRIST IN YOU *IS* YOUR VICTORY! (See Ephesians 1:3, 2:6, 1 Corinthians 15:57, Colossians 1:27).

However, this victory only comes to those who make a decision of faith (see James 2:14,17). Head knowledge of Jesus being the Messiah means nothing without an act of faith—a one-time decision (see Hebrews 10:10). Even the demons know that Jesus is who He said He is, the only difference is *they* are not placing their faith in Him for forgiveness (see James 2:19). They're already damned to hell. We aren't. We still have a chance. So will you believe Jesus is your Savior? If the answer is yes, then welcome! Welcome to my Family! *We* have overcome this world through Jesus' loving sacrifice!

Now, the enemy and his demons also know that our victory flag was firmly planted at the top of the Cross. Their goal, however, is to hide this fact from us. They want us to think God is weak, angry, frustrated, vindictive, and disappointed. They want us to believe the Cross didn't work, and that *they* are still in charge! Our *battle*—not our war—is in our minds. Again, the war has been won, but there are still pockets of soldiers from the losing side all over the place.

Like a renegade group of sore losers, demons still take orders from their defeated general. They've been studying you from the time you were conceived and they know how to get at you the best. In the spiritual realm—in your thinking—they *are* fighting you, so please recognize this!

The good news is you can fight back! You have impenetrable armor! You have weapons! Our armor and weapons come from the Spirit of God indwelling us! (See Ephesians 6:10-17). SO BE CONFIDENT, LOOK FORWARD, SCOWL, AND DON'T BE AFRAID! We have complete power over the enemy! Jesus tells us so:

> *"I have given you authority to trample on snakes and scorpions and to overcome all the power of the enemy; nothing will harm you." (Luke 10:19)*

I believe Jesus was speaking spiritually when He said snakes and scorpions. Why? Because He spoke spiritually more often than not, and people thought He was crazy when He did so. Most of the stuff He said that was confusing, if you look at it spiritually it makes perfect sense.

However, in context for this verse, He was sending out people to give the world a prequel to the Cross' effects. So He *could* have been speaking literally for them *during* that mission. But for us, on this side of the Cross, to apply this literally? To handle snakes and scorpions and say, "Nothing will harm me!"? We're just asking for it and that's not wise.

There are some not-so-bright people out there—being influenced by the enemy—who actually handle poisonous snakes and scorpions up on stage at church while quoting this Scripture. A lot of them have died. So keep in mind, the Holy Spirit won't lead you to do such things. *Listen* to Him.

But anyway, Jesus wants all Christians to know that the enemy cannot touch us! (See 1 John 5:18). Christ in us is our power! (See Luke 10:19). All the enemy can do is accuse us, bark at us, bring up our past, and attempt to knock us off course in our thought life. But we can fight back! We *should* fight back! We don't have to stand there and take it! Here's some tips on how to fight like a Christian:

1. **Recognize the spiritual realm.** We tend to blame people, money, the government, and religion for the problems in this world, but the power of sin and the forces of hell are hard at work. Yes, people make bad choices which impact us negatively, but if you'll begin to think of all situations *spiritually*, you'll start to react differently. I'm not saying become a religious fruit-loop, I'm saying do as Paul said and, "Set your mind on things above, not on earthly things" (Colossians 3:2). *Think* spiritually. Recognize what you see is not all there is.
2. **Don't be so suspicious.** There are demons in this world whose main job is to constantly tempt us to be uber-suspicious and hyper-critical. Friend, give people a break. Give people the benefit of the doubt. Everyone doesn't have to be exactly like us, and just because they're not, that doesn't mean they're secretly sinning. People's sin is not our business anyway. If that sentence upsets you, then this paragraph is *for* you. Back off, and let others have a chance to breathe and live their lives. We don't have a heaven or hell to throw anyone into. To combat suspicion and criticism, begin to *think* of them with love and goodness. *Think.* Remember, the battle is in our minds.

3. **Overcome nagging thoughts, doubts, and fears with the truth and your testimony.** Since the enemy can't touch us, he works overtime accusing us in our thought life. In the book of Revelation he's actually *called* the accuser (see Revelation 12:10). Most of the time, you should just ignore him like you would a barking dog. But other times, STOMP at his dumb butt and he'll scamper off! Bark back! It's good to speak the truth about who God has made you to be! Tell him, "I am the righteousness of God! I am a holy saint, set apart, spotless and blameless!" (See 2 Corinthians 5:21, Colossians 1:22). Also, give your testimony! Tell others what Jesus has done for you! (See Revelation 12:11). The enemy hates this!
4. **Overcome hate with love, and evil with good!** (See 1 Corinthians 13:4-8, Romans 12:21). When the Holy Spirit revealed this battle plan to me, it took me a while to trust it *and* to pull it off. He currently has me on the 90-year plan of having my mind renewed, and I'm getting better each day. To be honest, I had a hard time finding a healthy balance with this because of my codependency issues. However, *this* is the atomic bomb used in spiritual warfare! JUST LOOK AT THE CROSS! MY GOSH! THE LOVE AND GOODNESS BEING POURED OUT BY JESUS DURING THAT HEINOUS ACT? IT'S THE EPITOME OF THIS! The more you feel hated, the more you should love! The more evil that comes your way, the more good things you should be doing! This is how you fight back! Put up your dukes and FIGHT!

So today, my friends, know this: The best way to fight like a Christian is to love God, love others, and love yourself. People are not your enemy, yourself is not your enemy, and God is definitely not your enemy—the enemy and his crew is your enemy! The power of sin is your enemy! But both have already been defeated through Jesus who lives in you!

SO STAND UP TODAY AND FIGHT BACK! Fight, BACK! Love! Forgive! Hope! Give! And be yourself, gracefully.

A prayer for you: *Well good morning, Heavenly Father! It's a great day today! I'm feeling good! When I get the chance to teach on spiritual warfare it excites me! This teaching is my way of fighting back! You and I both know that for so long I allowed the enemy's lies to keep me in a state of low self-worth and fear. NOT ANY LONGER! I pulled his card and he's done! HE'S SO WEAK! Thank you for teaching me this! Right now, I lift up all who are reading this, directly to you. So many of them have believed the lies of the enemy about you, others, and even themselves. Today I ask that you begin to show them how spiritual things work. Yes, it's a mystery, but through your guidance, you teach us everything we need to know. You teach us the truth and how to fight back properly. Help us to stay focused on fighting like a Christian and turning from the wrong ways of fighting. Teach us more about the power that lies within us! YOU! In Jesus' name I ask these things, amen.*

Day 45

What Is the Unforgivable Sin?

"They will be punished with everlasting destruction and shut out from the presence of the Lord and from the glory of his might"

2 Thessalonians 1:9

The only unforgivable sin is rejecting the forgiveness of Jesus, by grace, through faith. There are many people who would disagree with me, and that's fine. This is a very touchy subject that the enemy uses to create tremendous amounts of fear and anxiety. However, when we allow the Holy Spirit to teach us the truth, all fear and anxiety in regard to committing the unforgivable sin, goes away (see Philippians 4:6-7, 1 John 4:18).

Of course, there are many who don't understand what Jesus has truly done, those who claim we can sin our way *out* of being forgiven. That doesn't hold water. With such a theology, we are alleging the Cross wasn't all it was cracked up to be—as if our wonderful actions and attitudes complete it. This self-focused belief system can basically be summed up in this: *we are forgiven of all our sins until we commit one.*

What happens when we have this mindset? We lie about our sinning, downplay it, and *compare* our sinning. We become modern-day Pharisees, acting as if God grades on a curve. Nope. We must be perfect, Jesus said so Himself (Matthew 5:48). Perfection can only happen by way of receiving a new, perfect spirit—*not* by what we do or don't do (see John 3:7, Colossians 1:22, Romans 6:6-7, Ephesians 2:8-9, Matthew 7:21-23).

Another group will say we are forgiven of our sins *only* if we confess them. They will use 1 John 1:9 as the hill they die on. However, this also doesn't match up with the truth of the gospel either. Just think about it, how impossible is it to keep track of all our sins? And worse, what if we forget one? Will God forget a sin because *we* forget a sin? No. This is neurotic and creates severe stress *or* hypocrisy for believers. "I'm just going to go ahead and sin because I can confess it later." At its core, this ideology is demonic. Let's look at 1 John 1:9 to see the proper context:

"If we confess our sins, he is faithful and just and will forgive us our sins and purify us from all unrighteousness."

1 John 1:9 was written to the Gnostics. The Gnostics were, and still are, a group of people who thought the word *sin* was not a real thing. They believed they had never sinned a day in their lives. What is the basis of the gospel? Admitting you have sin to *be* forgiven of. John was telling them they need to confess, as in *agree*, that they actually *have* sin which needs to be forgiven. This is why he said they will be cleansed of *all* of their unrighteousness. He didn't say, "If we *keep* confessing, we'll *keep* getting cleansed." This is bonkers to say the least.

Heck, to back up my point, in the very next chapter, John says that he is writing to them so that they *won't* sin, but if they do, they have an advocate, Jesus (see 1 John 2:1). He doesn't say, be sure to confess those sins too. Further, if you read before and after 1 John 1:9, you'll understand the context: believe you are sinful so that you can be forgiven once and for all through faith in Jesus. Afterwards, you are *not* sinful, you are a holy saint.

So what *is* the unforgivable sin people are claiming to be such? Over the course of my 36 years of life, I've dealt with many religious people. According to the majority of the most self-centered and legalistic, there are two main unforgivable sins. One of them actually is the unforgivable sin, but the self-righteous people have misconstrued it to fit into their church-box of manipulation and control through fear and hierarchies. The other sin has simply been taken out of context. Let's look at both:

1. Blasphemy of the Holy Spirit
2. Suicide

First of all, blasphemy of the Holy Spirit *is* the unforgivable sin. This is exactly what the Gnostics were doing in the book of 1 John. Blasphemy means, "to speak ill of." If you speak ill of someone you are not believing what they have to say, therefore, you are rejecting them.

The whole premise of Christianity is based on belief alone—faith (see John 1:12, 3:16, Hebrews 11). If you don't believe that Jesus is the Son of God who can and will forgive your sins, you will speak ill of that. You will *reject* that. The self-absorbed person who's claiming to be the world's best Christian will assert that blasphemy is saying a swear word, "It's taking the Lord's name in vain! Once you do that, you're out for good!"

Who came up with this stupid crap? As if a curse word will automatically keep you from being God's child? I'll tell you who came up with it, Satan did! Then he put it in the mind of an uber-religious person and it spread like California wildfire!

How many people have given up on going deeper into their relationship with God because they said His name in vain *believing* they are now disqualified from being a Christian? Lots! They think they've blown it because someone lied to them about what blasphemy actually is!

"I've already committed the unforgivable sin, so why even try?" This is what they think! *Then* they never fulfill the good plans God has for them! IT'S *OUR* FAULT! We *must* be clear about the truth of God's unconditional love through Jesus!

And no, having foul language is not a good thing; it's not organic as a heaven-ready saint. Saying G.D. as a Christian is like being a cat who barks—it's not natural. Cursing at *all* is like eating out of the trash when we have a steak dinner sitting on our table. But I'll tell you this, we don't *get* saved by stopping our foul language, and we don't *stay* saved by *staying stopped* with our foul language. We get saved by grace through faith and this is a one-time event! We believed Jesus saved us and He did! (See Ephesians 2:8-9, Hebrews 7:25, 10:10, 10:14, John 3:16-18).

So where are we getting this "swear word" blaspheme verse as the unforgivable sin? When it's taken out of context, in Mark 3. Satan loves it when we cherry-pick from Scripture, especially when we twist it into something ungraceful. Jesus said this:

> *"Truly I tell you, people can be forgiven all their sins and every slander they utter, but whoever blasphemes against the Holy Spirit will never be forgiven; they are guilty of an eternal sin." (Mark 3:28-29)*

When you don't understand what blaspheme means, and when you pull this up and out from the page, I can see how a person might be afraid to say a curse word. However, if you start up in verse 20 and read down *to* these two verses, you'll realize what Jesus is talking about. The religious people were saying He was demon-possessed! What's that called?... SPEAKING ILL OF! Blasphemy! They were bad-mouthing Jesus! Jesus was telling them this mindset would keep them from being saved! Why? BECAUSE THIS WOULD KEEP HIS SPIRIT FROM JOINING THEIRS! If you *don't* believe Jesus is who He said He is, you will *keep* your sinful spirit, and His *Holy* Spirit will not come and live with your *new* spirit! BLASPHEMY IS REJECTING THE HOLY SPIRIT INTO *YOUR* SPIRIT! Blasphemy prevents you from being supernaturally reborn! It's not a swear word, it's your belief! They didn't believe He was the Messiah, they believed He was working for the devil!

When a person believes such, these following verses will *not* happen for them! If you reject belief in Christ, these do not apply to you, which will *keep* you on your way to hell:

> *"For we know that our old self was crucified with him so that the body ruled by sin might be done away with, that we should no longer be slaves to sin—because anyone who has died has been set free from sin." (Romans 6:6-7)*

In this verse, your *old self* is your sinful spirit you're born with. When you believe Jesus has saved you, that spirit immediately gets crucified in the spiritual realm, it's buried, and then you get resurrected as a new, perfect spirit! Only then can the Holy Spirit of Christ *join* your spirit, which is *after* you're cleansed from all sin! Here's another:

> *"Therefore, if anyone is in Christ, the new creation has come: The old has gone, the new is here!" (2 Corinthians 5:17)*

The *old* that has gone is your old spirit! This is not referring to your incorrect actions and attitudes—but your spirit! It's been done away with! You can't get rid of your old spirit if you speak ill of Jesus by saying He can't save you! The *new* is your new, perfect spirit, joined with Christ! Let's look at another!

> *"I have been crucified with Christ and I no longer live, but Christ lives in me. The life I now live in the body, I live by faith in the Son of God, who loved me and gave himself for me." (Galatians 2:20)*

The first *I* in this verse is the old, sinful you. The second *I* is the new, perfect you. YOU ARE A SPIRIT! So now, your perfect spirit *has been* reborn of God's own Spirit! I'm not talking about your perfect thoughts and choices, I'm talking about your identity! Your identity is *God's own child*! NOTHING CAN CHANGE THIS ONCE IT'S HAPPENED!

You receive a spirit born of God when you do *not* reject the Holy Spirit of Christ into your spirit (see 1 John 3:9, Romans 6:3-4). Once you receive His Spirit, you're ready for heaven and then joined by God, all at once! This only happens by way of faith in the power of Christ's forgiveness! (See 1 John 5:4, 1 Corinthians 1:18).

Do you not see it? Blasphemy has nothing to do with a swear word and has everything to do with belief in the forgiveness of Jesus Christ! We have to stop telling others the wrong stuff about blasphemy! People are going to hell and lives are being ruined!

...And I digress. Now, let's talk about suicide being unforgivable. Just think about how inconsiderate and *wrong* it is to tell someone this is an unforgivable sin. Here a person is, completely distraught, even to the point of not wanting to live any longer, and *we* want to say that killing themselves will cause God to send them to hell? We have the *audacity* to claim that our loving Heavenly Father will pile on top of *that* pain, eternal punishment? HOW DARE US!

Imagine if your child committed suicide. Does such a terrible choice cause them to never have been your child in the first place? NO! SO JUST THINK ABOUT HOW GOD FEELS? This makes me shake my head in disgust! I don't get mad about much, but this religious manipulation is one of those things! We are *not* saved by our bravery! We are *not* saved by our ability to snap out of a severe depression! WE ARE SAVED BY OUR FAITH IN JESUS! *JESUS* SAVED US AND HE *KEEPS* US SAVED! You cannot be un-born of God! You either *were* born again, or you *never* were! PERIOD! The sin-centered people out there cannot fathom this! Why? BECAUSE THEY LOOK AT THEIR "LACK" OF SIN AS THEIR SAVING AND IT'S SICK! They look at all of their wonderful religious deeds as if God needs them! HE DOESN'T! HE NEEDS US RE-BORN! *These* will be the goats He separates from the sheep! These will be the people saying, "Look at what all I did in your name!" and Jesus will reply, "Depart from me, I never knew you!"

I can already hear a grace-confused person yell at me, "Yeah right, Matt! The Bible is clear that there is a sin that leads to death! If you actually *read* your Bible, you'd know that! I'll be praying for you harder because you need it!"

Friend, please, I understand the Bible says there is a sin that leads to death, but that *sin* is unbelief in Jesus' forgiveness. If we read the verse in context, you'll realize the truth:

> *"If you see any brother or sister commit a sin that does not lead to death, you should pray and God will give them life. I refer to those whose sin does not lead to death. There is a sin that leads to death. I am not saying that you should pray about that." (1 John 5:16)*

John is clearly saying we should pray for the sins of others that do not lead to death. What might that be? *Anything* except for praying them *out* of unbelief. Why should we not pray for this? Because it's impossible to pray someone out of unbelief. The death John is talking about here, as a spirit, is our final death…hell. You and I can always pray for the struggles of others, and we should. We can pray that doors would be open for them *to* believe, but no matter how hard we pray for someone, we can never pray them *out* of unbelief. And once they get to hell, we can't pray them out of that place either. Even God won't do this. He lets everyone decide to believe on their own.

So today, my friends, know this: Believe Jesus has forgiven you, please. This is the only unforgivable sin. Once you do, your old spirit dies, you get a new spirit that is perfect, and then His Spirit comes to live with you forever. Please, believe.

A prayer for you: *Father, I want to thank you for teaching me the truth of the gospel; that your Holy Spirit would be combined with mine* *for free at my believing and receiving. You and I both know that I lived in fear for so long over this, and it was because of the lies of people and the devil. But you've taught me that your grace is enough and I'm secure. I'm not afraid any longer. I know who I am. Thank you. Right now, I lift up all who are reading this, directly to you. So many of them have believed the lie that they've been disqualified from being your child because of some swear words. Reveal to them how silly that is. And there are others who are reading this who have loved ones who've committed suicide and they're not sure if they made it to heaven. God, ease their minds today. Let them know if there was any point in time that person believed Jesus had forgiven them, they are with you right now. Sure, you had more life for them to live on earth, and they made a horrible, permanent choice; but Jesus' sacrifice on the Cross banished ALL of our sins forever, even the permanent sin of suicide. The enemy won that battle, but it still didn't stop you from sealing them up with your Spirit for good—from the moment they first believed. You knew what they were going through, and you were with them. Thank you for such unconditional love! Thank you for your Spirit! In Jesus' name I pray, amen.*

Day 46

Smile!

"A glad heart makes a happy face!"

See Proverbs 15:13

As believers in Christ, in our hearts, we have been given joy! Joy is a part of our spiritual DNA! (See Galatians 5:22-23). Our hearts—everything we truly are—the *real* us, has been infused with the Creator of the universe! (See Colossians 3:3, 1 Corinthians 6:19). *He* is a very joyful Person! Where do you think we got this emotion from?

Therefore, since joy is a part of us, we should have smiles on our faces quite often. Joy—not happiness—is based on a state of mind. *Our* state of mind is in Christ! (See 1 Corinthians 2:16). So by simply being ourselves—joyful at heart—smiles will happen all the time, no matter our circumstances!

If you're not smiling, you've forgotten who you are: a heaven-ready saint, a child of God! (See Colossians 1:22, John 1:12).

Smiles are powerful! Smiles are attractive! Smiles can bring you favor with other people and get you noticed! Smiles lower blood pressure and relieve stress. Smiles can alter a bad mood and ease emotional pain. Smiles are gifts for other people. Smiles *show* other people the real you!

Just think about it, when someone smiles at you, something happens in your soul. You can't help but smile back! It's nearly impossible! You would actually have to *try* to not smile back. Smiling is a universal language. Smiling is a weapon against the enemy, it can get *rid* of enemies, and it makes you look good in pictures!

Have you ever been around a person who never smiles? I mean, it would absolutely kill them to crack a nice grin? Either they're too grumpy, arrogant, or self-conscious *to* smile, or they want to be sure *you* know *they* don't like you? What kind of feelings do you get from that? Not any good ones! You just want to say to them, "Hey grouchy pants! *Smile*, would you? It would help your stiff-as-a-board butt!"

Some people are even too legalistic to smile. "I don't want these heathens to think it's okay to live how they live. You couldn't pay me to smile in their direction." Or, "They ain't been to church in months, I ain't smiling at them." Get *off* of it! We should always be conscious of those around us, and smile at every opportunity we have! It's no wonder they stopped going to your church! Nobody wants to be like you! They might want Jesus, but they don't want to become a Christian so they can be cantankerous and miserable like your non-smiling rear! SMILE, WOULD YOU? GET OVER YOURSELF! Show them it's fun to be a Christian! Smiles are fun! Being a child of God is fun!

And you might say to me, "Matt, I want to smile. But right now, there's not much to smile about. I'm really hurting."

Friend, I know life hurts sometimes...I know. I feel you. Sometimes our pain can last for very long periods, it seems as if the storm will never pass. During those seasons we might not feel like smiling, but do it anyway. Crack a smile...you can do it. Just lift up each side of your mouth, and show your teeth...go ahead. Do it right now...I'm waiting . . .

Now, wasn't that nice? Yeah it was! Listen, I'm not saying be fake, I'm just saying...smile. Look around you, look *within* you, and smile. You're gonna be okay. The stuff you are worried about, in the grand scheme of eternity, it's small. God is working all things together for an eternal good and He's with you. That's something to smile about!

So today, my friends, know this: Smiling is a very serious matter! By forming a habit of a simple smile, all day long, your life will be revolutionized! I know this sounds like entry-level faith, but it's so much more. I'm not trying to have a pep rally here, I'm trying to get you to realize countless smiles are inside of your heart. Let them out! Smiling changes your thinking! Don't be weird about it, just smile regularly! When you smile, negative situations don't seem so bad, your pain subsides, and you're reminded of who loves you infinitely...Father, Son, and Holy Spirit. *They are smiling at you right now. You make them smile all day long.*

A prayer for you: *God, thank you for my ability to smile, I know it comes from you! Like Buddy the Elf, you love smiling, it's your favorite! For so long I hid my smile, or I had a fake smile, but not any longer. You've shown me so many things that cause me to smile naturally—even when I'm in deep pain. I want to thank you for that! Thank you for such a simple thing, a smile! Right now, I lift up all who are reading this, directly to you. There are some people who think they're too holy to smile, help them to loosen up and not be such a religious stick-in-the-mud. At the same time, there are many of these dear readers who think there's nothing to smile about; reveal to them that's not true! Yes, there's lots of heartache in their lives, and smiling might be the last thing on their minds. But if they believe Jesus is their Savior, His smiling Spirit lives in them! From Him, they can smile! His Spirit infuses joy in all of us! We ALL have the ability to smile and to thank you for being with us in every situation! SQUEEZE a smile out of them! We can smile because we know you'll never leave us, and because you've made us your children forever. We love you. Amen.*

Day 47

Christians Don't Have Wicked Hearts

*"And I will give you a new heart, and I will put a
new spirit in you. I will take out your stony, stubborn
heart and give you a tender, responsive heart."*

Ezekiel 36:26

To decipher the lies about the human spiritual heart, let's first define *schizophrenia*. People with schizophrenia struggle with debilitating consistency in their thinking. In their minds, they argue with themselves all day long. They can never come to a solid agreement about certain subjects because of a mental condition which causes severe two-time talk. The church of today is plagued with *spiritual* schizophrenia. I'll explain how, but first, let's jump over to something Jesus said in Mark 3:25:

"If a house is divided against itself, that house cannot stand."

Jesus said this when He was describing a demon-possessed man in which He just removed a demon from. He *removed* the demon, so there was no longer a battle going on inside him. But Jesus was also referring to Himself as He *defended* Himself against the religious people! The

Pharisees were accusing Jesus of also being demon-possessed. He replied by basically saying "If I'm demon-possessed then why am I driving out demons from people?"

He was saying, "You can't be on both sides, you have to pick one." So for the Christians who are claiming we have a good heart and a bad heart, this makes no sense at all. It's called double-talk and it's rampant in our churches. It keeps the gospel unclear, our churches cliquey, and allows self-centered people to compare their "low" level of sin to other's "high" level—as if God grades us on a curve. He does not!

God requires perfection (see Matthew 5:48). For this reason, He gives all who believe in Jesus, perfect hearts. We can only receive our perfect hearts by way of allowing God to kill our old hearts—our old spirits (see Galatians 2:20, Romans 6:6-7). Only then will He give us new hearts, new spirits! (See 2 Corinthians 5:17). This happens from the moment we first believe! (See John 1:12, 3:16). The modern-day legalists confuse this amazing truth by way of two main things:

1. **Mixing Old Covenant Scripture in with New Covenant Scripture.** Before Jesus came and went, yes, all of humanity had wicked hearts—and unbelievers still do. David and the prophets talked about how deceitful the human heart is (see Psalm 109:2, Jeremiah 17:9, Ezekiel 36:26)—so did Moses in the book of Genesis, "For the intent of man's heart is evil from his youth" (see Genesis 8:21). Our hearts are naturally wicked because of our original forefather, Adam. When he sinned for the first time, we inherited sinful hearts (See Romans 5:12, 1 Corinthians 15:21). But now, on this side of the Cross, we get a new heart, one that is perfect like Christ. Just like it was unfair that we inherited sinful hearts from Adam, it's also unfair that we received perfect hearts from Jesus. The Old Covenant is now obsolete for believers in Christ *because* we have new hearts. For those who don't understand this, they will mix some of those Old Covenant verses about deceitful hearts *in* with the New. This creates a

flabbergasting quasi-gospel. It creates a house divided against itself which Christ warned against.

2. **Calling Christians sinners.** Christians are not sinners, we *were* sinners. Do we still *commit* sins? Yes, but we are not sinners in any way. Our identity has changed completely and our actions and attitudes are catching up! Because of our new hearts—our new identity in Christ—choosing to act on sin will never feel right, permanently. We now want what God wants and we can't get away from that. Sure, our flesh might get a quick thrill from sin, but the Holy Spirit always guides us *away* from sin, reminding us of who we are inside (see Galatians 5). Because of this, no matter how much we choose to act on sin, or how often, God *in* us steadily reveals the truth *about* us. "Matt, that won't work for you. Stop doing it. You weren't made for that." So the best thing to do is just don't sin! But *when* we sin, turn from it once again, and do *not* call yourself a sinner! YOU ARE A SAINT! There is not a single New Covenant Scripture which states a *Christian* is a sinner. Not one time does any apostle call a believer in Christ a person with a wicked heart. Therefore, believer, anytime you read a verse referring to sin, or sinful actions and attitudes, that is *not* describing you. It's describing non-believers, it's describing how a Christian used to be before becoming a Christian, *or* it's describing a Christian who has forgotten about their one-time spiritual cleansing (see Hebrews 10:10, 1 Corinthians 6:11, 2 Peter 1:9).

For number one, a grace-confused person will shout at me, "How can you say the Old Covenant is obsolete? Are you suggesting we should just throw it out?"

Friend, *I'm* not saying the Old Covenant is obsolete, the Bible is:

> *"By calling this covenant 'new,' he has made*
> *the first one obsolete" (see Hebrews 8:13)*

When something has become obsolete it's because it's now useless—something better has replaced it. What Jesus did at the Cross created something *better* than attempting to follow 613 laws and commands from Moses. The Old Covenant law and commands don't stop at just ten, and *nobody* could follow them perfectly even though they promised to! (See Exodus 19:8, Romans 3:20, 4:15, Galatians 2:16, 3:11). The first Promise Keepers convention was a bust! The Law is an all or nothing proposition! (See James 2:10, Galatians 3:10). Therefore, a mediator brought in a New Covenant. One that is much, *much* better:

"Christ is the mediator of a new covenant" (see Hebrews 9:15)

So no, don't throw away the Old Covenant, leave it exactly where it is! It's beautiful, it's perfect, it's right and true! But it's obsolete. For Christians, it's like a museum. The only use it has is to teach us the history of our *New* Covenant. It explains Creation, the Fall, the Patriarchs, Israel, the Judges and Prophets; it has Psalms and Proverbs which are full of wisdom. But more than anything, it teaches us the lineage of our Savior and what He has taken care of for us! Leave it, read it, know it—but keep it in context! It does not apply to us because of our faith in Jesus Christ!

As for the Mosaic Law, the Old Covenant—which includes the Ten Commandments—it also is of no use for any believer in Christ because our spirits are already righteous (Romans 7:4, Galatians 2:19, 1 Timothy 1:9). That sentence will upset a lot of legalistic demonic spirits, but I don't care, it's the truth.

We Christians live by a new way of morals, ethics, right from wrong, and freedom, and we get these things from...God's own Spirit living in our hearts! God's own Spirit leading us, counseling us, discipling us, and keeping us free! Check it out!

"But now, by dying to what once bound us, we have been released from the Law so that we serve

> *in the new way of the Spirit, and not in the old*
> *way of the written code." (Romans 7:6)*

> *"But when he, the Spirit of truth, comes, he will*
> *guide you into all the truth." (See John 16:13)*

> *"But the Advocate, the Holy Spirit, whom the Father will*
> *send in my name, will teach you all things and will remind*
> *you of everything I have said to you." (John 14:26)*

> *"It is for freedom that Christ has set us free. Stand*
> *firm, then, and do not let yourselves be burdened*
> *again by a yoke of slavery." (Galatians 5:1)*

The yoke of slavery Paul is referring to in Galatians 5 is the Jewish laws and commandments. If you read the full chapter and the two before it, you'll see.

Now, I want to be perfectly clear about something: the Old Covenant is still alive and well today, but we believers are dead *to* it. The Law is still useful, but only for unbelievers in Christ. And it's only useful to them because it reveals how much of a complete failure they are when it comes to godly perfection. That's what it did for us, and that's what it still does, for them.

Even the people who have never heard of the Law still have God's "perfection requirements" written on their consciences, so they too are without excuse (see Romans 1:20, 2:15). As a result, the Law *and* man's conscience are both meant to funnel non-believers into God's grace through faith in Jesus' perfection. Many people who claim to live by the Law can't even name the top ten, let alone all 613. This proves it's not *knowing* Law which makes us guilty, but instead, being born into sin, in our hearts.

Attempting to follow the Law for righteousness with God is the same as attempting to summit an impossible-to-climb mountain. The smart people give up at the bottom! For the Christian, the mountain is still there, we respect it, but we've said, "Whoa! No way am I even trying that! I give up! I'll take grace!" Paul tells Timothy this fact:

"We know that the Law is good if one uses it properly. We also know that the Law is made not for the righteous but for lawbreakers" (see 1 Timothy 1:8-9)

Who are the righteous? WE ARE! Who are the lawbreakers? The people who attempt to follow the Law! We *Christians* are righteous because of our faith in Jesus *not* in attempting to follow 613 rules! Just look!

"God made him who had no sin to be sin for us, so that in him we might become the righteousness of God." (2 Corinthians 5:21)

"You also died to the Law through the body of Christ" (see Romans 7:4)

"For through the Law I died to the Law so that I might live for God." (Galatians 2:19)

This next one is my favorite!

"For sin shall no longer be your master, because you are not under the Law, but under grace." (Romans 6:14)

And here's the proof of our spiritual perfection! Here's the proof of our hearts being heaven-ready and good!

"But now he has reconciled you by Christ's physical body through death to present you holy in his sight, without blemish and free from accusation" (Colossians 1:22)

Do you see *what* has made us righteous, holy, without blemish, and free from accusation?...Jesus' body! Jesus' blood! Yes, it's strange, but God has a blood-based economy. He doesn't forgive us by *asking* for forgiveness, but only by faith in Jesus' perfect blood! The words "ask for forgiveness" are not in the Bible! ONLY BLOOD CAN FORGIVE! The apostles *knew* this fact—they were Jewish! That's why they didn't write it in their epistles!

Without the shedding of blood there is no forgiveness of sin (see Hebrews 9:22). The Law required blood to be spilled by animals once a year at the Day of Atonement for the forgiveness of the Jews' sins—for the *past* year. That animal blood didn't remove their sins, but instead, *reminded* them of their sins (see Hebrews 10:3). It atoned for their sins, covered up, or "paid for" their sins, but did not remove them (see Hebrews 10:4).

But even still, when they walked out of the temple, after the priest would lay hands on the carcass *transferring* their sin to that animal (see Hebrews 6:2), that Jewish person *knew* they were good to go until next year! That blood brought them relief for their sin!

What I think is funny is that the Jews got an entire year of forgiveness, yet, the modern-day church thinks we need to get forgiveness daily. If that were the case, I'd rather be an Old Testament Jew!

On this side of the Cross, we've got an even better deal than a year of forgiveness—we get a lifetime of it! Further, Jesus doesn't atone for our sins, or cover them up—HE BANISHES THEM FOREVER! God chooses to not even *remember* our sins any longer! This is why you don't have a wicked heart!

> *"For I will forgive their wickedness and will remember their sins no more." (Hebrews 8:12)*

Oh, but it doesn't end there! Jesus' blood being shed also caused His death. *Death* brings in new covenants, new agreements, new inheritances! Just think about it, if you have a rich grandpa and you know you're written into his will, when will you get your inheritance? When he kicks the bucket, and not a moment before!

Therefore, Jesus' blood not only forgave us, but His death *from* that bloodshed brought in the New Covenant between God and mankind! Do you see it? FRIEND! THIS IS SO AWESOME! WOULD YOU JUST LOOK AT THIS?

> *"Because of this oath, Jesus has become the guarantor of a better Covenant" (Hebrews 7:22)*

The New, *better* Covenant is between the Father and the Son! It's their oath to one another! We are simply the beneficiaries to that contract! We got the inheritance when Jesus died!

We sucked at being promise keepers—the Jews did any way—but everyone else would have too. So because *they* couldn't keep their end of the deal—obeying 613 contingencies—God created a *new* deal and then swore by Himself at the Cross through Jesus' perfect blood! (See Hebrews 6:13). He *then* took it a step further and included the Gentiles! That's us! (Galatians 3:14, 3:28, Romans 3:29).

C'MON SOMEBODY! THIS IS BROTHER-HUGGIN', KNEE-SLAPPIN', GOOD NEWS!

God swore by *Himself* because He couldn't find anyone greater to swear by! The Father and Son are one! (John 14:11). The New Covenant is based on a promise between God and God! It's not based on a promise between us and God because our promises are jacked up! We lie! God *can't* lie!

IS THIS NOT THE MOST EXCITING THING EVER? I'll answer that, "Yeah! Yeah it flipping is!"

Why did He do this? Because God never changes. It's the same God, but a new Covenant. By way of this New Covenant from an unchangeable Father and Son, God showed us how much He truly loves us. He solved our sin problem, once and for all. He wanted to be sure we had an immovable anchor for our souls:

> *"Because God wanted to make the unchanging nature of his purpose very clear to the heirs of what was promised, he confirmed it with an oath. God did this so that, by two unchangeable things in which it is impossible for God to lie, we who have fled to take hold of the hope set before us may be greatly encouraged. We have this hope as an anchor for the soul, firm and secure."* (See Hebrews 6:17-19)

What does this have to do with our hearts? Everything. The New Covenant is God making His home in our hearts, permanently. This can only happen after we get new hearts. Our hearts are our spirits. Sure, we can use that word to describe "all that we are" but our hearts are our core. Our hearts are the real us.

Friend, the Old Covenant prophets longed for the day God would finally make His home in our hearts. Back then, God came and went based on righteous behavior and faith, but He *never* infused Himself with anyone's spirit! Now He does! How? Why?...JESUS!

It was Jesus who finally gave us the opportunity to have our old sinful spirits done away with for good. The New Covenant is *you* dying—your heart—and *you* coming back to life at the same time with a new heart while still in this body on planet earth (see Romans 6:6-7, Galatians 2:20, 2 Corinthians 5:17) Our agreement with God is no longer based on behavior and attitudes. *Every* incorrect behavior and attitude required death, and Jesus died (see Romans 6:23, Hebrews 9:22, 10:10). The Cross actually worked!

If you believe this, you get a new heart! This new heart is not wicked or deceitful! God cannot live in wicked or deceitful places!

You are not at battle with a good side of you and a bad side of you! YOU ARE COMPLETE! You've been supernaturally reborn! (See John 3:7, 1 John 3:9, 5:4). Be sure and know that you will keep your perfect heart as long as Jesus lives! (see Hebrews 7:25). Even better, God is committed to you forever because of your one-time moment of faith in Jesus:

> *"If we are faithless, he remains faithful, for he cannot disown himself." (2 Timothy 2:13)*

The Father will never disown Jesus. They both live in you based on the New Covenant. They are committed to each other, and to us. Our commitment to *them* is an absolute joke. If this Covenant was about us, each time we sin, blood must be shed and a death must occur. It's not about us. We are receivers and reflectors of God's love. We are branches, He is the vine. Our only job is to simply relax and be our new selves.

Do we sill commit sins? Yeah, but Jesus isn't dying over and over again up in heaven each time we do. He finished it. One final sacrifice. (See John 19:30, Hebrews 10:10). By way of that last offering, He has made our spirits perfect forever! (See Hebrews 10:14). Christian, you don't have a wicked spirit! You don't have a wicked heart! Never say that! Never believe that! Trust yourself! Trust God too! After all, you want exactly what He wants!

So today, my friends, know this: Christians don't have wicked hearts. We are not at battle with ourselves. We can trust our hearts because we have new hearts, and because Jesus lives with us *in* our hearts (see Colossians 3:3, 1 Corinthians 6:19, John 14:23). As for the unbeliever? Yes, following their heart would be a bad choice, but not for us. Are we learning more about our hearts each day? Yeah! Are we growing in the knowledge of God's grace? Sure! Do we have old, stinking thinking which is constantly being renewed by our heart? Absolutely! (See Romans 12:2, Philippians 1:6, 4:8). But as for our core, our heart, our spirit, *we* have been made perfect forever because of the Cross. Trust yourself, Christian. Your heart is good.

A prayer for you: *Heavenly Father, thank you for my new heart! Thank you for making your home IN my heart. Thank you for the promise you made with Jesus to give me my new heart—and to never leave me! This happened when I was just a boy, but because of false teaching, I didn't realize what you had done. It makes so much sense to* *me now! As I look back, I can see that you've been guiding me for nearly all of my life! You've impressed upon my soul who you are, and who I am! Thank you! Right now, I lift up all who are reading this, directly to you. So many of them have been taught they have two natures, reveal to them that's not true. Sure, we have unrenewed parts of our minds, but we are complete in you. Teach them that the power of sin is still real on planet earth—and so are demonic forces. But because of our faith in Jesus, both have been defeated! We can trust ourselves! Your Word says we've become obedient from the heart, not from old Jewish law! Your Word says we've been crucified with Christ, buried, and raised as new creations! It says we are no longer slaves to sin, but slaves to righteousness! Jesus said He came to give us life, and life abundantly! INSTILL THESE TRUTHS IN OUR MINDS! We already know them in our hearts, but help us to know them in our heads! Help us to be confident as we live out this New Covenant of your grace! We are so grateful! In Christ's name I pray, amen.*

Day 48

Do You Feel Like You're All Alone?

"I will never leave you nor forsake you." ~God

SEE HEBREWS 13:5

Loneliness can really hurt, that is, if you don't understand something: you are *never* alone. As a Christian, wherever you go there are four of you. Father, Son, Holy Spirit, and you! God understands you still crave human contact and companionship, He made you that way! But when you *feel* alone, that doesn't mean you actually are!

Feelings are fickle, they come and go, ebb and flow. You can be in a room full of people and still *feel* alone. So we can't live off of our feelings, we have to live off of the truth. God in us teaches us the truth! Jesus explains:

> *"But when he, the Spirit of truth, comes, he will guide you into all the truth. He will not speak on his own; he will speak only what he hears, and he will tell you what is yet to come." (John 16:13)*

When Jesus said this it was still pre-Cross, so the Holy Spirit hadn't yet made His home inside of any human being. He had been *with* people, and even *on* people, but not *in* people! As New Covenant believers, the Holy Spirit now resides in our spirit! So this verse applies to us!

The Spirit of truth *has* come and He is guiding us *into* the truth! The truth is, we are never alone! The truth is, we've been grafted into the Trinity! Our spirit is now a part of the Trinity! So it's not just a Trinity any longer because you are included! (See Colossians 3:3, 1 Corinthians 6:19, John 14:23, Ephesians 2:6).

The truth is, we can enjoy our lives even without human contact. Do we want to? No. But the enemy wants us to think something is wrong with us when we are alone, but there isn't. Relationships—the amount of relationships you have—do not define you. If you think this way, you will slip into codependency. Codependency is allowing people to do bad stuff to you just so that you can keep them in your life. God doesn't want that.

The truth is, God doesn't want us to force any human relationship—nor get our identity from it. Or worse, continue to allow unacceptable treatment to *keep* a human relationship. HE WANTS US TO HAVE HEALTHY RELATIONSHIPS! He wants us to have organic relationships based on love and respect—both for others *and* for ourselves. This becomes easier as the Holy Spirit teaches you the truth of your infinite value. Soon enough, He'll give you the skills to take a stand against the poor choices of people—and to enforce change in the right way.

This might cause you to lose relationships and that's okay because your value will start to come to life! Understanding your worth will result in the creation of healthy relationships, as the decrepit, one-sided relationships fall away.

Friend, you are so valuable, Jesus died for you. You are so valuable, the Father gave you Jesus to pay off your sin-debt with Him for good! (See John 3:16).

And would you look at something else from that verse above—John 16:13? Can you see that the Holy Spirit is not speaking on His own? *He* is in relationship with the Father and Son. Therefore, He who is speaking the truth to your heart is hearing what they have to say about you too—and it's all good stuff!

So you can know that even when things look bad, you are still good! You are a holy saint! You are set apart and sanctified in full! Your spirit is spotless, blameless, and free from all accusation because of your faith in the Cross! (See Romans 6:18, Hebrews 10:10, 10:14, Colossians 1:22, John 1:12). This relationship you're in with God, the Trinity, will continue to guide you into truth. But not only that, they will comfort you and help you in your time of pain and need. Just look at what Jesus said:

> *"But the Helper, the Holy Spirit, whom the Father will send in my name, will teach you all things and will remind you of everything I have said to you." (John 14:26)*

Again, this *has* happened to you *if* you believe in Jesus as your Savior, and it's *currently* happening to you as well! God is helping you and reminding you of everything He constantly says to you! He's telling you that you're not alone. He's telling you that you're fine. He's telling you to relax and don't worry. He's telling you to be confident. He's building you up, not tearing you down.

How do you know if it's His voice? First of all, you have to know that God is love. Love is not just a characteristic of His but *what* He is (see 1 John 4:8). Here's more of what His voice sounds like:

> *"He's loving, joyful, peaceful, patient, kind, good, faithful, and He's not erratic." (See Galatians 5:22-23)*

> *"He isn't envious, He doesn't brag on Himself, and He's not pompous. He'll never dishonor you, He looks out for you, He's not easily angered, He keeps no record of your wrongs. He doesn't get happy when bad things happen to you or others, but instead gets excited about His truth! He always protects you, always trusts you, and He never gives up on you. He never fails you!" (See 1 Corinthians 13:4-8)*

So today, my friends, know this: You are never alone! You have God with you and in you! He is interwoven with your spirit like wicker! Everywhere you go, He goes! He is faithful to you no matter what you do, and no matter if others are faithful to you or not. Please begin to understand that seasons of being by yourself—from certain people—is not a bad thing. It helps you refocus on God. It helps you get to know Him even more. It helps you *learn* more about your true identity! Jesus went off by Himself quite often, to spend private time with the Father. Also, when He was tested the hardest, He went away from all human contact for 40 days. It was during that time He was pressured by Satan the worst! (See Matthew 4:1-11, Luke 4:1-13). However, that testing in the wilderness only revealed how strong He was to that stupid devil! If you're currently alone, away from people, this is happening to you too! You are *not* alone! God is with you! You are strong! Your faith is being honed and tested! STAND FIRM IN THE TRUTH! BE CONFIDENT! YOU ARE BEING PREPARED FOR GREAT THINGS!

A prayer for you: *Heavenly Father, you have used human loneliness more than anything else in my life to get me to focus on you. You've used the rejection of loved ones and trusted people to test my faith. It's weird to say this, but I'm truly thankful. Your grace has always been enough. The enemy has attempted to make me feel as if something is wrong with me, but you've assured me that I'm perfectly secure in you. YOU define me, and HE does not. YOU have taught me that I can enjoy my life at all times! YOU have helped me break free from codependency when Satan has wanted me to sit idle! THANK YOU FOR THE TRUTH! Thank you for teaching me that I'm never alone! Right now, I lift up all who are reading this, directly to you. Dad, so many of them are in deep pain, they think they're lonely when they're not. Please reveal your truth to them, and please comfort them. I know you already are, but help them to open up their eyes to the fact that you're ALWAYS with them—even when they are rejected by people! Even when they are hurt! TEACH THEM HOW TO TRUST PEOPLE AGAIN! Teach them* *to trust YOU! Help them to refocus on hope! Some of these dear readers have even believed the false teaching of religious people; that, because of their mistakes, you've left them. WHAT LIES! What demonic lies! Reveal the truth, God! Reveal your commitment to them! Soothe these feelings of loneliness and rejection. Teach them how to enjoy their lives and not force relationships, or worse, allow unacceptable behavior to KEEP relationships. Show them what a healthy, loving relationship actually is. The same they have with you. Amen.*

DAY 49

AM I REALLY SAVED?

"Examine yourselves to see whether you are in the faith; test yourselves. Do you not realize that Christ Jesus is in you—unless, of course, you fail the test?"

2 CORINTHIANS 13:5

It's been a beautiful day on the golf course. The sun is just about to set and my round is almost finished. The fall air is cold, but not too cold, and the vistas of the Missouri countryside are gorgeous. Many different shades of orange, red, and green trees are the backdrop as I stand on the tee box and scan where I want to hit the ball—but suddenly, my pocket vibrates.

"Matt, I struggle with an addiction. Since I struggle, will God leave me?" A text comes through on my oversized phone, from a friend of mine. Had I thought about it, I would have gone with a smaller phone because getting this one out of my pocket is a chore each time.

However, based on this text, it looks as if my friend is having a tough time with some sin, and he is a Christian. So I reply with some comforting words. Did I ask him, "Well, what are you struggling with so that I can gauge whether or not God has left you?" No. I *comforted* him because that's what *God* does, for us. He comforts us when we are afraid of anything. Jesus told us this:

> *"But <u>the Comforter</u>, the Holy Spirit, whom the Father will send in my name, will teach you all things and will remind you of everything I have said to you." (John 14:26)*

Jesus was comforting the disciples because He was about to be tortured and killed. He was letting them know what they were about to get themselves into by spreading the gospel of grace; that they would *need* His comfort, because the religious people and unbelievers would be *against* such grace.

As a Christian, this "Holy Spirit" whom Jesus said the Father *would* send, is here, right now, today. He's in you at this very moment, whether you feel Him or not. That is, if you believe Jesus has forgiven you.

"But Matt, am I *really* saved? How do I know for sure?"

The verse at the top of this devotional tells you to *test yourself* to see if Jesus lives in you. So how do you do that? A couple things. Ask yourself these two questions:

1. Do I believe Jesus has forgiven me?
2. Do I struggle with sin?

For number one, that's simple. The answer should be a quick *yes*. But for number two, this is a tricky one because we have an accuser who hounds us day and night (see Revelation 12:10). The devil and his demons want us to think that *because* we are struggling with a particular sin pattern we aren't really saved—but honestly, the opposite is true.

If you *weren't* saved there'd be no struggle! If you *weren't* saved, the Holy Spirit of Jesus would not be in *your* spirit causing you to feel strife each time your flesh decides to act on that temptation. The struggle is evidence *for* your salvation—not against it.

As a child of God, *you* don't want to sin. Your old immature thinking does, but *you* don't. You are a perfect, heaven-ready spirit (see Colossians 1:22, Romans 8:9). The reason why we can't grasp this fact is because we've been told we *want* to sin. We don't! We've also been told we have two natures—WE DON'T! We have one nature, God's nature! (See 1 Corinthians 2:16, 1 John 3:9, 2 Peter 1:4).

One of the reasons why we think we have two natures—and even I was duped—is because of the NIV Bible. I like the NIV Bible, I'm not downing it. But unless we are reading the original manuscripts, *all* Bibles have some errors in them when it comes to translation. English cannot express the original writings perfectly—it's impossible. But in the early 1980s, the NIV version, in order to be more readable, changed the word, "flesh" to "sinful nature." The original word is *sarx* which means *flesh*—not sin, not nature, and definitely not sinful nature. So the confusion began.

Christians do not have two natures as if we are at battle with ourselves. We have *one* nature, and *one* flesh. If you read the NIV version and you keep seeing the words "sinful nature" rather than "flesh," it would be very easy to think you are trying to kill off your sinful nature, but you aren't. You don't *have* a sinful nature. God can have nothing to do with sin, and He lives in you. Why would He clean house and still allow sin to remain in your spirit? It makes no sense.

Further, we aren't even trying to "kill off" our flesh, but instead, walk *by* the Spirit! (See Galatians 5:16). God likes our flesh! He made it! Our flesh is but a tool, it does what *we* tell it to do, not the other way around. We are to make ourselves *living* sacrifices each day, not dead ones. Paul tells the Christians in Rome about this epiphany:

"Present your bodies <u>as a living sacrifice</u>, holy and acceptable to God, which is your spiritual worship." (See Romans 12:1)

God is *not* trying to kill off your body. There is nothing wrong with it. Your flesh was made in God's own image! (See Genesis 1:27).

"Yeah, Matt, but I gotta die daily!"

Friend, no, you don't. The words "I die daily"—when read in context—you can see that Paul is *not* saying he kills himself each day. That's been twisted. The more accurate version is "I face death every day," and Paul said this because he literally faced death every day as he traveled the world to spread the gospel. That's why he said he even fought wild dogs (see 1 Corinthians 15:31-32). He dealt with the *threat* of dying all the time, he wasn't trying to kill off his old self. Paul knew that his old self died once, not multiple times (see Galatians 2:20, 2 Corinthians 5:17).

"But Matt, I've been told I have to pick up my cross and follow Jesus *every* day!"

I understand the rationale behind this, however, we only pick up our cross—figuratively speaking—once. Do you have a cross on you right now? No. We supernaturally, by faith, pick up our cross and follow Jesus to *His* Cross, once. Then, *at* the Cross, by grace through faith, our spirit gets crucified in the spiritual realm, buried, and then resurrected with Christ one time—not daily (see Romans 6:6, Galatians 2:20, Ephesians 2:8-9, Hebrews 10:10).

You are not being crucified daily, God loves you! Why would He want to kill you every 24 hours? Even Jesus is not being crucified daily, so what makes you think that you are? As a matter of fact, the reason why we can never lose our salvation is because Jesus will never die again! Just look:

> *"Therefore he is able to save completely those who come to God through him, <u>because he always lives</u> to intercede for them." (Hebrews 7:25)*

Do you see that? Jesus is always living, therefore, so are you! Christ is not dying daily in heaven, and *you* are not dying daily on earth. YOU'RE NOT! YOU ARE ALIVE! SO LIVE! Be who God *has created* you to be! You do not have a sinful nature or a dark side! You actually want what God wants and your struggle with sin is the evidence of God in you!

Even the publisher of the NIV version of the Bible has since changed the words *sinful nature* back to *flesh*, and that's because it's the truth. If we think we are at battle with *ourselves*, then we are going to constantly be at *war* with ourselves—which is what Satan wants, inner turmoil. God is a God of peace, not inner turmoil. You *are* saved, if you believe you are saved.

"Matt, you're a liar! In order to be saved you have to repent and be baptized! Acts 2:38 says so!"

Friend, I agree that we have to do both—repent and be baptized—but we must *define* both. Repent simply means *"turn from, do a 180; stop, go the other way."* It means: *change your mind.*

What do we need to repent of?...Drumroll please...UNBELIEF! We *must* repent of unbelief in Jesus as the Messiah! The first 10 chapters of Hebrews mentions no sins except for the sin of unbelief! More than anything else, God wants us to believe Him about Jesus. Belief is what saves. It's always been this way, even before Jesus. Heck, even *before* the Jews were given the Mosaic Law, which included the Ten Commandments, God justified all humans by them simply *believing* Him (see Genesis 15:6). Today, it is the same (see John 1:12, 12:32).

So, repentance of unbelief saves us *not* repentance of attitudes and actions. Changing our behaviors and thought patterns are carts *after* the horse. No amount of life change can save you. You can repent of bad choices and nasty thoughts until your repenter falls off—that *still* won't save you. Only Jesus living inside of you will. Which brings me to the second part of Acts 2:38, baptism.

Baptism simply means *"placed inside of."* In Romans 6, Paul speaks about being baptized into Christ the whole time, but not once does he mention water. So yes, we must be baptized into Christ, but that happens the very *moment* we are saved—the very *moment* we first believe. Baptism allows our spirits to be placed inside of God forever, that union is then marked with an unbreakable seal (see Colossians 3:3, 1 Corinthians 6:19, Ephesians 1:13, 2 Corinthians 1:22).

Water baptism is simply a celebration of your spiritual birth, it doesn't *make* you born again. You can dip an unbeliever in water 100 times in a row, they still won't be saved. So sure, get baptized! But get baptized for one reason only: TO CELEBRATE!

But please know, what Peter said in Acts 2:38, in context, has nothing to do with changing your behaviors or getting dunked in a hot tub at church to *receive* a new spirit. If that were the case—a law being made for water baptism—then we must also have a flame above our heads for proof of our salvation. Why would I say that? Because in the very same chapter, that happened.

This brings us to one conclusion: you cannot *see* someone's belief.

Acts is a history book. It is recorded *actions* of the disciples. It is not an epistle of doctrine. Just the same as the Old Testament is a collection of history books—not epistles of doctrine. It belongs where it's at, but must be kept in context and proper position. We live under a *new* covenant (see Hebrews 8:13), therefore, we must dive deep into the roots of such. The fact of the matter is, Acts also tells us about a couple falling over dead because they lied about money (see Acts 5). If we are using Acts as doctrine, our churches should be littered with corpses.

So how do you know if you are really saved? Simple: *You want what God wants—and you do!* I heard a preacher say up on stage one time, "Sin is fun! If somebody says sin is not fun, they are lying!" No, *he* is lying. Sin is not fun at all. We weren't *made* to sin. Our flesh might get a quick thrill from it, but afterwards, the real us is disgusted with it. Friends, we are holy! We are blameless! We are sin-free saints! WE DON'T *LIKE* TO SIN! SIN NEVER FEELS GOOD! IT GOES AGAINST ALL WE ARE AS GOD'S CHILDREN! If you believe that, you are saved. Now, since we *are* saved, let's live that way.

A prayer for you: *Well good morning Heavenly Father! I'm feeling great today! Thank you for another day alive as a saint! Right now, I lift up all who are reading this, directly to you. For those who are confused about their salvation, let them know how secure they are. Your Word says, in Hebrews 6, that the hope we have which anchors our souls* *is based on a promise between you and Jesus—not us! You are the only true promise keeper! We are the beneficiaries to that promise! You also say in 2 Timothy that even when we are faithless, you remain faithful, because you cannot disown yourself. That's because you live in us! Thank you so much for the confidence you've given me in your promises! Help us all to walk out our spiritual perfection today, and choose to not act on any sin. But even if we do, we know that we are still secure because we have an Advocate, Jesus. In His name, I pray, amen.*

Day 50

How to Deal with Depression as a Christian

"I will never leave you nor forsake you." ~God

See Hebrews 13:5

Bear with me while I quote some terrible teaching:

"You're depressed? You just gotta have more faith! The reason why you feel like you do is because of your lack of *faith*! Name it and *claim* your healing! *Speak* to that spirit of depression! Your faith isn't big enough, that's why you've not *received* your deliverance!"

"You must have sin in your life! A true man or woman of God would never be depressed because they repent of *all* their sins daily! *Repent* and you'd stop feeling like you feel!"

"Pull yourself up by your bootstraps, boy! A *strong* man of God would never complain about feeling depression! This must be a sign that you're not saved!"

"Depressed? You just gotta have the Holy Ghost! If you *had* the Holy Ghost, He'd never let you feel sad! Speak in tongues so you can get Him!"

"You are depressed because God has left you! You sinned too much! You are living in sin and you've missed church for months! READ YOUR BIBLE AND SERVE GOD! No wonder you are depressed, it's because you are of this world! You are getting what you deserve!"

...Fortunately, I had to stop myself from continuing to write such horrendous statements as these. I could easily continue. Why? Because I've heard all of them. This is called religious abuse and it is rampant in our churches. It's no wonder so many people want nothing to do with church, and why they can't stand Christians. I don't blame them.

People are hurting. People are in pain. People are struggling. People are sad and depressed, *Christians* even. First of all, I want to say that not all churches teach such demonic doctrine. Some actually have the gospel correct and teach both parts:

1. Believe Jesus has forgiven you, for free, and He actually does, once. (See John 1:12, Hebrews 10:10, Ephesians 2:8-9).
2. *When* you believe Jesus has forgiven you, your old spirit dies, it is buried with Christ's Spirit in the supernatural realm, and it is *raised* with Christ's Spirit in the supernatural realm, instantly. Your spirit is then perfect just like Him, forever, because it is *in* Him. (See Romans 6:6, Galatians 2:20, 2 Corinthians 5:17, Colossians 1:22, 3:3, 1 Corinthians 6:19, Hebrews 10:14).

Christians have brand new spirits. That's the gospel. We aren't *getting* brand new spirits, we *have* brand new spirits while still *in* these physical bodies. All of us is blameless—spirit, soul, and body (see 1 Thessalonians 5:23). Our flesh will soon be discarded because it won't be needed any longer and we'll get new flesh. The only reason why you have it now is so you can temporarily be a part of this physical universe (see 2 Corinthians 5:1, Galatians 5:16).

Our spirits want what God wants and our minds are being renewed to this truth. We could have really immature thinking *or* really mature thinking. Either way, we are complete and not defined by what we think or do. This is why a great divorce must happen in our mindsets before we can truly understand the gospel. Being a Christian is a noun *not* a verb.

You could have received your new spirit 45 years ago and just not realized it because of trash teaching by aggressive people who act like they have no self-control. Or, you could have received your new spirit yesterday and you don't have any real education on who you are inside. Don't worry, the Spirit of God in you will teach you who you are. Jesus explains that it is His Spirit who now guides us, *not* religious laws, commandments, or rules:

> *"But the Counselor, the Holy Spirit, whom the Father will send in my name, will teach you all things and will remind you of everything I have said to you." (John 14:26)*

The Holy Spirit of Jesus *teaches* you and *reminds* you the truth of who you are! This is why gutter teaching will never match up with you. It's because you don't live in the gutter in the spiritual realm, so when someone talks to you that way, it will rub you wrong. Some people allow this to happen all their lives and they think it's okay because it's coming from a person on stage—IT'S NOT! IT'S NOT OKAY! YOU ARE ROYALTY! Don't allow yourself to be talked to that way! Paul told the Christians in Ephesus who they have become:

> *"And God raised us up with Christ and seated us with him in the heavenly realms in Christ Jesus." (Ephesians 2:6)*

This verse is past-tense. God is not *raising* us up, He *has* raised us up! We, right now, our spirits are sitting with Christ in heaven! And I need to correct myself here, because we are not just sitting *with* Christ, but *in* Christ! You've been immersed in the Trinity! You are now a *part* of God! That is, if you believe you are.

"But Matt, I don't feel like I am."

I know. I know it doesn't always feel like it. Most of the time, we feel nothing. Although I do have to say, there are times when I feel God... when I *feel* heaven. It could be in my darkest hours, or during my most mundane tasks, or singing in worship—but I feel it. I *feel* my royalty and it is something very special.

But those feelings are few and far between. God didn't create us to live according to our feelings, but instead, according to our *knowing*. There is no part in the Bible which speaks about feelings dictating our identity in Christ—but it does say all over the place, "Do you not *know*?" and "I write this so that you may *know*." Our spirit is our identity. This we know.

For this reason, depression can hit you at any moment *in* your feelings. Feelings ebb and flow, they come and go like a breeze. Further, depression could also be coming from a physical issue in you, from your flesh. The chemical things happening in your flesh can't be "faithed away" or "repented of"—IT'S IN YOUR BODY. So you might want to consider seeing a physician if you struggle with consistent depressed feelings, and shockingly, a medication might help you.

"Matt, you're telling people they can't be healed by God and that they need to pop pills!"

No, I'm not. God can do anything He wants. He can fix any physical ailment, obviously. He is causing our hearts to beat this very second, so if He wants to tweak the chemical make-up in our body, that is His prerogative. But sometimes He chooses *not* to fix what's wrong for a better *overall* result for mankind. So, in that case, see a doctor. Pray, exercise, eat right, do everything the crisis demands, and see your doctor. There is nothing wrong with that.

"But Matt, I have a relative who is hooked on pills."

I'm sorry to hear that. We shouldn't be controlled by anything, this is why we need to *listen* to the Spirit's guidance. He will never lead us into addiction, He will lead us into balance (see 1 Peter 5:8). I know all about addiction, it ruined my life as a child, and it almost killed me as an adult. But for those who don't have a problem, sometimes a glass of red wine is healthy; and sometimes taking medication to balance out something that is off in your brain is wise. It's not your fault.

Friends, depression is real. Chronic sadness is *real*. These things are not meant to be covered up with a Christian pep-rally or yelled at by an overbearing person at church—they should be brought to Dad. Talk to Him. Cry. Bawl your eyes out. Yell! FEEL! He wants you to. Don't be afraid to feel the pain. It's okay. But when you feel the pain, keep letting God know that you trust Him. Keep letting Him know that you want to understand more about who you are inside. Ignore the enemy when he tempts you to handle your depression in the wrong ways—YOU WEREN'T MADE FOR THAT. You were made for love, joy, and peace, not sin.

Give it time, give it truth, and soon enough you'll be able to separate your feelings from your knowing. You *know* that you are more than okay with God, you *know* that He loves you exactly as you are, and you *know* that you are already seated in heaven with Him. No matter how you might feel today, this is the truth. Things will get better, but in the meantime, know that God is with you, arms wrapped around tight.

A prayer for you: *Heavenly Father, thank you for helping me with my feelings. Thank you for teaching me that my feelings don't define me, you do. Thank you for being there for me, and for teaching me the truth about who I am inside. Right now, I lift up all who are reading this, directly to you. God, so many of them are in severe pain. Let them know you are with them. So many have been lied to by religious people who just don't understand you, so please, reveal the truth. Your Spirit in them will never lead them to angst or stress, so when religion is used to hurt them, make your red flags obvious. Let the buzzer go off on the* *inside of them when the lies of Satan are coming from the pulpit. Teach them the truth about who they are, which is unconditionally loved, royal children. Even if they don't feel like it right now, reassure them they are. In Jesus' name, amen.*

Day 51

The Truth About Baptism and Repentance

"Repent and be baptized, every one of you, in the name of Jesus Christ for the forgiveness of your sins. And you will receive the gift of the Holy Spirit."

Acts 2:38

Do you want to become a Christian? Do you want to be saved from hell, and have God's own Spirit come and live in you forever? Then say this prayer with me and believe it as true:

"God, I'm a sinner. I believe Jesus died for my sins and I want to be completely forgiven right now. Please forgive me."

Congratulations! You are now a Christian and no longer a sinner! Yes, it's really *that* easy! Honestly, there's not even a certain sentence or phrase you must say, you simply have to believe you are forgiven by Jesus and you are! (See Galatians 3:2, Romans 10:17).

However, the grace-confused person will be quick to comment, "Yeah right, Matt! They gotta repent and be baptized! The Bible says so in Acts 2:38!"

To that I'd reply, "They did. Repentance and baptism *just* happened. They repented of unbelief in Jesus' forgiveness, and when they did so, they were supernaturally baptized into His Spirit."

The problem is, the self-righteous folk have turned repentance and baptism into laws based on actions and attitudes *rather* than what it was originally meant to be: two different one-time events which happen simultaneously based on faith and grace.

If we define repentance and baptism according to Scripture you'll see! If we *stop* taking the word of angry "representatives" of Christ, and instead look into the Bible for ourselves, freedom will happen! Freedom from fear, and freedom from legalism!

First, let's unpack baptism. How about we stop fooling ourselves by saying H2O will wash away our sins? There's no amount of any liquid in all of the universe that can wash away sins. Therefore, true baptism according to the gospel is a *supernatural* baptism.

All baptize means is "to place inside of." Paul refers to baptism in Romans 6, and not once does he mention water. Why? Because he's talking about *our* spirit being placed *into* Jesus' Spirit. This is exactly what Peter was referring to in Acts 2:38. Peter was not creating a law out of being dunked in water, he was being literal. He was talking about their spirits.

Peter was saying, "You must be baptized into the Spirit of God in order to be saved." This only happens by way of grace through faith (see Ephesians 2:8-9).

Again, baptism simply means "to be immersed in." Paul goes to great length explaining authentic baptism in Romans 6. He tells the Christians in Rome they should stop sinning because they are no longer made *to* sin (Romans 6:2). But not once does he say their sinful actions will wear out God's grace. Then he tells them why:

> *"Don't you know that all of us who were baptized into Christ Jesus were baptized into his death?" (Romans 6:3)*

What does that even mean? It means that *we too* have died *with* Jesus—that is, our spirits. From the moment we first believe, our spirits are placed *inside of* Jesus' Holy Spirit—and vice versa:

> *"For we know that our old self was crucified with him so that the body ruled by sin might be done away with, that we should no longer be slaves to sin—because anyone who has died has been set free from sin." (Romans 6:6-7)*

The body ruled by sin was our old, sinful spirits. These two verses are not talking about our physical bodies dying, but our spiritual bodies! The one we were born with! This spiritual death, burial, and resurrection happens from the moment we first believe, whether we feel it or not! Salvation is not based on our feelings, but on the truth!

He says the same thing in Galatians 2:20 as he talks about his old *I* and his new *I*.

> *"I have been crucified with Christ and I no longer live, but Christ lives in me. The life I now live in the body, I live by faith in the Son of God, who loved me and gave himself for me."*

And again, to the Corinthians:

> *"Therefore, if anyone is in Christ, the new creation has come: The old has gone, the new is here!" (2 Corinthians 5:17)*

The self-absorbed person will read that verse and immediately think of their actions and attitudes—as well as the actions and attitudes of others. But Paul is talking about identity! Paul is talking about a *spiritual* death, burial, and resurrection! Paul is talking about being reborn for a second time, in your spirit! 2 Corinthians 5:17 is about us being placed inside of the Holy Spirit of God after our old spirit is killed off! Paul tells the Colossians the same truth about baptism:

> *"For you died, and your life is now hidden with Christ in God." (Colossians 3:3)*

But this won't be enough proof for the behavior-centered person. They will be quick to point out an event which happened in Acts 19. However, if we do a brief exegesis of that passage, the truth of the gospel will burst off the pages. Here it is:

> *While Apollos was at Corinth, Paul took the road through the interior and arrived at Ephesus. There he found some disciples and asked them, "Did you receive the Holy Spirit when you believed?"*
>
> *They answered, "No, we have not even heard that there is a Holy Spirit."*
>
> *So Paul asked, "Then what baptism did you receive?"*
>
> *"John's baptism," they replied.*
>
> *Paul said, "John's baptism was a baptism of repentance. He told the people to believe in the one coming after him, that is, in Jesus." On hearing this, they were baptized in the name of the Lord Jesus. (See Acts 19:1-6)*

The legalist's sinful senses will start to explode like Pop Rocks at reading this—but hold your horses for a minute. Let's break this down. These people, whom Paul *just* encountered, were still believing according to the *Old* Covenant. John the Baptist's ministry was built on Mosaic Law and that's all they had ever heard of.

John preached, "Stop sinning or else!" His entire ministry was based on behavior repentance toward obeying the Jewish law!

Paul explains to them that John the Baptist's teaching was the *opposite* of Jesus' by telling them, "John's baptism was a baptism of repentance." He then tells them about the new way, "Believe in Jesus," right *after* he corrects them about John's old way of behavior modification for righteousness (see Acts 19:4). He was saying, "*Now* we receive baptism into God's own Spirit by way of grace through faith in Jesus!"

These people had never received information about Jesus and they just did! This is *how* they finally received the Holy Spirit, which is by hearing with faith!

"Matt, how can you say that John's ministry was the opposite of Jesus'?"

Friend, I'm not saying it, John the Baptist spoke this from his own mouth:

"He must become greater; I must become less." (John 3:30)

Many fake-martyr Christians will take this verse out of context and apply it to themselves, "I GOTTA BECOME LESS! YOU GOTTA BECOME MORE, LORD!" when that's wrong.

This is John saying that his ministry of legalism—of trying to make people obey 613 laws and commandments—must go away *so that* Jesus' ministry of grace by faith can enter. His ministry had to cease in order to make room for the Messiah because the Messiah would take away our sins forever *through* Himself. John said so from the first moment he laid eyes on Jesus:

The next day John saw Jesus coming toward him and said, "Look, the Lamb of God, who takes away the sin of the world!" (John 1:29)

Remember, John knew that repentance of sinful actions and attitudes was hard to do. Not just 10, but 613 different rules to follow was very burdensome! John also knew that the forgiveness received by animal blood each year at the Day of Atonement was getting old! HE WANTED PERMANENT FORGIVENESS! HE WANTED RELIEF! Jesus would bring both into the picture.

So Paul was telling the people in Acts 19 that there was a new way other than John's way—Jesus' way. After hearing this, they believed, *then* the Holy Spirit joined them just the same as He joins every believer.

I don't want to get off subject here, but briefly, when these new believers received the Spirit, Paul put his hands on them and they also spoke in tongues. Neither of these things are required to receive the Holy Spirit. When Luke wrote this, he was *recording* events—he was writing down the *acts* of the apostles—not creating laws to *get* the Spirit. The truth of the gospel is *no* physical act nor supernatural gift *causes us* to receive God's Spirit. We get Him for free.

With all of this being said, what's the use of water baptism? To answer that, let me ask you another question: What's the use of having a birthday party? TO CELEBRATE YOUR DAY OF BIRTH!

Water baptism is a celebration of your *spiritual* birth! It is an outward expression of something that *has* happened inside of you. It's not something you do to achieve God's Spirit, but instead, it's an act that celebrates God's Spirit being *in* you. Unless you first believe the instant you go down into that water, you're already saved.

Just think about it, you can dunk a non-believer in water all day long while chanting, "I baptize you in the name of the Father, Son, and Holy Spirit," but still, that would never cause them to receive God's Spirit. We only get placed into the Spirit by way of believing in Jesus' sacrifice for our sin! So sure, get baptized in water! But do it to celebrate and not for any other reason!

Now to repentance. The very word *repent* has been infused with demonic steroids by Lucifer himself. For centuries, he's whispered lies into the ears of the self-righteous and fearful the like. This six-letter word wreaks havoc in the lives of all who don't understand God's grace.

According to the gospel, all that is required to be saved is repentance of unbelief in Jesus' forgiveness—*not* repentance of incorrect actions and attitudes. That would be Judaism. Remember, repentance of incorrect actions and attitudes was the ministry of John the Baptist as well as Moses and all of Israel.

But still, the self-centered "well behaved" person will attack me over this subject, "It sounds like you are just saying we can sin, sin, sin away! You're telling people we can sin however we want!"

No, I'm not saying that at all. I'm saying we have *new* wants and *new* desires *because* we have God's Spirit infused with our new, perfect spirits. As beings who are now one with God, we actually want what He wants! We don't even *want* to sin!

Sure, our old way of thinking might—our mind didn't get saved, our spirit did—but as soon as we *do* sin, it's like stepping on a tack. We always regret it. Even if we continue stepping on that tack and saying it doesn't hurt—even for a lifetime—we know deep down that *sin* will never be okay with us.

"You're just being light on sin! You're just giving people a *license* to sin!"

No I'm not. I hate sin. I hate it when *I* sin. It was *my* sin—past, present, and future—that killed Jesus. None of us *need* a license, we're all sinning just fine without one. However, repentance of incorrect actions and attitudes does not *earn* us a license either—not even a permit.

Lots of unbelievers have polished lives. But polished, low-sin lives *still* cannot achieve God's Spirit. Only repentance of unbelief can. The entire book of Hebrews is written about one main sin, unbelief. The Hebrews—those who were following Mosaic Law—didn't have the problem of outwardly-bad sin like us Gentiles. So the author didn't even bother going over all of those sins.

Instead, the writer of this letter had a bullseye on rejecting faith in Jesus as the Messiah. The Jews wanted to keep getting forgiven at the temple by way of animal blood even *after* they had heard about Jesus—but that would no longer work. They needed to believe!

"If we deliberately keep on sinning after we have received the knowledge of the truth, no sacrifice for sins is left, but only a fearful expectation of judgment and of raging fire that will consume the enemies of God. Anyone who rejected the Law of Moses died without mercy on the

testimony of two or three witnesses. How much more severely do you think someone deserves to be punished who has trampled the Son of God underfoot, who has treated as an unholy thing the blood of the covenant that sanctified them, and who has insulted the Spirit of grace?" (Hebrews 10:26-29)

This passage is *not* written to Christians! The author is saying to the unbelieving Jews, "You've heard about Jesus so you are without excuse! The blood of animals cannot forgive you any longer and the Law of Moses is obsolete!"

He, or she, was saying, "If you think punishment was bad by way of the Old Covenant, how much worse do you think the punishment will be for rejecting the New Covenant of God's grace through Jesus?"

Friends! All we must do is repent of unbelief! Actions and attitudes ebb and flow and cannot generate righteousness! We have a righteousness which comes by way of faith! (See Romans 3:22, Philippians 3:9, Galatians 5:5). The author even tells the Jews to move forward *past* the elementary teachings of repentance from dead works! (See Hebrews 6:1).

"But Matt, you gotta repent of *all* your sins! All of them!"

Yes! We do! From the moment we first believe, we *have* repented of all of them because our sinful spirit was killed off! If you're claiming that repentance of actions and attitudes is what gives us our righteousness—or *sustains* our righteousness—then how do you know you've done it properly? How do you *know* you've repented of *all* your sins? How are you even keeping track of them? How do you know you've done *enough* behavior and attitude repenting? HOW DO YOU KNOW?...Friend, you don't.

The devil sure wants you to think you're doing a good job at repenting—or a terrible job—but we are fooling ourselves if we think that changing the stuff we do and don't do is earning us kudos with our Creator. We can repent until our repenter falls off, that still won't make us right with God. Only through spiritual death and rebirth are we right! And that only happens by way of faith.

I gotta say something that might come across as harsh, but I know this is true because I used to live this way: Repentance of actions and attitudes for righteousness with God might be the most anti-Jesus mindset a person can possibly have. Why? Because it's saying, "The Cross was not good enough. I have to make it good enough."

So today, my friends, know this: Repent and be baptized if you haven't! Do it right now, this very moment! Don't wait any longer! Today could be your last shot! Believe Jesus has saved you from your sins, and you've done both! Afterwards, plan on having a water baptism to celebrate, and allow your new spirit to help you change your incorrect actions and attitudes. After all, you've been baptized into Christ and you are now holy!

A prayer for you: *Heavenly Father, thank you for teaching me the easiness of your truth. Baptism and repentance are both very simple! In your Word, in 1 Corinthians, even Paul said he didn't come to baptize but to preach the gospel—he also said he was glad he DIDN'T baptize many. Just as you've revealed to him, you've revealed to me, that water saves no one and neither does behavior change—only faith in Jesus can! Right now, I lift up all who are reading this, directly to you. So many of them have been lied to about the truth of baptism and repentance. Today, I ask that you reveal the authentic relaxation found in the gospel. Help them begin to understand that the Cross was enough, and their faith in that event was too! Teach them anything which begins with "I do" or "I don't do" in order to "get right" with you is wrong. Jesus already did it all. Our only job is to say, "Thank you!" and to receive His Spirit! In His name I pray, amen.*

Day 52

When Praying for Your Enemies Is Hard

*"Do not gloat when your enemy falls; when they
stumble, do not let your heart rejoice"*

Proverbs 24:17

Let's all be honest with ourselves, when those who hurt us *fail*, the flesh gets a bit of a thrill out of it. However, as heaven-ready saints, we are not of the flesh, but of the Spirit (see Romans 8:9). We've been made new on the inside, so this old way of thinking must be put in place from time to time. We should *pray* for our enemies, not be excited about their misfortune.

The great news is, the only way to do this is to be yourself—to walk by the Spirit! You don't have to keep "crucifying your flesh." Honestly, that only happened once, and it happened to Jesus not you. Sure, your spirit was crucified, but that only happened one time as well, then you came back to life in Christ! (See Romans 6:6-7, Galatians 2:20, 2 Corinthians 5:17).

Your flesh has never been crucified, and it doesn't need to be. There's nothing wrong with your flesh, it's just a tool for your spirit. It is a temporary vessel for you to be able to walk around on planet earth. If you crucified your flesh, you would literally die, so we need to stop saying that. Be easy on your body, it's not your enemy. It is good! (See Genesis 1:27, 1 Corinthians 6:19).

You don't have to constantly be at battle with *the* flesh either, but instead, walk by your true nature. There's nothing more frustrating than trying to tame the flesh. *The* flesh—not *our* flesh—isn't our physical body but the power of sin coming to life through us and others. It can't be tamed and it doesn't *need* to be tamed. So rather than try your hardest to do so, just be the real you, then you'll do as you please (see Galatians 5:17).

Even better, when you are being who you truly are as God's own child, you won't have to look to any of the Jewish laws or commands for structure and guidance. Instead, God's desires are now written into your supernatural DNA, so you *know* what to do and what not to do, organically, from the heart. His holy character is now built into *your* natural reflexes and instincts! (See Hebrews 10:16, Galatians 5:22-23).

As a result of this, you will naturally put the desires of the flesh to the side. Paul explains how this works to the Christians in Galatia:

"So I say, walk by the Spirit, and you will not gratify the desires of the flesh. For the flesh desires what is contrary to the Spirit, and the Spirit what is contrary to the flesh. They are in conflict with each other, so that you are not to do whatever you want. But if you are led by the Spirit, you are not under the Law." (Galatians 5:16-18)

Two things to point out:

1. **Walking by the flesh causes you to *not do* whatever you want as a saint.** Remember, you actually want what God wants. The legalist sees this verse one way, the saint sees it another.
2. **There's no need to legislate being yourself.** As you can see, you're not under a single law or commandment of the Old Testament, including the 10 Commandments, which are 10 of 613 given to Israel by Moses (see Deuteronomy 4:2). Therefore, your godly behavior comes forth naturally and is never forced

by way of pressure or legislation. You can't pass a law to force an apple tree to grow apples, it just happens as it is itself. Same with you, with the fruit of the Spirit (see Galatians 5:22-23).

Friend, by being who you are in spirit, you will be able to pray for your enemies simply and easily even in the midst of being hurt by them. This mindset is based on *knowing* that your enemies are loved by God too, and *choosing* to pray for them—not feeling like it—but choosing.

As an act of your will, you will ask God to bless your enemies and you'll mean it. The Spirit of Jesus will strengthen you to be able to pull this off without effort (see Philippians 4:13).

Understanding who *we* are modifies our thought processes toward others because we begin to realize their importance to our Creator as well. God made them too. Jesus died for them too. In turn, we can pray for them genuinely.

For years, I would have quoted the following verse for such a topic as this. But as I learned more about the New Covenant, I soon found out that I'd be taking it out of context. Jesus said:

> *"But I tell you, love your enemies and pray for those who persecute you"* (Matthew 5:44)

The heart behind this verse might be true in regard to what we should do as Christians. However, this verse *in context* does not apply to us as believers. Why would I say that? Because most of Matthew 5—from verse 17 and on—was written to the legalistic Jews who thought their wonderful behavior was earning them righteousness with God.

This verse was one of the nails in the coffin of Mosaic legalism in which Jesus used to rightfully bury the Pharisaical hypocrites. He was speaking to his critics in the crowd, *not* comforting those who actually believed in Him as Messiah.

For proof of this, all you have to do is look at the chapter as a whole and then read the end of it. Jesus said, "Be perfect like God is perfect" (see Matthew 5:48). From verse 17 on, the Sermon on the Mount is a death sentence. Even for today, it's meant to cause those who follow Mosaic Law to say, "Well, crap. I'm a complete failure."

It's meant to funnel the legalist toward grace. It's meant to teach: we must be born again in spirit in order to receive supernatural perfection—following rules can't do this! Only by believing in Jesus' complete forgiveness does this happen.

However, if we are going to cherry-pick Scripture to make an honest point, I think cherry-picking *this* particular verse for *this* particular subject is fine. The heart of God *is* to love His enemies! The heart of God *is* to pray for those who persecute Him! Jesus did both at the Cross, and He now lives in us!

So today, my friends, know this: Yes, praying for your enemies is very hard—in the flesh! But we walk by the Spirit! We can do all things through the Spirit of Christ who strengthens us! Keep doing it! Keep blessing others! Keep praying! Keep being yourself! God is paying close attention to everything! It could be *your* prayers that change the lives of even your enemies! Keep showing them the goodness of God!

> **A prayer for you:** *Good morning, Dad. I just want to thank you for being such a good Father to me. You're so patient and kind, and you always pick me up when I fail. I love you so much, and I'm glad to be your son. Right now, I lift up all who are reading this, directly to you. So many of them have been hurt by others, some are still BEING hurt by others—please, help them. First, help them to learn WHO they are as a heaven-ready person. Once they understand this, they'll begin to understand how they should truly act and live. Afterwards, teach them how to establish healthy boundaries in order to protect themselves. Begin to renew their minds into learning how to handle their feelings. Teach them that their feelings don't dictate their identity, and neither do their feelings dictate whether or not they should pray for their enemies. We CHOOSE to forgive others, we CHOOSE to pray for them. These are acts of our will NOT our feelings! Help us to bless those who*

cause us harm and to pray for them. But also help us to remember our infinite value to you. Give us balance in all things! In Christ's name I pray, amen.

Day 53

Jesus Will Not Blot Out Your Name

"The one who is victorious will, like them, be dressed in white. I will never blot out the name of that person from the book of life, but will acknowledge that name before my Father and his angels."

Revelation 3:5

Revelation 3:5 has been used by false teachers for centuries to create fear and anxiety in the believer. They will begin by telling a Christian how bad of an individual they are, why God is extremely disappointed in them, and how they've "backslidden" terribly. Then they'll put the rotten cherry on top of their disgusting Sunday sermon as such: "God Almighty will *rightfully* blot your name out of the book of life!"

Oh how wrong can a person possibly be? In this instance, eternally.

Revelation 3:5 was meant to be a comforting verse for Christians, not a scary one. If a saint would actually read it for themselves, they'd see the word "never." By the way, every Christian is a saint. Saint simply means "set apart" and that's what our faith in Jesus has done! We've been set apart as sheep from goats! (See Matthew 25:33). Our faith in the event of Calvary has caused us to be set apart, holy, and blameless! (See Hebrews 10:10, Colossians 1:22).

But let's look deeper into the passage in question. You will see it *assures* us that Jesus will *never* blot out our name from the book of life:

> "*The one who is victorious will, like them, be dressed in white. <u>I will never blot out the name of that person from the book of life</u>, but will acknowledge that name before my Father and his angels.*" *(Revelation 3:5)*

Whether the book of life is symbolic or not, we know what it means. It's referring to our reservation in heaven. The good news of the gospel is, once our names are in it, they can never be blotted *out* of it—it says so right there! Read it again if you have to!

Other than this reassuring verse, how can we be certain our names will never be taken out of the book of life? Many biblical reasons, but I want to point out two things the Holy Spirit has revealed to me about His New Covenant with mankind:

1. **Our names will never be blotted out because Jesus will never die again.** Hebrews 7:25 explains, "Therefore he is able to save completely those who come to God through him, because he always lives to intercede for them." What is the punishment for sin—*every* sin—from jealousy to murder? Death (see Romans 6:23). What did Jesus do at the Cross? He died *then* He came back to life. When He died, He paid off every believer's sins—past, present, and future. Yes, even future sins. Remember, *all* of your sins were in the future when Christ died. He is not bound by time, we are. He holds the remote to the DVR of the universe, we don't. So, once Jesus paid the penalty for our sin through His death, He rose again. Coming *back* to life matters because He does not have to die again to pay off any more of our sins! He

finished this task—death for sin—with one, final, *perfect* death, and He's never going to die again! (See John 19:30, 1 Peter 3:18).

2. **Our names will never be blotted out because the Father and Son will never break their promise to one another.** The New Covenant is based on a promise between God and God and we are the beneficiaries to that promise. Hebrews 6:13-20 explains. God could not swear by anyone greater so He swore by Himself. Our salvation is secure because of two unchangeable things—Father and Son—both are unable to lie, therefore, both are unable to un-save us from eternal punishment. Jesus promised to die for our sins, the Father promised to remember our sins no more (see 2 Corinthians 5:21, Hebrews 8:12). So *our* job is to simply open up our hands, receive this gift, and say, "Thank you!" (See John 1:12, Ephesians 2:8-9). It's not about us, it's about them and our faith in *their* promise to one another. Yes, we try to make it about us, and when we do, terrible things happen. However, it is in their agreement to each other that we finally discover the anchor for our souls!

Sadly, the behavior-focused person—not the identity-focused person—will attempt to prove me wrong. They'll say, "No way, Matt! You're just telling people they can sin and not be punished! Revelation says we will be judged for our sins and our names will be taken *out* of the book of life!"

Friend, none of that is correct. First of all, I'm not telling people to sin nor am I downplaying sin. Sin is bad. Our sin caused Jesus to have to die. We, as new creations, are no longer made *to* sin, but we *will* sin because of where we're currently at—on a fallen planet.

John even said, "If any of you *does* sin, you have an advocate with the Father, Jesus" (see 1 John 2:1). So obviously we will sin—we will fail in our actions and attitudes—but those failures cannot change our heavenly DNA! We've been spiritually reborn *of* God! (See John 3:7, 1 John 5:4).

To answer the other part of this person's statement: Correct. I *am* saying we *won't* be punished by God for our sin. Why? Because the Cross was suffice. Now, will we suffer earthly consequences for sin? Sure, but not heavenly.

What's the punishment for sin according to our Creator? Again, as I said above, it's death (see Romans 6:23), and the author of Hebrews tells us Christ died *once* for *all* sin (see Hebrews 10:10). Friend, Jesus isn't dying in heaven each and every time we sin. Do you see it? Do you see that it's finished? That *one* sacrificial death of the Messiah was enough!

So who will *not* be in the book of life? Only those who reject Jesus' one-time spiritual sanctification by grace through faith:

> "*all whose names <u>have not been written</u> in the Lamb's book of life*" (see Revelation 13:8)

The only people who will be judged for their sins are those who have *never* been written in the book. It's not people who have been written in and then removed, but those who were not in there in the first place. Here's more proof of unbelievers being judged according to what they have done—not us:

> "*And I saw the dead, great and small, standing before the throne, and books were opened. Another book was opened, which is the book of life. <u>The dead were judged according to what they had done</u> as recorded in the books.*" (Revelation 20:12)

I've underlined, "The dead were judged according to what they had done." Who are the dead? The dead are those who do *not* have Christ. Jesus tells us:

> "*For God so loved the world that he gave his one and only Son, that whoever believes in him <u>shall not perish but have eternal life</u>. For God did not send his*

> *Son into the world to condemn the world, but to save the world through him. Whoever believes in him <u>is not condemned</u>, but whoever does not believe stands condemned already because they have not believed in the name of God's one and only Son." (John 3:16-18)*

We are not condemned! We have eternal life! Our eternal life is Christ's life because He will never die and He lives in us! (See Romans 6:4, John 10:10, 20:31, Colossians 3:3-4, 1 Corinthians 6:19).

Because *Jesus* will never die again, neither will we—that is, our spirits! We are spirits!

Further, Revelation 20:12 says the dead were judged *according to what they had done*. What are the deeds of people who are not in Christ?...Sin. This verse is speaking of the final judgement of *sins*, and *we* don't have any! Jesus has taken them all away! Just look!

> *The next day John saw Jesus coming toward him and said, "Look, the Lamb of God, who <u>takes away the sin of the world</u>!" (John 1:29)*

> *"so Christ was sacrificed once <u>to take away the sins of many</u>; and he will appear a second time, not to bear sin, but to bring salvation to those who are waiting for him" (Hebrews 9:28)*

Do you see what we have to look forward to when Christ returns? GUARANTEED SALVATION! Not fear, not condemnation, but Home! Jesus is currently building up His Family and *you* are a part of it! Don't be afraid any longer! He has taken away your sins for good!...That is, if you believe He has.

So today, my friends, know this: Jesus' blood blotted out your sins forever—THEY ARE GONE. Therefore, your name will stay written in the book of life forever. God is not neurotically adding your name and then deleting you name, so be confident! *Be* confident. God cannot lie and Christ will stay risen for eternity—and so will you!

> **A prayer for you:** *Heavenly Father, thank you for sending Jesus here to pay off my sin-debt once and for all time. Thank you for giving me such a gift! Right now, I lift up all who are reading this, directly to you. Dad, there are so many of them who have been taught to be petrified of you—and they shouldn't be. They've also been scared of a demonic word called "backsliding"—which is not even in the new Testament. Teach them the truth! This very word goes against your grace and is anti-gospel! Teach them it is self-centered, not Christ-centered, for a person to honestly believe a child of God can somehow slide back from you. No matter how severely incorrect their actions and attitudes may be—or how often—you will never allow this to happen! Proper choices and thoughts didn't save them, your promise to Jesus did. Help them to go further into your truth! Help them to look at YOUR commitment to THEM—not THEIR commitment to you. Our commitment is a joke! Empower their souls with the truth of the Cross! I command any religious demon to leave them alone, in Jesus' name! Give them peace in their thinking. Give them confidence. Help them to never be afraid of you and to KNOW their name is infused with YOUR name, forever. Amen.*

Day 54

Debunking Christian Myths Part 2

*"We are hard pressed on every side, but not crushed;
perplexed, but not in despair; persecuted, but not
abandoned; struck down, but not destroyed."*

2 Corinthians 4:8-9

There is a very well-known Christian teacher whom I love. This person has helped me tremendously over the years. However, as I go deeper into the knowledge of God's grace—the New Covenant—there are some red flags the Holy Spirit throws up in regard to their teaching.

This morning I read something they wrote about God's protection, our righteousness, obedience to Him, as well as spiritual fruit—and it did not set right with me. God takes us from glory to glory; that means our minds are constantly being renewed with His truth about *our* new identity as saints (see 2 Corinthians 3:18, Romans 12:2). Once we know who we are, everything changes. The Holy Spirit is trying to convince us of who we are every single day. Why? Because He knows once we actually believe it, we will live *out* our true selves!

However, if you're still green to the good news of the New Covenant, which is the only Covenant available to anyone, some teachings can cause serious anxiety for you. Especially when the Old Covenant is mixed in with the New Covenant.

Remember, the Old Covenant deal is gone and the New Covenant is here to stay! (See Hebrews 7:22, 8:6,13, 9:15). Therefore, be sure to know this: it's the *same* God of the Old Covenant, but a *new contract* with mankind based on Jesus' perfect sacrifice at the Cross.

GOD IS SATISFIED IN FULL BECAUSE OF WHAT JESUS DID. OUR BEHAVIOR CANNOT MODIFY HIS APPEASEMENT—GOOD, BAD, OR INDIFFERENT.

When we make the mistake of mixing in Old Covenant teaching with the New Covenant—teaching that makes God seem *not* satisfied—confusion and angst is soon to come forth. The enemy loves when this happens and God does not (see Romans 8:15, 2 Timothy 1:7). For this reason, we must be clear as best we know how. So, the gist of this person's teaching went as such:

> *God wants to protect you. However, He will not and cannot protect you if you are not obedient to Him. Neither will He protect you if you are not making good, healthy choices. You won't have any righteousness, peace, and joy if you are not obedient to God.*

Now, to give this person the benefit of the doubt, this could be some of their older writings which haven't yet evolved or matured. True Christian theology gets worked out through the Holy Spirit's guidance over time (see Philippians 1:6, 1 Corinthians 3:1-2, 13:11, Hebrews 5:12-14, 6:1). Some stuff is foggy, some stuff is strong. He teaches us *gracefully* what we need to know day by day. But for these statements, they were so off base I was tempted to get out a pen and scratch through it.

Friends, the truth is God protects us at all times no matter our behavior! *All* of our bad behavior was dealt with on Jesus' bloody back! God's plan to deal with our shortcomings *through* Jesus actually worked! He is not *kinda* satisfied with what Jesus did, but fully! (See Romans 3:25, 5:9).

This is what the New Covenant is all about! As God's kids, through our faith in Jesus, His eternal protection will not change! Further, what kind of good father would not protect their child just because they're making choices which are not up to par?

Secondly, our righteousness is a free gift that comes by way of our spiritual rebirth *not* by way of behavior. The opposite of that sentence is *Old* Covenant! The opposite is Judaism! Religious demons will try to convince you otherwise, but this is the truth. Our "good behavior" is a joke! God requires absolute perfection! (See Matthew 5:48).

The good news is, godly righteousness is only imparted to us by way of our sinful spirits dying and then being raised back to life *infused* with the Holy Spirit of Christ! This is the only way we are right with God which is complete identity change into *spiritual* perfection. That is, supernatural rebirth while still in these physical bodies by way of grace through our faith in the truth of Jesus' forgiveness (see Romans 6:6-7, 2 Corinthians 5:17, Galatians 2:20, Ephesians 2:8-9).

And lastly, peace and joy is a fruit of the spirit, neither of which grows in our lives through obedience to God, but simply by being who we truly are as His children.

Let's look at Scripture to back this stuff up:

1. **God's protection is not based on our behavior but on His promise to us through Jesus.** Ephesians 1:13 says, "In him you also, when you heard the word of truth, the gospel of your salvation, and believed in him, were sealed with the promised Holy Spirit." From the moment we first believed, our spirits were sealed up with God's Spirit. Who can break this seal? Nobody! Not even us! Therefore, nothing can harm our spirit, ever. As for behavior, God is not blind to our poor choices—but, He protects us *even* when we make them. If we continue to make poor choices, we will continue to sow *seeds* of poor choices. On this planet, what you sow is what you'll reap. Bad things can happen in our lives *because* of bad choices, but God isn't *causing* those

bad things to happen—our bad choices are. God is *not* punishing you for doing unwise things. Instead, His Spirit is correcting you with patience and love! He is guiding you and counseling you! But punishing? No way. JESUS WAS ALREADY PUNISHED ENOUGH *FOR* YOU (think New Covenant). God is rich in mercy, He's our Dad. So He is always protecting us and working things out for something eternally good—*even* when we are ignoring Him and not being who we really are.

2. **Our righteousness is a free gift inherited the moment we first believed Jesus forgave us.** Romans 5:17 states we have received an abundance of grace from God and a free gift of righteousness through Jesus Christ. 2 Corinthians 5:21 says we *are* the righteousness of God, because of Jesus! Our rightness with God does not fluctuate just the same as our lineage does not fluctuate. We've been born into a Holy Family and nothing can change this! However, just because we are now blameless in our spirits we can still not *act* as such. Look at it this way: a prince can get amnesia and then find himself on skid row begging for food, but just because he has forgotten who he is that doesn't change the fact that he's royalty! The same goes for us when we choose to act on sin! Those choices don't change who we are, they simply keep us from enjoying *being* the saints we are.

3. **Peace and joy do not happen in our life because we are "obedient," but because we are naturally peaceful and joyful people.** That word *obedient* has a connotation of, "You better do this or else!" The New Covenant does not work that way. Christ has set us free from all obligation to anything which comes by way of force, law, or rules (see Galatians 5:1, Romans 8:2). Have you ever walked outside to a tree and said, "You better be obedient and grow some fruit!" I would hope not, and why wouldn't you? Because you know the tree will grow fruit without being told. It will grow its fruit without being forced, guilted, or shamed as it simply lives its life. Same with us saints. As we simply be

ourselves as heaven-ready people, we will not only grow peace and joy, but also, love, patience, kindness, goodness, faithfulness, gentleness, and self control! (See Galatians 5:22-23).

A prayer for you: *Heavenly Father, thank you for another day of life! It's GOOD to be alive on planet earth! What a blessing! Right now, I lift up all who are reading this, directly to you. Today, I ask that you begin to reveal the truth of the gospel to them—the New Covenant. Teach them that you are completely satisfied with Jesus' sacrifice at the Cross! Teach them our faith in that event causes us to always be protected by you! Our faith in that event causes you to use all things together for good, even our terrible mistakes! Our faith in that event has made us righteous forever! Our faith in that event has infused your Spirit in us, causing us to organically grow good spiritual fruit! Thank you so much for everything! We love you! Amen.*

Day 55

Children: The Real Victims of Addiction

"Train up a child in the way they should go: and when they are old, they will not depart from it."

SEE PROVERBS 22:6

"Matthew, your mom is here. Do you want to go see her?"
"Yeah...I guess," I say hesitantly, as I walk forward out of the room, led by an employee of the children's shelter.

Mom didn't always come to visitation day. Grandma did, Dad did, but rarely did she. Most of the time Grandma and Dad just couldn't find her because she was at a crackhouse in Hibiscus Park, or who knows where.

As a ten-year-old boy, walking into the visitation room and hugging Mom was always awkward. I resented her very much because I knew that if she wasn't so busy with her addictions, she could easily get us back. But no matter, Mom had finally come to visit, so I had to put on a fake smile and act like I was happy to see her.

When the supervised visitation was over, they'd shuffle me back to the main area with the other kids. I'd always go to my room after visitation day and lay on my bottom bunk. While breaking down in tears of sadness and anger, I remember how unfair it felt to be in that place. "It's all her fault! I'm here because of *her*!" I hurt. I hurt *so* bad.

Fast forward to today. As I write this, I'm a 36-year-old man. It is 5:23 am on Friday, November 10th, 2017. However, 26 years ago feels like yesterday. I can even remember the *smell* of that children's home—I hated it. I hated that place, I hated the mean kids who tried to fight me every day, I hated the employees who should have been arrested for what they did to us—everything about it, I hated.

Let me be clear: my spirit hated no one but my old way of thinking sure did. When you are abandoned by your own mom, and then treated like a second-class citizen because you are a ward of the state…well, I'll just say this, the enemy starts to work on your thought life at a very young age.

Thankfully, the Holy Spirit has taught me to forgive and love. Not forget, but forgive and love. If I choose to focus on it, the pain from back then can be just as real, right now, today. Satan wants that, God doesn't.

The memories we have from childhood are more vivid than the ones we form as adults. We are sponges at that age. That's why, if we aren't careful, the very same things that hurt *us* so badly, we too can hurt our own kids with, so badly.

That's what happened to me.

When I used to drink, Saturday mornings were the worst part of my week for two main reasons:

1. Debilitating hangovers
2. Embarrassing regrets

Sure, I drank nearly every day of the week, but Friday nights were the heaviest drinking times for me because I didn't have to get up for work the next day. Therefore, all bets were off, I'm getting smashed.

I always planned on getting drunk quickly, even if I tried to fake it at first by going slow. But once that fuse was lit, forget about it. I'd continue to drink until I passed out, or I'd binge eat and *then* pass out.

My alcoholism had made me fat because of the huge amounts of caloric intake before bed. It didn't matter though, I was in denial.

In my denial, on Fridays, I'd ignore the hangover I *knew* was coming the next morning. Not only that, because we problem drinkers have incredibly short memories—wink, wink—I'd also overlook the stupid crap I knew I'd be saying and doing while drunk. No matter, "I'm drinking! So mind your own dang business! It's legal!"

Where was God this whole time?...In me. Right where He is right now. I had been a Christian since single-digit age, so the Holy Spirit was in me in full. However, I ignored Him as He tried to counsel me about my inability to drink like a gentleman. For this reason, my heavy drinking would never be okay with me; an inward battle happened each time I did it. There would never be a possibility of actually *enjoying* getting drunk, no matter how much my unrenewed thinking tried to convince me otherwise.

"Matt, why'd you drink? If your mom was an addict, why would you become one?"

It snuck up on me. What started out as a way to socialize and relax, morphed into a monster. Honestly, I wanted to feel different. Those of us who have a problem in our minds with an addiction to alcohol, we are trying to feel different. This is really the bottom line. You can call us weak, you can say we are people who lack self-control, but we just want to alter our feelings. Strangely enough, while deep in my own addictions, I finally understood my young mother's poor choices. Mom wanted to feel better.

Further, I'm not a weak person whatsoever when it comes to effort. I rarely talk about it in my ministry, but I'm a very successful business owner. From the age of 19, I've built up the largest home and business security company within a 45-mile radius of my hometown—second place is not even close. I have employees, I have a storefront, a fleet of vehicles, and Alarm Security is a household name. This has taken more work, self-sacrifice, and determination than anyone who's not done the same could possibly understand.

So it's not a self-control issue that I had, it was a mindset issue. It was my *thinking*. Truth be told, I will outwork anyone, but at the same time, I can't stop drinking once I start. I tried for years and I just can't do it with any consistency. Drinking is not for me, my off-button is broken, and I'm at peace with that.

As for self-control, *all* Christians have self-control. Self-control is built into us as a part of our supernatural DNA (see Galatians 5:22-23). When you received your new spirit—from the moment you first believed Jesus forgave you—you inherited *in* your spirit, what God Himself has: *the ability to control yourself.*

If a Christian says, "I have no self-control," that's a lie. God lives in us, and He has plenty of self-control to spare. However, self-control cannot be worked *out* of us through our own power. It has to be coming from a state of rest (see Hebrews 4:11). As we relax and stop trying so hard to overcome our addictions, the Holy Spirit works *through* us, producing self-control. Paul told the Philippian Christians about this spiritual epiphany:

> "For God is working <u>in you</u>, <u>giving you</u> the desire and the power to do what pleases him." (Philippians 2:13)

God *in* us is *giving* us the desire and power to stop making stupid choices. So I had to learn to relax and stop trying to do His job. That's not easy for me because I get things done!...But, I had to learn to feel my feelings, relax in Him, and simply be a branch connected to the vine of Christ (see John 15:5). By doing this—resting—God's wisdom in me came to life and I finally gave up drinking for good.

Most of the time I drank to get rid of boredom, or to celebrate a great work-week. But at other times, I'd drink because of the poor treatment coming from others and the pain which came from such. Getting buzzed was my way of ignoring or *masking* the suffering from being severely codependent. Because of my abandonment issues, I allowed a lot of bad things to happen to me when I shouldn't have. Codependency recovery is something that I'm also well-versed in. I've studied it *hard*, and if a toxic relationship is your drug, you might want to as well.

Most boozers struggle with people-pleasing. They can't change the bad choices of others, so they drink to make those frustrated feelings go away. The problem with this is when we sober up those frustrated feelings are even worse.

The good news is, the Holy Spirit's desire is to teach us how to *not* cover up our feelings about being taken advantage of. Instead, He educates us on how to establish healthy boundaries with firmness, respect, and love—both for the other person *and* for ourselves. God wants to get us to a place of balance. For this reason, He will counsel us *away* from enabling others *without* turning to an addiction to cope. This process is not easy, but possible through His strength! (See Philippians 4:13).

My parents didn't pass down any healthy relationship skills. From a young age, I was taught to handle my relationship problems with rage, yelling, abandonment, the silent-treatment, and brushing terrible behavior under the rug as if it never happened.

Because of this, I had no real expertise when it came to standing up to unacceptable behavior as an adult. To soothe myself, I'd drink. This only made things worse, as painful issues piled up like junk in an episode of *Hoarders*. I *had* to change how I handled my relationships with others—as well as myself! And I had to do this without drinking! As an adult child of an addict, history was starting to repeat itself in my own home, so on May 8th, 2014, I decided to never drink another drop. Had I known life would be so much better this way, I would have given it up a long time ago!

As for Mom and I, we have a somewhat normal mother/son relationship now. From the rubble of the war-zone that was my childhood, God has healed the pain. She is sorry and I know it. I've completely forgiven Mom, and I hope she understands that.

So today, my friends, know this: Our addictions are not fair to our kids. Rather it be alcohol, drugs, food, men, women, work, hobbies, religion—whatever—ADDICTIONS HURT OUR KIDS. *They* are the real victims. Our children suffer silently as they witness us being controlled by something in which we shouldn't be. Or worse, they begin to turn their pain and frustration inward. When this happens, there is a lot of stuff they will have to unlearn as they grow up. I was that kid. So please, *please*, if you are reading this and you are struggling with an addiction, ask God to teach you how to break free from it. Make no mistake, He will. The sooner you do this, the sooner your kids will get to see the real you, the sober you, the free you, the *loving* you. They are worth it.

A prayer for you: *Father, thank you for another sober day. My daughter, Grace, thanks you for another sober day for me as well. Friday used to be a day of Dr. Jekyll and Mr. Hyde. Thank you for teaching me how to be myself by walking according to your Spirit! Right now, I lift up all who are reading this, directly to you. Many of them are adults who had addicted parents. Because of the pain they felt as a child, some have never touched drugs or alcohol. They've made a wise choice and their kids have benefited greatly. However, there are others who have followed in their parent's footsteps and become addicted themselves. God, let them know you are not disappointed in them at all. Let them know you love them unconditionally, exactly as they are. Help them to feel your love right now. But at the same time, speak to their hearts and remind them of how they felt as a kid, and that now their own kids are witnessing and suffering the same. Reveal their children's pain to them. Help these dear readers to begin exuding the self-control that every believer has inside! In Jesus' name, I pray. Amen.*

Day 56

Why Should I Listen to God?

"I will instruct you and teach you in the way you should go; I will counsel you with my loving eye on you."

Psalm 32:8

Life can be frustrating, to say the least. Certain situations, circumstances, and people—in which we have no control over—can cause us to lose sleep and walk throughout our day resentful. However, God *in* us wants us to listen to Him so we can enjoy His peace. This peace won't come easy because we live in a fallen world.

There are three main factors stoking the fire of our frustrations, causing us to forget who we are. In turn, we can *act* unbecomingly. As you'll see, *people* are not on this list, just look:

1. The power of sin.
2. Satan and demonic forces.
3. Unrenewed parts of our thinking.

First of all, I'm writing this devotional to the saints—to Christians. If you're not a believer, this won't make a whole lot of sense. If you want to become a believer, say this prayer, believe it as true, and you will instantly become a holy child of God too:

"Heavenly Father, I am a sinner. I believe that Jesus is your Son, and I believe I need His forgiveness. Please, forgive me of my sins. Thank you."

Congrats! You are no longer a sinner! You've become a heaven-ready person! Now, continuing on with my devotional.

For number one on the list above, the power of sin, I'm not talking about *committing* sins—I'm talking about a force. Like the power of gravity, the power of sin is also invisible and affects absolutely everything on planet earth. Because of this power, you can be in a room all by yourself with nothing happening at all—no temptation or person is around you—yet, you still get a sinful *thought*. "Where did that come from?" you might think. That's the power of sin.

If you don't understand this power, or if you've been religiously abused into thinking you're not saved if you have bad thoughts, the power of sin can influence you *away* from listening to God. From the opening book of the Bible, the power of sin is introduced:

"Sin is crouching at your door; it desires to have you, but you must rule over it." (See Genesis 4:7)

As you can see, sin is an *it*. Also, as you can see, we are already being told to rule over it. Paul tells the New Covenant believers the same:

"Therefore do not let sin reign in your mortal body so that you obey its evil desires." (Romans 6:12)

Again, sin is called an it. Sin is not you, Christian. It's a parasitic *power*. This power wants you to *not* be who you really are—sinless in spirit—but it has no power to *alter* who you are. As a person who Christ literally possesses, you are:

> *"Loving, joyful, peaceful, patient, kind, good, faithful, gentle, and you have self-control." (See Galatians 5:22-23)*

God will always reveal this to you, so listen to Him.

For number two, Satan and demonic forces, they too want you to ignore God's guidance—which is the truth about who you are. They *hate* you. Their desire is for you to live a frustrated life not knowing the truth about yourself. They want you to try harder to be good, or to forget that you *are* good.

These forces cannot touch you, but they can constantly accuse you in your mind. The reason they can't touch you is because God won't let them. You are sealed up, forever protected from hellish forces! (See Colossians 3:3, Ephesians 1:13, 1 John 5:18).

I say again, CHRISTIANS CANNOT BE POSSESSED BY DEMONS. CHRISTIANS CANNOT EVEN BE *TOUCHED* BY DEMONS. We are holy, blameless, and set apart! We are members of God's household! (See John 1:12, Colossians 1:22, Ephesians 1:5, Romans 8:17).

There is not a single verse in the Bible where a *Christian* is having a demon cast out of them. This is garbage and a learned behavior, it needs to stop. Once we know the truth of the power of God in us, we'll stop allowing these moronic forces to lead us away from God's guidance. All the enemy can do, all any *demon* can do, is accuse you. They lie to you *about* you. They see the real you in the spiritual realm, and they are afraid of you! (See James 2:19, Mark 5:6-10).

Satan wants to kill, steal, and destroy everything in your life—this primarily happens in your mind (see John 10:10). Jesus called him, "The father of lies," and in the book of Revelation he's called "the accuser" (see John 8:44, Revelation 12:10). All he can do is yap his mouth! The main lie he feeds you is the lie about yourself—that you're *not* holy. A close second is that you should not handle your problems how God wants you to, and really, how *you* want to. You want what God wants!

Number three on this list is our unrenewed thought life. When you received your new, perfect spirit, you didn't receive a new, perfect mind. Sure, some people will claim, "I was miraculously delivered!" and that's fine. I'm not against that, I just think it's abused.

A more real way of looking at poor thinking is being transformed by the renewing of your mind, over time. This happens little by little, day by day—it's not instant, whatsoever. We learn and grow *by* who we are in spirit. What's *in* us comes *out* of us as the years go by! (See Philippians 2:12). Paul tells the Romans, the Philippians, and the Colossians this truth:

> "Be transformed by the <u>renewing of your mind</u>." (See Romans 12:2)

> "Whatever is true, whatever is noble, whatever is right, whatever is pure, whatever is lovely, whatever is admirable—if anything is excellent or praiseworthy—<u>think about such things</u>." (Philippians 4:8)

> "<u>Set your minds</u> on things above, not on earthly things." (Colossians 3:2)

This is a process. Your renewed thought life takes time (see Philippians 1:6). You have psychological factors that will change over the course of your lifetime as you come to know the truth about your spirit! Be easy on yourself, and listen to God as He teaches you new things each day!

So today, my friends, know this: You should listen to God because He loves you! You should listen to God because He knows the truth about you! The power of sin, demonic forces, and unrenewed thinking stand no chance against the real you! Listen, learn, and grow!

A prayer for you: *Heavenly Father, thank you for your voice. Your voice is a KNOWING to me. I KNOW it's you when you speak to my spirit. I KNOW it's you when I'm up against sin, enemies from hell, and my old thought life. Please continue to guide me into peace, comfort, confidence, and a sound mind. I know you will! Right now, I lift up all who are reading this, directly to you. Dad, so many of them are struggling. They've been dealing with the same situations and people for a long time now, they just want some rest. Give it to them today! Let them know their rest is found within themselves! Let them know they've already been made new! Let them know you're with them and in them! Let them know the peace which surpasses all understanding will guide them in all of their choices! Teach them more about your ocean of grace as they swim through it today. Amen.*

Day 57

How Many Times Have You Been Saved?

> *"For it is by grace you have been saved, through faith—and this is not from yourselves, it is the gift of God—not by works, so that no one can boast."*
>
> Ephesians 2:8-9

I love Chonda Pierce. Some of the stuff she says in her stand-up comedy routines makes me laugh so hard my stomach hurts. Recently I was watching her and she said something that not only made me laugh, but made me think:

> "I got saved 342 times growing up. If there was lightning outside, I got saved. If there was a cute boy at the altar, I got saved again. I ain't stupid."

Ha! That's good stuff! It's funny because it's true in how Christians think *when* we are taught wrong about our salvation. I understand Chonda's background because I've seen the documentary about her life, *Laughing In The Dark*. She grew up in a very scary home—her dad was a preacher, a very legalistic one—and legalism creates fear. Legalism is demonic.

The enemy wants nothing more than for us to believe we are *not* who we really are as God's children. He wants us fearful, confused, and afraid. He doesn't want us to know that we *are* saved. Christians are saved people! Saved from what? From hell.

If he can cause us to be unsure about our true supernatural identity, he can then wreak havoc in our lives. We will stress out and strain harder—trying to earn or even sustain our salvation—based on what *we* do or don't do.

The devil knows we will live out who we believe we are. If he can get you to *think* you are going to hell, he knows you will live that way. The Holy Spirit, on the other hand, is always attempting to teach us that we are secure forever! He too knows we will live out who we believe we are! But until we allow Him to latch onto our thought life with His grace, we will say, "But what about—" all day long.

As the Spirit of Christ Himself, He gently chips away at our "But what abouts." Our incorrect theology of "I gotta do!" "I gotta stop!" "I gotta this and that so God will stay pleased with me!" To those things He says, "Stop worrying. *I'm* enough. *I'm* in you." Jesus wants us to remove the *I's* from our "But what abouts" and replace them with Him.

For some, even reading about this subject will muddy up the waters in their mind. Why? Bad teaching. *Fearful* teaching. Conditional grace theology. Behavior centered presentations rather than identity focused lessons. And I get it, I've been there. The way I *got* there was by trying so hard to keep my salvation I just about killed myself. When a Type A personality gets a hold of legalism, bad *bad* stuff happens. Debilitating burn-out happens.

Really, that's all it takes. Spiritual burn-out. Trying *so* hard to keep what you already have until you realize you aren't even the one keeping it—and you never have been—this wakes a person up!

We are saved once! Jesus saved us! Jesus keeps us saved! What He did was more than good enough to accomplish this feat, and to *maintain* this feat! When we got saved most of us didn't even realize what He had truly done! But He did it anyway!

So for the people who push the idea of us being able to lose our salvation, they are wrong. We have it, or we don't. These same confused folk will say, "Yeah, we might get saved once, but we have to be forgiven daily!" They don't understand that our one-time saving is the same event as our one-time forgiveness. Being saved *is* being forgiven. We don't get saved multiple times nor do we get forgiven multiple times.

Because they are focused on themselves and not Jesus, they have many more rebuttals to everything I just wrote. Here's a few of them, and my own replies:

1. **They will claim God will spit us out of His mouth based on Revelation 3:16.** The entire book of Revelation is symbolic. From beginning to end it reveals what will happen to those who have placed their faith in Jesus, and ultimately, those who reject Him. It also lets us know what will happen to the forces of hell. Guess what? WE WIN! So when a person claims God is spitting Christians out of His mouth, that's just not true. This passage is a picture. Because of the New Covenant, even if God *did* spit us out of His mouth, He'd slurp us right back up. This verse is saying, "Don't be passive. Be *something*. Be hot *or* cold, but don't be in the middle, lukewarm." The previous verse even says so, "I know your deeds, that you are neither cold nor hot. I wish you were either one or the other" (Revelation 3:15). Nobody enjoys a lukewarm drink. We want a cold drink when it's hot, and a hot one when it's cold. This verse is saying, "Please, use your deeds to make a difference for heaven's population." It's *not* saying, "Get to work or you will lose your salvation." Remember, we got our salvation for free to begin with (see Ephesians 2:8-9).
2. **They will say if we deliberately keep on sinning we will lose our salvation based on Hebrews 10:26.** First off, all sins are deliberate, and all Christians sin. We can attempt to belittle our sin, compare our sin to others—or worse, try to hide it—but God does *not* grade on a curve. We must be perfect! Jesus said so

Himself! (See John 8:11, Matthew 5:48). The good news is, our perfection only happens by way of spiritual death and resurrection through believing in Jesus' forgiveness (see Romans 6:6-7). Godly perfection does *not* come through behavior repentance. Polishing up a turd does nothing. It's gotta be flushed. You must become new on the inside, in your spirit. So in context, Hebrews 10:26 was written to the unbelieving Jews, not to Christians. Yes, several parts are written specifically to Christians (they are addressed as *beloved* or *friends*), but not this verse. Further, why do you think the name of the book is called *Hebrews*? The author talks about Hebrew issues—not Gentile issues—primarily the Jewish sin of unbelief in Jesus as Messiah. Some of the Jews *did* believe in Jesus, but some refused. This is an evangelistic passage to the unbelievers. It was for those who had taste-tested the gospel and said, "No, thank you." It was for those who heard about such grace but fell away from it—those who *never* fully accepted Jesus! Legalism sounded better to them, *Mosaic* legalism. The author was saying, "You've heard about Messiah with your very own ears, yet you want to keep going back to the temple to get forgiveness from animal blood. That won't work any longer. Jesus was the final sacrifice for sin." That's why they wrote, "No sacrifice is left!" If you keep reading all the way to verse 31, you'll understand the context. This passage is not talking about Christians sinning their way out of being forgiven. If that were the case, Jesus' blood was very weak.

3. **They will claim we can turn our backs on God.** John nips this in the bud in 1 John 2:19. He says, "They went out from us because they were never really a part of us," as in, they never really believed in Jesus. Lots of people like to dress up and play church. They want a sin management program and a conservative country club to join. However, outside appearances and going to a specific geographical location does *not* mean a person has accepted Christ's forgiveness. They might have accepted

religion, but not a graceful faith in the Cross. Be sure to know, countless amounts of people have headed for the hills *away* from church, but not *away* from Jesus. He went with them. They are not un-churched, but de-churched. They've had more church than they can possibly stand so they leave and never come back. They couldn't put on a show for one more second, attempting to impress the hierarchies. Church was a lot more difficult than first advertised. However, just because they left, that does not mean they weren't saved. It just means they want nothing to do with judgmental people and legalism any longer. They want freedom. Not freedom to sin, but freedom from those who think their sins are not as bad. They were looking for help with their pain, but their pain was doubled up with conditional love and ultimatums—so they left. They were taught *church*, not the New Covenant, and not their new identity. But even though these saints don't grace the doors of a building on Sunday, this doesn't mean they've turned their back on God. Why? Because God will never turn His back on them! He is *in* them! Just look! "If we are faithless, he remains faithful, for he cannot disown himself" (2 Timothy 2:13).

There are many more excuses the grace-confused people will use, it's very sad. And you can tell if they are *really* confused about God's grace because they will get mad *about* His grace. Crazy, right? They are upset about the very thing keeping *themselves* eternally secure.

"You better be careful with that grace!" they'll say. Yet that grace is the branch they are sitting on, high above hell and from their own demise.

Friend, the gospel is this: "He is able to save completely those who come to God through him, because he always lives to intercede for them" (Hebrews 7:25). The reason why we will stay saved—once and for all time (see Hebrews 10:10)—is one main reason.

JESUS WILL NEVER DIE AGAIN!

If He dies, yes. If He doesn't die again, no. Your life is His life! So be confident in His ability to stay alive! He is God! You are saved! That is, if you believe He has forgiven you. Do you?

A prayer for you: *Good morning, Dad. I want to thank you for teaching me the truth of my identity, I am your son! I'm no longer a slave to the fear of hell, but instead, I'm confident in what Jesus did for me—and is still doing for me—staying alive! Nothing can change this, not even me! Right now, I lift up all who are reading this, directly to you. So many of them have been manipulated with religious fear. Let them know your Spirit does not bring fear to them, especially about their salvation. Instead, you bring peace, comfort, confidence, and a sound mind! You let us know we are your kids! Teach them the truth of the New Covenant! Teach them that no behavior—good, bad, or indifferent—can change who you've made us to be! SAINTS! We are secure forever! Thank you so much! We love you. Amen.*

Day 58

The Father Will Never Give up on You

"See what great love the Father has lavished on us, that we should be called children of God! And that is what we are!"

See 1 John 3:1

God the Father is relentlessly pursuing you. That is, if you don't believe in Jesus. God the Father is relentlessly *loving* you. That is, if you believe in Jesus.

When Christ was killed on the Cross, Satan celebrated. I can almost hear him, with both fists raised high above his head, "Yes! He's dead! What will God do now? Send another Messiah? They will kill Him too! Hahaha! THIS IS SO GREAT! These sins *have* to be punished, and this Messiah, who was meant to take away the sin of the world, is dead!"

Little did he know, God's loving plan for all of humanity would be buttoned up three days later. The sin of the world *was* being taken away, through Jesus' own blood. The Father was making a way for Himself to become one with all who would believe. It was *His* love that caused Jesus to be sent here in the first place:

> *"For God so loved the world that he gave his one*
> *and only Son, that whoever believes in him shall*
> *not perish but have eternal life." (John 3:16)*

God the Father is bigger than the Bible. Yes, the Bible is His words written through the hand of man, but not everyone will read a Bible or listen to a preacher. That doesn't matter. Our Father still pursues *every* human being. He finds a way—He *makes* a way—for us to know He's real.

This started out with the Jews. The Jews looked to signs and wonders for reasons to believe, so that's exactly what Jesus gave to them. Muslims look to their dreams as the crown jewel of enlightenment. For this reason, Jesus is appearing to those who follow Islam, as they sleep, in unprecedented levels. Many are turning from Mohammed and Allah, to Christ, due to seeing Jesus in visions.

The Father makes a way. The Father never gives up on us. And once we turn to Him—once we *believe* Jesus is His Son who forgave us—we become a permanent member of His family and nothing can change this...not even us. Just the same as your flesh cannot be unborn from your earthly father, your spirit cannot be unborn from your Heavenly Father. You are born. Birth cannot be undone.

There is a story in the Bible Jesus tells about two sons and a father. Although it's about two *different* sons, it's famously named, *The Prodigal Son*. Those actual words are not in the Bible, but *people* have called it that. The self-righteous folk lean in closely on the behavior of one of these sons, but not so much on the other.

Another title the publishers have put before this passage is, *The Parable of the Lost Son*. But which son was truly lost? Which son did not know the father?

In Luke 15, the story goes as such. A father has two grown sons, one of them asks for his inheritance before the father has even died—and he actually gives it to him. It doesn't say whether or not the *other* son got his inheritance at the same time, but if one did, I'm sure the other would have as well.

After the father gave it to him, he took off to foreign lands, living lavishly, partying, and spending money on sex. Soon enough, he didn't have a dime to his name but was too full of shame to go back home. Instead, the man got a job cleaning up after farm animals. Jesus said, "He was so hungry, he longed to eat the food of the pigs" (see Luke 15:16).

Finally, he had a come-to moment. "I know what I'll do! I'll go back home and ask Dad to hire me! I know exactly what I'll say! 'Father, I have sinned against heaven and against you. I am no longer worthy to be called your son; make me like one of your hired servants'" (see Luke 15:17-20).

Coming up the road with his head hung low, the father saw him from far off. Did he turn away in disgust? Did the father send someone to see if he had "truly" repented of all his mistakes? Did his dad sit back and wait for him to prove himself worthy?...No. No he did not.

He ran. He ran toward his son as fast as he possibly could.

He *squeezed* his son with all of his might, bursting into tears of joy.

The son had never stopped being his son. The son's poor choices and disrespect for the father never stopped the father from loving him—it never made him *not* his son. The son's squandering of his inheritance and living in a manner not becoming of his lineage *still* could not cause him to be un-born from his father. The *whole* time, he was still family. His actions never changed his identity.

The father was waiting all along, for him to realize this. As he waited, nothing his son could have done, would have *ever* been able to change his unconditional love for him.

The father threw a party to celebrate! However, his other son was not happy about his excitement. Born into the family just like his brother who had made bad choices—yet forgot who he was—*this* son, "the good one" was mad and jealous as can be:

> *The older brother became angry and refused to go in. So his father went out and pleaded with him. But he answered his father, "Look! All*

these years I've been slaving for you and never disobeyed your orders. Yet you never gave me even a young goat so I could celebrate with my friends. But when this son of yours who has squandered your property with prostitutes comes home, you kill the fattened calf for him!" (Luke 15:28-30)

Do you see it?...Who was the *real* lost son? Who didn't *truly know* the family to which he was born? Who never came to understand the authentic character of his father? Who had no idea about the unconditional love of his very own parent? Who *was it* that didn't know Dad would never give up on any of his kids, no matter their behavior?

Was it the son who ran away from home, or was it the one who *stayed home?*...It was both. Neither son knew just how deep and wide their father's love for them actually was. They couldn't fathom such a love! Even though they were born into it, even though they could never change it, it was too great of a love to understand.

So today, my friends, know this: Father God will never give up on you. If you haven't believed in Jesus' forgiveness just yet, He is hard at work giving you opportunities to do so. No, it's not truly hard for Him; and it's not really work—but He is very active in your life, calling you to believe. Friend, *believe*. Dad wants you to be forgiven so you can spend eternity with us, starting right now. And if you *have* believed in Jesus as your Savior, once, you will never be able to change, sustain, increase or decrease the Father's love for you. He loves you because He loves you. You've been born into His family, you are His child, and you will *never* be able to fully understand His love. His love is as expansive as the cosmos. Even in a trillion years, you'll still be going deeper, and deeper, into it.

A prayer for you: *Father, I love you. I don't even know what else I can possibly type to express my love for you, as my Dad. Your commitment to me makes me choke up nearly every time I think about it. I know you can feel how grateful I am—how proud I am to be in you, and you in me. If there is anything I can do to show you just how much*

I love you, reveal it to me and I'll do it. Keep taking me deeper into your love. Teach me more and more about it each day. Right now, I lift up all who are reading this, directly to you. So many of them have been lied to about you. They've been told that their behavior or thoughts can cause them to be un-born from our family—reveal how untrue this is. Today, give them a new revelation of what you've done for us through Jesus. Open up their minds to the truth of how everlasting your love is for your children. And for the unbeliever, let them know the same. The offer is on the table, and it's a good deal. All they gotta do is believe they need to be forgiven by Jesus, and they are. Grace and faith were such great ideas, Dad. Thank you for both. Thank you for everything. Amen.

Day 59

Don't Hide Any Longer

He answered, "I heard you in the garden, and I was afraid because I was naked; so I hid."

-Adam, speaking to God, Genesis 3:10

"Hey, is there any way we can meet up and talk?" I said, over the phone to a friend of mine.

"We can talk now, if you want," he replies.

"No, I'd like to see you in person if that's okay with you."

"Sure, we can do that."

The next day, I showed up early to the cafe, attempting to get my bearings. The conversation which was about to take place was something I had been hiding from for a long time now. Sitting there, waiting, I felt like a turtle on its back, slowly waving each leg in sequence trying to turn over. What was about to be discussed already had me in prayer, I started talking to Dad on the drive over.

"God, help me. Give me the words to say, and speak through me. Please, let healing happen. Bless this conversation and help me to be confident. I feel physically nervous, but I'm not worried about that because I know you're with me. I know something good will come out of this, even if he doesn't accept my apology."

As my friend came in he greeted me, "Hey man. How are you?" He sat down across the table, still bewildered about why I wanted to see him.

After our brief pleasantries, I didn't hesitate to get to the matter at hand.

"I know you're wondering why I wanted to sit down with you and talk—and this isn't easy for me. I hide from being vulnerable, I'm not very good at expressing my weaknesses."

"Well, what is it?" He didn't say this, but his face did.

"I just had to tell you in person that I'm sorry. I'm sorry for how I treated you. I'm sorry for how I attacked you. I'm sorry for everything. I was *so* wrong with what I did and I now know it. I've actually known it for a while now, but I just could never bring myself to say this to you."

The fact was, I knew I was wrong when I verbally attacked my friend, years before. At the time, I was in a very bad place, a *frustrating* place. I was transitioning from completely ignoring God—as well as my own heaven-ready identity—to actually allowing Him to live through me. This was strange and I did not know how to handle it. The Holy Spirit was teaching me new things every single day, and as my mind was being renewed to the truth, I didn't know how to *release* this new information properly.

I know *now* how I'm supposed to do it—which is with love, respect, and grace—but back then I couldn't wrap my spiritually immature mind around such. I was like a bull who had just realized he was a bull. The China shoppe was being destroyed and I had no clue how to relax. Sadly, my good friend was a victim of my sharp horns.

This person had blocked me on social media, as well as my phone number, and rightfully so. I even had to reach out to him from a number he didn't recognize. I know I had hurt him and I wanted to make sure I was clear about my remorse.

After my apology, he quickly replied, "Oh, it's no big deal," and kindly tried to change the subject. I expected this from him, because he's such a nice guy, so I reiterated the importance of our meeting.

"No, it *was* a big deal. I need you to know that you were right for shutting me out. I was not doing good at all, and you were nothing but kind. I'm sorry." I intentionally lock eyes with him, "I'm *really* sorry."

Right then I could see he finally knew how serious I was. The sympathy in his expression told me he realized I wasn't just trying to save face—I was trying to be as genuine as I possibly could be...and he got it.

"It's okay. I forgive you."

With those words, I felt the tension float up and away as the Holy Spirit blew in a small cloud of trust. We chatted and laughed for another 45 minutes or so, and then both went our separate ways. I forgot just how much I liked talking to him. He's a good man and I'm glad we are *real* friends once again. It was a good meeting. It was a very good day.

None of this would have been possible without me becoming defenseless. Being defenseless is not part of my personality. Yes, it's part of my spirit—a heavenly trait I've inherited from Dad—but my *mind* has learned to guard my ego like a lion over a fresh kill. I hide from being defenseless, and I shouldn't. My stupid ego—my unrenewed thought pockets—is not needed in any way. It would be best if it walked into oncoming traffic, but that won't be the case until I'm gone from planet earth.

Being exposed as weak easily inflames my thinking with fear. But it is *in* my weakness godly things happen in my life. It is *in* my weakness—when I allow it to be revealed—I feel more like myself than ever before. I don't have to be addicted to being a pillar of strength and God's Spirit teaches me this truth day by day.

I felt *really* good as I sat vulnerable across from my friend. Even though I was nervous, it was as if I had impenetrable armor on. It was *in* my weakness that I felt strong! It was *in* my weakness that God's Holy Spirit mended a broken friendship! I didn't *have* to call him! I didn't *have* to let God fix this!

...But, I didn't want to hide from being vulnerable any longer. I didn't want to grieve my Dad. He would have still been proud of me either way, but He kept saying, "Matt, call him. Trust me. Don't worry about how he'll react, just trust me."

When I trusted He who is in me, restoration happened. But even if restoration wasn't reciprocated from my friend, Dad would have still said, "That was awesome. Thank you. I'm going to use that for a greater good than you can possibly understand. You did well, son."

So today, my friends, know this: You don't have to hide. It's impossible to hide anything from God anyway, so why not come out into the open so healing can take place? Whether you are hiding the fact that you binge eat a whole box of Double Stuffed Oreos in one sitting—or like me, you hide from being sensitive and defenseless—expose yourself. Just do it. When you do, God takes you further into the halls of His grace. The more you expose your weaknesses, the more you'll realize just how strong you truly are! The more you expose your weaknesses, the *deeper* God's love for you goes.

A prayer for you: *Heavenly Father, thank you for teaching me how to become weak. It is in my weakest times that something strangely powerful happens—I reveal YOU. When my underbelly is exposed and I'm worried I might be devoured, you stand guard and say, "I'm protecting you. Don't be afraid." Teach me more about yourself. Teach me more about YOUR strength within me. Teach me who I am. Teach me more about your grace and live through me. Right now, I lift up all who are reading this, directly to you. Dad, so many of them were taught to hide growing up. Many were even FORCED to hide because of aggressive parents or parents who used guilt as a way to punish them. They've LEARNED to hide stuff, and you want to teach them differently. YOU are a good, good Father, and you never shame us or use scare tactics. We are secure. For some, hiding stuff is not only rampant in their own lives, but they also hide things for others. Release them today from such pressure. Let them know they can step out into the open because you're there! Whether they are hiding a physical or emotional affair, or credit card bills; it could be an addiction or they could EVEN be hiding extreme criticism and legalism. Whatever it may be, empower them to become vulnerable! If they believe in Jesus as their Savior, that power is already in them! Teach them today how to let it come out! In His name, I pray, amen.*

Day 60

By His Stripes We Are Healed?

"But he was pierced for our transgressions, he was crushed for our iniquities; the punishment that brought us peace was on him, and by his wounds we are healed."

Isaiah 53:5

In the Old Testament there was a prophet named Isaiah. Hundreds of years before Jesus was born, Isaiah foretold about a man who would take the sin of the world into His body—it was Jesus. The punishment for every single sin a person ever commits is death—from gossip to murder (Romans 6:23). This prophet was Jewish, so he knew that without the shedding of blood, you could *never* be forgiven (see Hebrews 9:22). The words "ask for forgiveness" are not in the Bible. This is because a death must happen to *be* forgiven. Confession doesn't forgive either, only a one-time confession that we *need* the forgiveness of Christ (see 1 John 1:9).

As a Jew, Isaiah was used to getting his own forgiveness at the Day of Atonement. This was a single day of the year in which the Jews received forgiveness for their sins for the *past* year—all of them. After they came out of the temple, they had relief. They were good to go for another 365 days.

The forgiveness was received only when their sins were transferred into the body of animals by way of a Levitical priest (see Numbers 18:1, Hebrews 6:2). To be clear, this animal couldn't be their 10-year-old heifer who was on her last leg, oh no. It had to be their *best* animal—a spotless and healthy creature (see Leviticus 27:10, 1 Peter 1:9).

However, "it was impossible for the blood of bulls and goats to take away sins" (Hebrews 10:4). The key words focus on in that verse is, *take away*. The animal blood was simply a reminder of how poorly a person performed over the course of the previous 365 days (see Hebrews 10:3). It was a *shadow* of what Jesus would do through His own perfect body! (See Hebrews 10:1, Colossians 2:17). But even better, Christ would *take away* our sin once and for all time with one last sacrifice! (See John 1:29, Hebrews 7:25, 8:12, 10:10).

Afterwards, the Day of Atonement would no longer be needed because the world would finally have the real thing!

Think about it, if my wife is pregnant and that's all I can talk about, *then* my child is born, but rather than go to the hospital to receive my new child, I stay home and stare at ultrasound pictures. This is what happened to the Jews who kept attending the Day of Atonement after the events of Jesus' life, death, burial, and resurrection! (See Hebrews 10:26).

Isaiah didn't know His name, but the Holy Spirit revealed exactly what Christ would do. In Isaiah 53, he goes into great detail about what would take place in the life of this Messiah. He penned, "He'll grow up like a tender shoot," and that very thing happened! Baby Jesus grew into boy Jesus, and then boy Jesus grew into the man. Christmas Day celebrates the beginning of this tender shoot's life.

Isaiah continued, "He had no beauty or majesty to attract us to him, nothing in his appearance that we should desire him." Could there be a more accurate description of how simple Jesus' life was? The very name *Jesus* is as common as the name *Joe*.

Verse three reads, "He was despised and rejected by mankind, a man of suffering, and familiar with pain." The foretelling of what would happen in Jesus' 33 years, through Isaiah, is uncanny. God even revealed to him how his own people would treat dear Jesus. "We held him in low esteem." But that's not all he had to say about those who refused to believe:

> *"Surely he took up our pain and bore our suffering,*
> *yet we considered him punished by God, stricken*
> *by him, and afflicted." (Isaiah 53:4)*

Surely He took their pain and suffering! Surely. Yes, even the Jews who were trying to kill Him, and finally did. One of the Jewish leaders, Nicodemus, was so intrigued by Jesus, he snuck off at night to meet with Him (see John 3). But even so, the colleagues of Nicodemus had Him cut up and ground into a bloody pulp. Isaiah 53:4 reveals that they honestly believed Jesus deserved to be crucified—that God was backing them up...they were wrong.

"He was pierced for our transgressions!" Isaiah announces in verse 5. But what is a transgression?...It's sin. He was pierced and killed for our *sin*. All of the stuff which cannot enter into heaven, He removed by way of a bloody death! He changed up our deal with God! (See Hebrews 8:6,13). A new Priest has come! The Levites are out! They've been replaced by a Priest who will never die! (Hebrews 7:25). He hails from the Tribe of Judah—a priest has never come from that group of Israelites! But it doesn't matter because a new covenant was put in place *by* the Messiaaaaaaah! He brings good tidings of salvation by way of grace through simple faith! BELIEVE! YES! IT'S THAT GOOD! YES! IT'S THAT EASY! (See Hebrews 4:14-16, Ephesians 2:8,9, John 1:12).

It's so easy it's impossible for many. "Nope, we gotta do our part," they'll say. They'll go right back to Judaism. They'll go right back to the temple.

Friend, Jesus *did* your part. Just open up your hands and say, "Thank you."

"Yeah right, Matt! He died for us so we gotta get to work and die for Him!"

Friend, no...just relax and be yourself (see Hebrews 4:11, Galatians 5:22-23). Sure, your mind is being renewed by way of Christ's Spirit—but *you* are complete! (See Romans 12:2, 2 Peter 1:3). All of the dying stuff is over. You symbolically followed Jesus to the Cross and you were supernaturally crucified, by faith.

So just...live. Be you. He *likes* you.

That word *pierced*, in Isaiah 53:5, is literal and accurate. Piercing was the job of a long, sharp, nasty nail. Other versions of the Bible read, "Crushed!" "Whipped!" "Bruised!" "Chastened!" One interpretation even claims Jesus was *scourged*. If you've seen *The Passion of the Christ*, you've seen a scourging.

As Jesus was tied up to a post, the Romans used a whip with metal shards on the end of each chord. WHEN THEY SLAMMED THE WHIP AGAINST HIS BACK, THOSE COARSE BITS OF METAL DUG DEEP INTO HIS SKIN AND LATCHED ON! Then they ferociously *ripped it away*! Fragments and chunks of the Son of God spread all around them! THEY DID IT AGAIN! AND AGAIN!

Fleshy portions of the Messiah fell into the crevices on the ground! His perfect blood—never tainted by sin—poured out of the holes in His back...saturating everything. Blood splattered in the faces of the guards! *Screams* from the crowd bellowed as people watched in horror!

...And Christ went limp..."GET UP! GET, *UP*—YOU *STINKING* FILTHY JEW! WHERE IS YOUR GOD NOW?"

Blow after *blow* after *blow* ..."STOP! PLEASE! STOOOOOOP IT!" Loved ones wailed for mercy! But they didn't stop...they showed no mercy...they kept going. *Our* sin was being dealt with at that moment. *Our* sin was being paid for in full. Our sin was being taken away by Jesus through one final death. Afterwards, He sat down in heaven, never to have to die again:

> *"Fixing our eyes on Jesus, the author and perfecter of*
> *our faith. For the joy set before him he endured the*
> *cross, scorning its shame, and sat down at the right hand of*
> *the throne of God."* (Hebrews 12:2)

This is how we stay saved as Christians, it's because Jesus died once for *all* sin. He is not dying again and again, up in heaven, after each stupid transgression we act on (see Hebrews 7:25).

Now, I say this with all due respect. But there are some people who are part of a "name-it-claim-it group." With vigor and enthusiasm—and even innocently—they'll shout, "By His stripes, I *claim* this job!" "By His stripes, I *claim* this new car!" "By His stripes, I *claim* this healing!"

Friends, claiming anything by His stripes is not the gospel. We cannot boss God around and then use the name of Jesus to do so. How about we just *ask* Dad, and trust Him? Romans 8:15 says we now have the right to call God, "Abba," which means, "Daddy." So what do you say we go from *claiming* stuff, to simply being content in all things while *asking* our loving Father for what we want? He already knows before we even ask (see Matthew 6:8), He just craves for us to talk to Him.

Dad longs for us to trust Him through prayer, and by being our true selves, His kids. He wants us to know, "I'm with you, always." He doesn't want you frustrated by claiming things over and over. He wants you at peace.

God is not against us having stuff, getting that job, or mending your broken relationship. He's not against you breaking that addiction, and He's not against miraculous healings. He is God and He can do anything He wants, whenever He wants—and He's always right. Thankfully, He loves us no matter *what* He decides about our requests!

But this verse, which was meant to explain what Jesus would do to our *spirits* has been misused for far too long. Can we please get back to the truth? Sure, Jesus can heal anyone at any time, and we *should* ask (see James 4:2, Philippians 4:6). But Isaiah 53:5 is not referring to our *physical* bodies, but instead, our *infected* spirits—our sinful spirits.

This verse is addressing our broken, damaged, spiritual selves. The one we were born with. Most people think we become sinners after our first act of sin, but that is not true. We are *born* sinners, because of Adam (see Romans 5:12). Humanity's original ancestor was created like God—perfect. But he chose to act on the power of sin which was presented to him by Satan. As a result, sin was infused with Adam's supernatural DNA—his spirit—and so were all of his would-be descendants, us.

The good news is, even though that one man caused us to be born sinful—Adam—by one *other* man—Jesus—*He* caused us to become non-sinful in spirit! He caused us to be perfect just like Him *in* our eternal bodies! (See Romans 5:19).

Therefore, it was by His stripes our *spirits* are healed! It was by His stripes we have the opportunity to go from having a disgusting, puss-filled, maggot-infested, sinful, dead, carcass of a spirit—HELL BOUND—to instantly being healed! To instantly being perfect and heaven-ready!

Why? Because we are joined with Him *in* spirit! God is not looking for dead spirits to improve their behavior or go to church! He wants us to be remade, in full, once. This happens when we believe that Jesus saved us.

To take this one notch higher, *if* you believe in Jesus as your Savior, you haven't simply been *healed*. You've been supernaturally killed off and reborn as a saint! *You* are a spirit! Your spirit *will* go on into eternity, with or without God. Your flesh will die but your spirit will not.

Isaiah thought our spirits just needed to be healed, but they needed to be born again! (See John 3:7). We had to be born of water—the sac we came into this world through Momma—and we had to be reborn of spirit! In John 3:5, Jesus is not telling Nicodemus about being dunked into H2O, but an embryonic pouch *and* God's own Spirit! Only the *Holy* Spirit joining *our* spirits can cause this rebirth, and it happens the first moment we believe *even* if we didn't feel anything. Your salvation is not a feeling, but a fact. Paul explains this to the Romans:

> *"For we know that our old self was crucified with him so that the body ruled by sin might be done away with, that we should no longer be slaves to sin—because anyone who has died has been set free from sin." (Romans 6:6-7)*

Do you see it? We've not simply been healed from sin—we've died to sin! Our spirits no longer contain it! By faith, we've died, we were buried, and then we were resurrected *with* Jesus already *in* our physical bodies *and* spirits!

With Christ in us, we don't even want to sin—it's like touching a hot stove—it makes no sense when we do so. But as flawed humans on a fallen planet, and with the *power* of sin and demonic temptations still floating around—WITH PEOPLE EVERYWHERE—yes, we touch that stove sometimes. But our Father will not disown us (see 2 Timothy 2:13). He doesn't even *convict* us any longer. Jesus was already convicted and the punishment was death.

So now, God's Spirit is loving us *through* our sinful choices with never ending grace (see Romans 5:20, 1 Corinthians 13:4-8, Galatians 5:22-23). He counsels us and patiently guides us away from danger. We still get to choose what to do! We get to decide if we will walk by our true selves or fake it! Either way, behavior cannot change your identity. Attitudes cannot change your identity.

Friend, saint, this is something we all have to deal with and it's not easy...but very possible. We are new creations in Christ! Through His body we are now at peace with God! We are completely reconciled with our Creator! Holy! Blameless! Spiritually set apart! We are already sitting in heaven with Jesus at this moment—He is not bound by time—we are! Yet, we are still righteous today! We are children of God! That is what we are! (See Philippians 4:13, 2 Corinthians 5:17,21, Romans 5:1, Colossians 1:22, 2 Peter 3:8, Ephesians 1:4, 2:6, John 1:12, 1 John 3:1).

> **A prayer for you:** *Heavenly Father, thank you for Jesus. Thank you for sending Him here so that I can be a part of you and Him for good. If Isaiah could have only known how accurate he was as he wrote, "He was oppressed and afflicted, yet he did not open his mouth; he was led like a lamb to the slaughter"—it would have shocked him! I know your Spirit guided his human hand on that scroll the very day he penned this passage. As I read it today, thousands of years later, I'm very grateful! Right now, I lift up all who are reading this, directly to you. God, reveal*

to these dear readers that the very same Spirit who was WITH Isaiah is now IN them. The event he wrote about—Jesus taking away our sin—CAUSED US to be able to have your Spirit infused with OUR spirit, permanently! You're not just WITH us, but IN us! We have something so much better on this side of the Cross! Because of Jesus' loving sacrifice, you are committed to us forever! That is, if we believe, once. Thank you for your promise to Jesus, and His to you. Amen.

Dear friend,

Thank you so much for spending time with me through this book. I hope I was able to bring you a sense of peace and confidence in knowing more about what Christ has truly done. My prayer is for you to grow into even deeper revelations of your identity as a believer. Lastly, it would mean the world to me if you'd leave a kind review on Amazon.com, Goodreads.com, Barnes & Noble's website, or wherever you've purchased this book. Your opinion is very important and encouraging to me. I always look forward to reading reviews.

May God continue to bless you greatly, with even more knowledge of His love for you through Jesus!

In Christ,
Matt

Additional Books by Matt McMillen

60 Days for Jesus, Volume 1: *Understanding Christ Better, Two Months at a Time*

"I really like Matt's writing style. He makes understanding the gospel simple and real. I have found his daily devotions to be very helpful in guiding my walk with Christ. I highly recommend his book." -*Amazon Customer*

ADDITIONAL BOOKS BY MATT MCMILLEN

60 Days for Jesus, Volume 2: *Understanding Christ Better, Two Months at a Time*

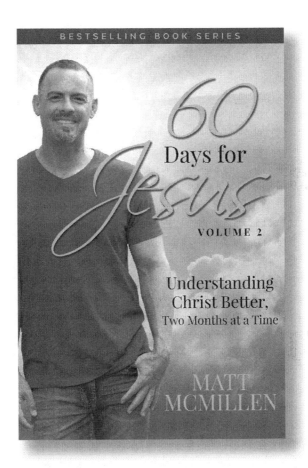

"This book is exactly what I needed to understand more about Jesus. I couldn't put it down. Thank you, Matt McMillen, for sharing your story to help strengthen others!" -*Amazon Customer*

True Purpose in Jesus Christ: *Finding the Relationship for Which You Were Made*

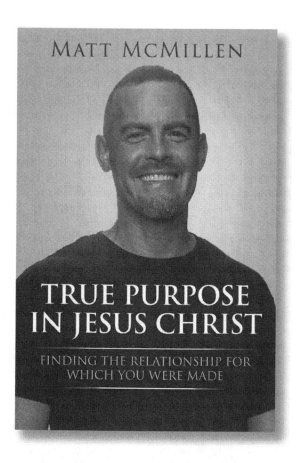

"One of the best books I've ever read! Matt's honesty about his life and what Jesus did to redeem him is amazing! He uses Scripture throughout his book to back up everything he talks about. I bought 20 books so I could share with the lost. Absolutely life changing! Thank you, Matt, for writing this book!" *-Amazon Customer*

ADDITIONAL BOOKS BY MATT MCMILLEN

The Christian Identity, Volume 1: *Discovering What Jesus Has Truly Done to Us*

"Matt brilliantly explains the supernatural transformation that happens when we become believers in the finished work of the cross. His writing style makes this easy to understand as he answers some of the toughest questions that are on so many Christians' minds today." -*Amazon Customer*

ADDITIONAL BOOKS BY MATT MCMILLEN

The Christian Identity, Volume 2: *Discovering What Jesus Has Truly Done to Us*

"Matt McMillen's books are amazing! You will learn so much and understand how to live your Christian life according to our Lord Jesus Christ. I've read all of his books and have shared them. I love his writing." -*Amazon Customer*

Made in the USA
Columbia, SC
11 December 2020